It's Not About You

IT'S NOT ABOUT YOU:
Paradoxes of Christian Leadership

By
Elizabeth Beasley

PRESS

Published 2023 by DWM Press
www.dwmpress.com

Printed in Wales by Gomer Press.

29 28 27 26 25 24 23   1 2 3 4 5

ISBN: 978-0-99-805164-2

All quotations from the Psalms, unless otherwise indicated, are from the Episcopal Church, *Book of Common Prayer, and Administration of the Sacraments and Other Rites and Ceremonies of the Church* (New York: Seabury Press, 1979).

The Scripture quotations contained herein, unless otherwise indicated, are from the New Revised Standard Version Bible copyright © 1989 by the Division of Christian Education of the National Council of the Churches of Christ in the U.S.A. Used by permission. All rights reserved.

To Kirk

I appeal to you therefore, brothers and sisters, by the mercies of God, to present your bodies as a living sacrifice, holy and acceptable to God, which is your spiritual worship. Do not be conformed to this world, but be transformed by the renewing of your minds, so that you may discern what is the will of God—what is good and acceptable and perfect. For by the grace given to me I say to everyone among you not to think of yourself more highly than you ought to think, but to think with sober judgment, each according to the measure of faith that God has assigned.

—Romans 12:1-3

"Not my will, but thine, be done."

—Luke 22:42 RSV

CONTENTS

ACKNOWLEDGMENTS ix

INTRODUCTION 1

Part 1: To Begin . . .

1. WHAT IS A RULE OF LIFE? 15

2. DON'T HURRY:
   The Pace of Time 33

Part 2: The Basics

3. GOD AND PEOPLE:
   Navigating Two Worlds 57

4. PRAYER:
   The Essential Task 63

5. PASTORAL CARE:
   "Talk Story" 87

6. RELATIONSHIPS:
   Boundaries, Friendships, and Other Thorny Issues 103

Part 3: Central Tasks of Ministry

7. WORSHIP:
    Opening a Lens on the Realm of God   121

8. READING AND STUDY:
    Read, Mark, Learn, and Inwardly Digest   145

9. PREACHING:
    The Word   167

10. PARADOXES OF PREACHING:
    Passing Life Through the Fire of Thought   183

Part 4: A Pause in Time

11. SABBATH:
    When Time Stops   201

12. KEEPING SABBATH:
    What Do We Do?   215

Part 5: Daily Life

13. MONEY:
    Relinquishing Money's Hold on Us   231

14. THE BODY:
    An Asset and a Liability   251

15. THE PERSONHOOD OF THE PARSON   263

    NOTES   279

    RESOURCES   291

ACKNOWLEDGMENTS

"SINCE WE ARE SURROUNDED by so great a cloud of witnesses . . . " (Heb. 12:1)

No one is ever in ministry by oneself. The whole nature of ministry is that one serves God in the midst of others. One interacts with congregations, mentors, colleagues, denominational officers, seminary professors and other teachers. One is also part of what is called, in the Anglican tradition, "the communion of saints": the whole line of faithful people who have come before us and who provide us with inspiration. From all such people we might receive education, inspiration, assistance, and fellowship.

As I wrote this book, I became increasingly aware of all the influences with which God has graced me: mentors who helped me through ordination processes, college and seminary professors, colleagues in ministry, bishops (I have worked for ten of them!), and especially the congregations among whom I have served. If I attempted to name all the people and all the congregations, I would inevitably leave out someone.

I know that anything I have ever "accomplished" in a congregation has been with the help of others. A parish minister cannot operate on one's own: ministry depends on a fluid and grace-filled interaction between clergy and congregation. It is an awesome privilege to be parish clergy.

I will, however, name one person: my husband, Kirk, to whom this book is dedicated and without whom I could not have written it.

To all these people, and to the congregations, I say simply, "Thank you."

Chapter 1

INTRODUCTION

A rule is stimulating if it presses, prods, and goads us towards sanctity; and what is sanctity but the absorption of our aims in God's?
                                   —Walter C. Klein, *A Priest Forever*

I HAVE SOME GOOD NEWS and some bad news for you. The news is the same, but whether you consider it to be good or bad depends on what you consider to be the foundation of your ministry.

The news is this: It's not about you. Life, church, ministry, or anything else: they are not about you.

This news is true whether or not you are a clergy person or any other Christian leader—or, indeed, anyone else in society. Advertising, television, media, school, workplace, and other societal institutions all tell us, It's all about you. We hear that the success of anything we do depends on us and on our own powers. Even a subsidiary of a major denomination several years ago

1

sent a postcard announcing their new website. The message on the postcard was "It's all about you."

Clergy, as well as those who spend a major portion of time in Christian leadership, are particularly susceptible to believing this message because of a paradox inherent in the practice of ministry. We have a variety of tools for ministry, gleaned from our studies and our experience, but the primary tool we have is simply who we are as individuals. All our study and all our experience are delivered through the vehicle of our own personality. In addition, we so often are, or appear to be, the focus of attention in our congregations or other ministry settings, when in truth Christian leaders are only a vehicle for a greater message and reality that we are attempting to convey. The real foci of ministry are God and the people among whom we serve.* We are meant to facilitate communication between the two, but the paradox of ministry can lead us instead to direct people's attention toward ourselves, even to such an extent that we become a stumbling block in their communication with God.

This paradox is accentuated by the flexibility and lack of structure that are inherent in the practice of ministry. To a large extent we are able to set our own schedules; our work day often takes us to a variety of places; and on any given day we never know what is going to happen. For many, such variability is a benefit in a demanding position. I, for one, have never liked punching a time clock. Clergy may work long hours, but other than certain fixed appointments (such as worship services), the time we spend working is flexible.

---

* Throughout this book, I will say that Christian leaders serve "among" the people. It is tempting, and even popular, to say that we serve the people, but we do not. We serve God, in the context of a particular group of people.

This very flexibility, however, leads to basic questions that every person in ministry has to face at some time: How do we structure our days? How shall we spend our time? In the absence of guiding principles to help us answer these questions, and in the face of people directing their attention and focus toward us, we can fall prey to several temptations that accentuate this focus on ourselves: for example, spending too much time and energy on social media platforms, fretting about a parishioner who dislikes us or complains about our ministry, or seeking out roles that will "advance my career." Finding a way to structure our days according to certain principles, and in response to our primary commitments and promises, can forestall such temptations.

People who serve in ministry part-time, as an increasing number of people do, especially need to find a way to structure their days because of the multitude of demands they face. One diocese for which I worked used to call part-time clergy "part-salaried" in recognition that people in ministry being paid for a part-time position often end up working full-time.

One way to address the question of how to structure one's day and at the same time deal with the paradox of Christian leadership is to develop a rule of life. "Rule of life" is a phrase traditionally associated with monasticism, for it was in monasteries and monastic orders that rules of life developed. The most famous is the Rule of Saint Benedict, developed by Saint Benedict of Nursia in the sixth century for monks living in community under the guidance of an abbot. From its origins in sixth-century Italy, the Rule of Saint Benedict then spread throughout Europe over the next few centuries and subsequently throughout the world. It was not the first monastic rule of life to be written, but over fifteen hundred years, it has remained the most influential.[1]

A "rule of life" might be developed by anyone. A rule of

life helps people to establish a structure for their lives that allows them to be true to their beliefs and commitments. For Christians, the rule reminds us that our daily lives must be oriented toward a sacred purpose: that of worshipping God and following Christ in all that we do. People in ministry especially need a rule of life because of the flexibility and the paradox mentioned above, both of which are inherent in ministry. We need a rule not only to structure our days, but also to remind us that all we undertake is for God and that we are dependent on God's grace.

Some pieces of a rule might be imposed from without. For clergy, this is especially true, in that most ordination rites detail the basic tasks and expectations of ordained ministry. These tasks will form the general structure of our rule, but we have to fill in the details. The very flexibility that is one of the joys of being clergy means that little actual structure is given to us. One has to fashion the rule oneself, in keeping with one's own patterns, commitments, life circumstances, and personality. Lay people commissioned for certain roles in the church often themselves make promises and commitments in a commissioning service; these promises can form part of a rule of life, in addition to one's baptismal promises.

Some of the specific details for a rule of life will be set by others. Certainly being part of a worshipping congregation will dictate times for worship each week. In Anglican practice, as another example, clergy traditionally have been expected to say the Daily Office each day; they will say a service consisting of Scripture-reading and prayer both at the start of the day and in the early evening, whether by themselves or with others. One might also bear in mind that many rules of life—most notably, Saint Benedict's—were intended for communal living. We do not live for ourselves alone, nor is any of us the sole arbiter of truth. In fashioning a rule of life, we would do well to draw on the wisdom of those who have come before us and to take into account the people among whom we live.

In this book, I will describe the paradoxes of Christian ministry that lead to the necessity of a rule of life and will mention, as examples, some of the elements of the rule that I have developed for myself. I recognize that this in itself is a paradox: to use myself as an example in a book entitled *It's Not About You.* Nevertheless, I decided to write from my own experience to illustrate that fundamental paradox in ministry: the tool God has given us to work with is ourselves.

I am not, however, perfect, no matter how tempted I am to try to be. I offer these reflections as examples of what I have found to be helpful for living my life as a Christian and as a priest. Many of the details of my rule of life have evolved through trial and error, and even sin. In other words, I sometimes have discovered what works and what I believe to be right by first doing what was not right and what made my life more difficult and lacking in integrity.

These reflections also come from working with ordained clergy and with people preparing for both lay and ordained ministry. With those preparing for ministry, I have been, in several places, one of a team of people who had the weighty and often painful responsibility of reviewing the suitability of people for ministry. Among all these groups, I have observed what helps people do well in ministry and what behaviors become stumbling blocks. On occasion, I have had to work closely with or even investigate clergy who "crash and burn," whether because of personality and mental health issues, or through unethical behaviors that forced them to leave the ministry, or through an untimely death. As I look back on all these cases, I can see that each of these clergy focused unduly upon themselves. Some tried to make themselves indispensable in their ministry. Some amplified their own importance. Some resented not receiving the attention they felt they deserved, for whatever reason. In short, each of them succumbed to the notion "It's all about me."

In summary, the topics explored in the chapters of this book come from what Christian leaders over two millennia have found to be the essential activities that form the structure of the ordained person's life. Many of these same activities form the foundation of lay ministry positions as well. I give specific examples and reflections from my own life and ministry, and from people among whom I have worked, as to how a rule of life might be structured to include these activities. Throughout the book, I include exercises intended to spur reflection so that readers might work toward developing a rule for their own lives.

A Word about Titles

THE VARIOUS CHRISTIAN DENOMINATIONS use a number of titles for their clergy, such as *pastor, priest, preacher,* and *minister.* Strictly speaking, these terms are not interchangeable, for each carries a nuance of meaning that arises from the particular role that the denomination emphasizes. Liturgical traditions, such as Anglican, Roman Catholic, and Orthodox, use *priest* because of its sacerdotal connotations. The word *pastor* suggests an emphasis on the role of caring for others. Traditions with a strong emphasis on the ministry of the word use the word *preacher.*

Minister seems all-inclusive and is useful, because these days many traditions recognize that one does not have to be ordained in order to be, in some sense, a minister. In this book, I will use all these terms, or simply the word *clergy*.

Another word, however, has a long history of use and also fits the way I will be describing the ordained ministry, and that is the word *parson*. Barbara Brown Taylor suggests that the term *parson* means a "representative person"; she writes, ". . . a priest is a representative person—a *parson*—who walks the shifting boundary between heaven and earth, representing God to humankind, representing humankind to God, and serving each in the other's name."[2] Clergy are representative persons not only in these senses, but also in that we are meant to show what it means to live as a Christian. We play a key role in a community of people—both the people in our own parishes or ministries, and also in the wider community—in that we are representative of the Christian faith. Even though this latter role may seem increasingly insignificant in a secular world, clergy still show to the world a living representative of Christ's message and being.

In fact, anyone filling a role of Christian ministry must be aware of being a representative of Christ in the world. Examples of roles for which laity might now be trained and commissioned include hospital chaplains, pastoral caregivers, and worship leaders. Such ministers might view these roles as purely functional: in other words, they might believe that they are simply doing a job. The people among whom they minister, however, will see them as representing Christ and the Church.

In this book, therefore, I speak primarily about and to ordained clergy, but the message applies to, and I intend the book for, anyone in a role of Christian leadership, especially one of a pastoral or liturgical nature.

A Word about Timing

I BEGAN THIS BOOK LONG BEFORE the COVID-19 pandemic began, but I completed much of it during the lockdowns brought about by the pandemic. Ministry in some ways became substantially different: where I was serving in ministry, churches closed for in-church worship; meetings moved online; and hospitals and nursing homes barred visits from chaplains and clergy. I wondered how much I needed to change this book in light of the pandemic.

I decided, however, that the basics of ministry remain the same, despite the pandemic. One of the points of this book is that ministry involves certain basic responsibilities and ways of living that are timeless. No matter what the outward circumstances, God and the people among whom we serve are still the foci of ordained ministry. We still must deliver pastoral care, whether in person or by some other means, such as phone calls and letters. We still have to provide worship in some fashion, even though this is much more difficult when churches are closed. And above all, we still must pray: communicate with and listen to God, and intercede for the people. During COVID-19 lockdowns, praying for all the parishioners by name is what I felt to be the most important thing I could do.

Because of COVID-19, or any other extreme situation, one might have to revise the details of one's rule of life—for example, how and when one provides pastoral care—but the basic responsibility remains the same.

Exercise: If you were serving in ministry during the initial stages of the COVID-19 pandemic, how did your ministerial tasks change? What became most important to you? Have these changes persisted as the restrictions eased in your area?

Sources

I USE A VARIETY OF SOURCES in this book. A number of them are
works by Christians from long ago. These sources might not be
popular now, perhaps because the book is out of print or because
the author's language would be considered outdated, whether in
the structure of the writing or in the inclusiveness of the author's
use of pronouns. (I have chosen not to change their language.)
These works are valuable, however, in describing the role of a
clergy person and in constructing a rule of life. These writers
are themselves "representative people": people who have come
before us in the Christian faith and who, in their struggles to live
a godly life, have dispensed wisdom and shared traditions from
which we can learn.

Sometimes even the title of a work from long ago is enough
to put off the potential reader. A good example is a book by
a priest of the eighteenth century in the Church of England,
William Law (1686–1761). I once told a friend, someone about
to be ordained, that I was reading Law's book *A Serious Call to a
Devout and Holy Life*.[3] Her response was "Why would one want
to?" I decided not to ask whether she was questioning why one
would want to read the book, or why one would want to lead a
devout and holy life. Law's work and life, however, are inspiring.
I once conducted a service on his feast day and found that the
congregation was inspired by Law's integrity.

Some of the sources I use arise within the Anglican tradition. This tradition has been one that emphasizes "right practice."
It focuses on patterns of life that help the Christian live well and
faithfully. A mentor of mine once described it as "redeeming the
time": living one's life in such a way and according to a structure
that relates one's activities to God.[4] Anglicanism therefore has

wisdom to contribute to a discussion of how to develop a rule of life and why it is a good idea to do so. At the same time, one does not have to be an Anglican in order to appreciate the need for a rule of life.

Some readers might object to older sources on the theory that life is different, and the Church is different, than in previous eras, and therefore ministry is different. They might claim that writers from previous eras, therefore, are irrelevant to ministry now. It is true that life and the world have changed a great deal in their outward appearances. Many of the means through which we express ourselves and communicate are changing. The raw material of ministry, however—what clergy have to deal with— are God and human nature. These have not changed. Therefore I have used sources, no matter from which era they come, that help us know how to structure a rule of life that allows one to live with integrity and faithfulness amid the demands and the paradoxes of ministry.

Structure of This Book

CHAPTER 2 SERVES AS AN INTRODUCTION to having a rule of life: what a rule is and why Christian leaders would benefit from having a rule.

The next chapter offers the very first "rule" that I ever made for myself in the ministry: "Don't hurry." In a world that has become increasingly fast-paced, with many competing demands on one's time, not hurrying would seem to be impossible. Yet rushing through life has detrimental effects on one's spirit, on one's relationships with God and people, and thus on ministry. I offer this first component as something that has helped me in developing a rule of life. "Don't hurry" is also a suggestion for how to approach this book in general: Take your time with it. Reflect on your life and your commitments. Pray about how you might live in order to be a faithful disciple of Christ and a wise leader for the people among whom you serve. Take your time to work through the exercises sprinkled throughout the book.

Each of the subsequent chapters of the book addresses a different facet of a rule of life. The topics are those elements that form the basis of ministry. Some are obvious elements of the working life of clergy: relationships with others, prayer, worship, reading and study, and sermon preparation and preaching. Yet not everyone would agree that all of these should be included in a clergy person's life; I once heard a priest in a position of some responsibility in the Church disparage the notion that clergy should study. Some clergy spend little time on sermon preparation. I have included two chapters on the topic of preaching because it is an activity so important to ministry and also is so rife with feeling that "it's all about me."

The chapters on Sabbath deal with the quandary of taking breaks from one's work, despite its ever-present demands, and they address the questions of what constitutes "time off" and how "time off" is different from Sabbath.

Other chapters address ordinary components of daily existence that nevertheless have significant impacts on ministry. They can become stumbling blocks for clergy if not addressed in an intentional manner. One topic is money. Another is one's physical well-being, especially how one treats food and exercise.

A final chapter on the personhood of the parson presents the ministry as a way of life that points past ourselves to God.

11

Part 1
To Begin . . .

Chapter 1

WHAT IS A RULE OF LIFE?

See then that you walk circumspectly, not as fools but as wise, redeeming the time...
—Ephesians 5:15-16 NKJV

WHEN I WAS PREPARING for ordination in the Episcopal Church, my bishop assigned me to "shadow" several priests, each for a month at a time. I followed them as they worked, participated in the worship services in their churches, and met with them regularly to learn from them.

Two of these priests served churches in very small towns. One town was economically depressed; the other boasted a substantial amount of wealth. Each of these priests in fact served as a pastor to the town. As I accompanied them on errands, I noticed how they would chat with everyone: the waitress in the restaurant, the postal clerk, someone we would run into on the street. Each priest had a distinctive personality and was highly suited to the ministry in which he was placed.

These two priests were inspirational to me. I learned from

this experience that parish ministry cannot be encapsulated in a list of well-defined tasks. While certain responsibilities clearly define the work life of clergy—such as preaching, leading worship, pastoral care, teaching, and administration—being parish clergy is more a way of life than it is a list of duties. Those two small-town priests whom I shadowed were successful in their ministries simply because of who they were, quirks and all. (I will note, however, that "success" in its usual, worldly sense is a questionable term in itself when applied to parish ministry.) These priests knew how to be with the people in their respective towns: how to listen to the people and show to them Christlike concern.

Clergy may learn in seminaries the historical, theological, and biblical backgrounds pertinent to our responsibilities, we may acquire a set of basic skills in internships and curacies, but in preaching, in pastoral care, in community work, in most everything we do, the primary tool we have for ministry is simply ourselves: who we are.

How we fulfill ministerial duties depends on who we are. This reality is both the beauty and the horror of ministry. It can make ministry immensely satisfying, because one's work, one's life, one's faith, and one's personality can be all of one piece; they are not disconnected from one another. On the other hand, we can easily succumb to the mistaken impression that "it's all about me." When our very personhood is our tool for ministry, when what we are often meant "to do" is simply "to be," as is often said about ministry, then how could we not come to the conclusion, even subconsciously, that we are so very important?

The problem is, ministry is not about us. As clergy, we are not the center. Ministry revolves around God, first, and people, second. We might hate that ministry seems to be about ourselves, or we might revel in this notion, but either way, the perception that we are central leads to a number of traps because it is a lie. Trying to live this lie is detrimental to our life and ministry. Clergy succumb to depression and anxiety at rates surpassing that of the general population.[1] We work incessantly and engage in constant activity because we have the mistaken notions that we are indispensable and that everything depends upon us. We decide to move on to another parish when we have been in one place long enough finally and truly to become part of the people, because being part of the people would require too much of us emotionally and spiritually. We become ambitious or bored and so delude ourselves with the notion that we belong in a larger church, or we should be a bishop, when in truth we may simply want, and think we deserve, the higher salary that may come with these positions.

So how do we escape the seemingly intractable paradox that ministry seems to be about ourselves when really it is about God and the people? While there is no cure-all, we must have a way to step aside from the lie that "it's all about me" and instead to keep returning, day in and day out, to what is true and important. "Be careful then how you live," the Letter to the Ephesians says, "not as unwise people but as wise, making the most of the time…" (Eph. 5:15-16 NRSV). Another translation puts it this way: "See then that you walk circumspectly, not as fools but as wise, redeeming the time…" (NKJV). To "walk circumspectly," to "be careful … how you live," means to pay attention to what we do and to order our life so that we refrain from getting caught up in activities and attitudes that have no lasting benefit and do not fit with God's ways.

The key contained therein is "to order our life." We need to put into practice those habits that return our attention to God. We need to develop a "rule of life" that keeps our focus on God and on the people instead of on ourselves.

17

To Begin . . .

What Is a Rule of Life?

AT ITS MOST BASIC, a rule of life is a set of guidelines for how one will live. It provides a structure for one's life and an order to one's days. It clarifies some sticky ethical dilemmas and conflicts in values and priorities before the questions even arise. It keeps us from basing our life on a set of external criteria that bear little relation to what is important. (For clergy, these external criteria are often summed up by what other people think of us.) And most important, the rule of life keeps our life on a spiritual footing.

I propose to examine each of these benefits in turn, but first I shall address the question of where a rule of life comes from.

A rule of life is based on one's commitments. If one is married, then one's marriage vows form the basis for how one lives in relation to one's spouse. I suspect most married couples do not together read through their marriage vows and then meticulously develop a structure for how they will live so as to be true to those vows; married life for most couples is probably much more fluid, and the couple develops a rule unconsciously.

For clergy, the rule of life arises from one's ordination vows, in addition to any other promises and commitments one has made, including promises made at one's baptism. As Walter C. Klein, an Episcopal Church bishop in the 1960s, wrote in his book *A Priest Forever*, "The character and content of the rule are dictated by its purpose, which is to implement our ordination vows. Our rule simply elaborates the promises we have made and insures our fidelity to them."[2] And it is a good idea to meticulously examine one's ordination vows in developing a rule of life, because ministry places so many diverse demands on one's time that it is easy to overlook activities and areas of life that are important.

Ordination vows consist of the promises that one proclaims

18

one will uphold. One makes these promises before God and a congregation, as well as perhaps a bishop or some other authority figure. In the Episcopal Church, one's ordination vows come in a section of the ordination rite called the Examination. The ordinand stands before the bishop, who reads several paragraphs outlining what it means to be a priest (or a deacon, or a bishop). Then the officiating bishop asks a series of questions, all of which the ordinand answers with "I do" or "I will," as appropriate. At the end of the Examination, the bishop says, "May the Lord who has given you the will to do these things give you the grace and power to perform them."[3]

Even though one's ordination vows supply the broad structures for a rule of life, we need to flesh them out. We need to figure out what habits and practices must be in place in order for us to be true to those vows. For example, in the Episcopal Church's Examination of a person being ordained a priest, the bishop asks, "Will you be diligent in the reading and study of the Holy Scriptures . . . ?"[4] The ordinand simply responds, "I will." But then one hits the daily grind of parish life, with meetings, pastoral care, and youth events, for example, as well as spending time with one's own family. With all these responsibilities, when is one going to find the time to study the Holy Scriptures, the foundation of our faith? Ideally, this means time other than the reading necessary for weekly sermon preparation. How do I fit into my weekly routine time to study the Scriptures?

The second part of this question raises even thornier dilemmas. It asks if one will be diligent "in seeking the knowledge of such things as may make you a stronger and more able minister of Christ?" But what will make me a stronger and more able minister? Just what things am I supposed to study? What should I avoid? One must answer these questions when composing a rule of life. If one does not make an effort consciously to answer them, one will end up frittering away one's reading time, if one reads at all.

Other questions also raise concerns about time and the choices one makes: "Will you undertake to be a faithful pastor to all whom you are called to serve . . . ?" "Will you persevere in prayer, both in public and in private . . . ?" One needs to figure out just how and when one will be that faithful pastor: Will one call on people regularly, for example? Or will one just visit people in hospitals during emergencies? Will the pastor expect people to make appointments, or can people just show up?

And how and when will one pray? Prayer is foundational to the work of clergy; I have often said it is the most important thing I do. Even so, neglecting prayer time is all too easy when meetings and sermon preparation and pastoral calls press on one's time. Prayer makes God our first priority, an attitude that is vital but difficult when everything else we are doing in ministry seems so much more tangible (such as the sermon that must be ready for Sunday morning) and so much more demanding (such as the person sick in the hospital who needs to be visited).

Klein outlines how having a rule of life helps to keep one true to one's vows:

> [Our rule] takes us to the altar and keeps us ready to serve there blamelessly and undistractedly. It locks us in our study and slowly shapes us into masters of theology. It dispatches us to the hundreds who need us and makes certain that we pray for the recipients of our ministrations. It leads us into the pulpit and prevents our arriving there with nothing to say.[5]

Exercise: Read the ordination vows for your tradition. What is it you have promised to do? Make a list of the promises. If you are not ordained, then read the vows you made at your baptism (or someone made for you) or, if you are a commissioned lay minister, read the promises in your commissioning ceremony. Consider any other promises and commitments you have made in your life. As you read this book, you will be considering how you can be true to these promises.

One question in the Examination seems to me the thorniest of all: "Will you do your best to pattern your life [and that of your family, *or* household, *or* community] in accordance with the teachings of Christ, so that you may be a wholesome example to your people?" The ordinand responds, "I will."[6] One can say these words—as I did, I am sure—quite innocently. But then one faces the question of how to live this promise in practice. What do the teachings of Christ look like in the pattern of a daily life? How does one possibly be a "wholesome example"? And what does one do if one's family stubbornly resists the pattern of life that one believes to be important?

To address these questions, we have to look more closely at what one is promising in the ordination vows.

A Way of Life

I ONCE WORKED FOR A BISHOP who called the Examination section of the ordination rite the "job description." It outlines what the priest is meant to do. He would tell people who felt some inkling of a call to ordination to read the Examination. "See if you think it describes what you feel called to do and what you want to do," he would say. "More basically, see if it describes you."

This last statement, "see if it describes you," is the crucial one. It begins to address the dilemma of how one patterns one's life to reflect the teachings of Christ. Being clergy is a way of life, not just a job. It is especially not a career or a profession. It is a way of living one's entire life, so that one's work, one's life, one's faith, and one's personality really *are* all of one piece. A rule of life, therefore, outlines a way of life.

Because being clergy is a way of life, to separate out what is work and what is not work is difficult. All of one's living is fodder for one's work. Even though a clergy person has to avoid identifying with "priest" or "pastor," one cannot forget that at all times, in everything one does, one is demonstrating one's faith. One's life reflects, one hopes, the teachings of Christ.

Before I was ever ordained, I served a year's internship in a church far from my seminary. I remember when I was serving in that internship, and when I was first ordained (and even still at times today), I struggled with the question, "Am I working right now or not?" The question has some pertinence to observing Sabbath or to being true to family responsibilities.

The question has arisen for me primarily with two activities. One is reading. I love to read. Some books are obviously meant for "work": books and magazines about the current state of the church, or books that a bishop might want clergy in the diocese to read. What about fiction? Reading a novel is one of my favorite ways of "escape," and especially when I begin a vacation, I always choose, with delight, some novel to read. But fiction is also great fodder for preaching. To preach well and effectively, a preacher needs to know and understand the human condition. Indeed, the human condition is a primary topic of religion. There is no better commentary on the human condition, I believe, than a good novel. So when I read a novel, am I working? Or not?

The other activity is socializing with people in the church or with colleagues. When having a simple meal with parishioners or with colleagues—which is "purely social," and "work" (such as the needs of the community, or the latest escapades of the national church, or the details of last week's sermon) does not even enter the conversation—is one working? Ideally, clergy have social connections with people who are outside the church. But even then, if one is truly living one's faith, then how I conduct myself even when I technically am not working should still be in accord with the teachings of Christ. If that "job description" in one's ordination vows truly describes who I am, who God made me to be, then I cannot so easily separate "work" and "not work." It matters how I live all my life, not just the work part.

Nevertheless, it is vitally important for clergy to have time when one is not working. Otherwise, one can easily lapse into the "it's all about me" mindset by overemphasizing one's own importance. I have found one way to distinguish between when I am working and when I am not. The nature of the activity itself is not so much the issue as whether I have to make a decision about something related to work. For example, if I decide to play the piano on my day off and play some hymns, and then begin to consider which ones I can use in which upcoming worship services, then I have started working. We will look more closely at this issue of when one is working in chapter 12 on keeping Sabbath.

Benefits of Having a Rule of Life

A RULE OF LIFE PROVIDES CERTAIN BENEFITS to the parson, not all of which are immediately obvious. Below are four benefits, from the most obvious to the least.

A rule provides a structure. When I served that year-long internship when I was in seminary, I arrived in August in the new city. The activities of the church I was serving began in September because the church operated on an academic calendar. I had little to do when I arrived, therefore, at least in terms of ready-made, obvious activities. I had plenty to do in terms of preparation and planning. My mentor did not give me a list of things "to do"; as I remember, he was on vacation when I arrived. As the year went along, he still did not attempt to structure my time, other than Sunday worship, our weekly meeting for supervision, and some regular church meetings. He told me when I was nearing the end of the internship that he had quite purposely not ordered my days beyond stipulating these few basic appointments in order to help me learn that we clergy have to order our own days.

Being parish clergy demands that a person be a self-starter. One has to be able to set an order and structure to one's day, or one will never be able to accomplish anything. A rule of life outlines how we will order our days and our week, and even our year. It helps provide the structure that allows us to balance work, prayer, personal life, and recreation.

The order we outline could be very general, or it could be quite specific. I know a priest who once gave to her bishop a schedule for her week. It had each hour of the day marked off and color-coded for work, eating, exercise, and prayer. On the other hand, I have seen some parish clergy, especially those newly ordained, struggle with ministry in general because they did not know how to order their days. They ended up frittering away their time, often in electronic or recreational pursuits. Left to our own devices, often our temptation is to default to whatever is the most comfortable thing for us to do. Because I worked in publishing before being ordained, and because I like to write and to design written documents, my default is to spend far too much time designing worship bulletins, newsletters, and flyers.

If it becomes evident, however, that a clergy person has a hard time structuring her days, and no one in the congregation is ever quite sure how she is spending her time, then the laypeople will start complaining and might even step in to try to structure her days for her. When a congregation's governing body starts attempting to set their pastor's schedule, it usually means a conflict is brewing, because they are wondering just how Rev. So-and-So spends his time.

It is helpful, therefore, for pastors to make public a general outline of how they spend their time, to help forestall such questions. A standard joke is that "clergy work only on Sundays," because this is usually the most obvious and most visible day that we work. Most of the other things we do—such as pastoral care, sermon preparation, and going to a community board meeting—are confidential, behind-the-scenes, or otherwise invisible to the bulk of the people in the congregation. This invisibility means that we are not directly responsible or accountable to anyone else; we do not have to account for our actions or whereabouts, except perhaps in general terms. This lack of accountability, in turn, can lead to the temptation either to waste our time or to become overscrupulous, and work constantly, in an effort to prove our worth.

Basically, developing a rule allows us to establish certain practices as habits. Some people consider "habit" to be a negative word; they think it implies a routine, a rut. Habits, however, can be worthwhile to develop because they help with discernment. Good habits allow me to choose ahead of time how I will act in particular situations. Then when I am in that situation, I immediately know what I should do. For example, if I have set as part of my rule of life that I take Monday as my Sabbath day, except in cases of pastoral emergency (such as, a parishioner is about to die), and I know that there are very good reasons for keeping this day sacrosanct, then I can tell people that I am not available on Mondays for whatever they might want me to do.

> **Exercise:** Do you have a structure for your days? Your weeks? How have you advertised or made public this structure?

A rule protects one's integrity. A second benefit of having a rule of life is that it helps one live with integrity. Integrity means to be true in one's actions to what one professes to be good and right. It is to practice what one preaches. It is the opposite of hypocrisy, which is to say one thing and do another. Hypocrisy is a sin that has been the death of preachers, priests, and congregations for centuries. We religious folk profess all sorts of things, but none of them is particularly easy to live by. Developing a rule of life helps us to remain true to what we say we believe. It helps protect us from our own sin.

People expect clergy to be role models. I have found that even people who have a negative view of religion and of clergy still expect clergy to abide by a higher standard of behavior. When I was first ordained, I used to balk at this notion that ordained people are supposed to live by a different, "higher" moral code. Over time, I adjusted to this idea and even came to support it, with one caveat. I have come to believe that ordained people and Christian laypeople both are called to live by a high standard of behavior. Those who are ordained, however, as well as laypeople in visible positions of leadership in the Church, have a greater responsibility to live up to this standard, because we are leaders and because people look to us for how to live.

I have friends who do not go to church, who dislike organized religion, who nevertheless expect, and rightly so, that who I am and how I behave will reflect what I say I believe. I believe that even those who dislike religion still have a desire that somewhere, someone is being not just an ethical person, but a truly good person. They want to see someone who professes faith in Christ actually to live up to what the religion preaches. Thus, it is important that we who are ordained do what we can to be true not only to our ordination vows, but to the profession of our faith in general; our ordination vows are meant to express the faith through a particular role in the church. A rule of life allows us to spell out ahead of time how we will live that will keep us true to what we profess.

In addition, having a rule of life helps us to become that pastor or priest that we say we want to be, and that our ordination vows call us to be, even if we start off unsure of what we are doing. The rule helps us to grow into the role and to be true to our calling. As Klein says, we might at first adopt a rule of life "on utilitarian grounds" in order to be more efficient and competent, only to discover its value in helping us to live faithfully.[7]

A rule prevents clergy from basing life on external criteria. Clergy are under constant pressure to base their lives and ministry on a variety of external criteria. Some of these are numerical: average Sunday attendance, the number of baptisms and confirmations, the number of new members, the size of the church's budget, the percentage increase in monetary giving. In the Episcopal Church, this numerical data goes onto an annual report form that is sent both to the diocesan office and to the headquarters of the denomination. Bishops might publicly praise those clergy whose congregations have shown the greatest increase in these numbers, while congregations that show decreases might be targeted for criticism or lack of support from the diocese. The clergy might even face the possibility of losing their position.

While increases in these numeric data might reflect a true vitality and depth of faith in a congregation, they might result from changed demographics of the area. One does not necessarily follow from the other. Better numbers might reflect truly good leadership, but again, they also might arise from people being attracted to a pastor who has strong charisma but little staying power. From overseeing a number of search processes, I have observed that search committees (by whatever name) are often attracted to clergy who are what I would term "flashy," rather than to those who are deeply faithful, who are capable of caring for the people in their congregations, or who might challenge their congregations to lay aside their sacred cows in favor of true discipleship and faithfulness. In other words, congregations tend to be attracted to the pastor who acts as if "It's all about me."

Other external criteria on which clergy often base our lives are more nebulous. The most nebulous, ubiquitous, and nefarious criterion is "what other people think of me." Clergy tend to be people pleasers, and we pay attention to how others respond to us. The standard joke about this tendency, which is all too true, is that a preacher will receive multiple positive responses to a sermon, but will ignore these and instead stew about the one or two people who exited church with complaints and criticisms.

In *Six Books on the Priesthood*, in a section on preaching, Saint John Chrysostom describes "popular esteem" as an "elusive, invincible, savage monster" that the preacher must subdue. If he does not, "he involves his soul in an intricate struggle, in unrelieved turmoil, and in the hurly-burly of desperation and every other passion."[8] Escaping this monster is very difficult for most clergy.

Clergy seek approval from certain other people as well as from parishioners. We are alert to praise or criticism from whoever in our denominational structure (assuming we have one) may have power over us, such as a bishop or district superintendent. A powerful peer pressure also operates in the ministry. It can be difficult for many clergy to take a view that differs from that of their colleagues, especially on a controversial topic. We compare ourselves to our colleagues and might feel that someone else is doing so much better in those numerical data mentioned earlier, or in starting a building program, or in getting one's name and picture in the newspaper, or in the number of followers on social media sites, to use some common examples. Notice the subtext of "It's all about me" that runs through these concerns.

Finally, even continuing education opportunities tend to reinforce the tendency to base our life on external criteria. Many denominations expect that their clergy will undertake continuing education, for good reasons. It might keep us from becoming stale in our preaching and teaching; it might help us learn new skills; it might help us better understand the people among whom we serve. Some conferences offered to clergy, however, simply consist of a speaker promulgating the latest fad for church growth, homiletics, or strategic planning, to name a few popular topics. Clergy are expected to jump onto the bandwagon of whatever the latest program might be, even if it is not truly beneficial. Often the proffered solution does not truly address the need.

The problem with clergy basing our lives on these external criteria is that such criteria change. They have no permanence. What is popular today will be passé tomorrow. The opinions of others are a devilish basis for evaluating one's ministry and especially oneself. People are both fickle in their allegiances and cowardly in their abilities to stand up for the people they believe have merit. This is simply the nature of human sin.

On a larger scale, the Church today is in the midst of massive change, to the extent that it does not really know what it is or why it exists. In the midst of such upheaval, clergy can feel at sea if we are basing our life on an external measure. We could be tempted to follow one trend in one direction, and the next month or year, follow another trend in another direction. We could think that some canned program will solve all our congregation's problems, only to discover that the initial changes it brings just fade away.

> **Exercise:** Are there external criteria, such as numerical data, that you have to report? Is there an external criterion by which you or anyone else could measure your ministry that especially weighs upon you?

We must beware that we are not "tossed to and fro and blown about by every wind of doctrine" (Eph. 4:14) or every wind of the personal opinions of people in the congregation. We have, instead, to look to our ordination vows and consider how we will live and what practices we will put into place that will allow us to stay both true to God and also solid and grounded in daily life in the midst of such massive change.

Some might say that the ordination vows themselves are external criteria. In many traditions, however, they are based on an understanding of ordained ministry that has existed for almost two thousand years. Some might say that their tie to antiquity in itself is reason to dispense with these vows: the Church and society are changing, after all. But two assumptions of this book are that ministry is about God and people and that neither has changed, ever. People might have changed in the details of how human nature manifests itself, but the basics of human nature, which is what ministry responds to, remain the same now as in biblical times. God might seem to have changed, but what have altered are people's images of God and the emphases that people place on certain divine manifestations.

A prayer in the Episcopal Church's Book of Common Prayer, in the service of Compline, said before bedtime, is pertinent here:

> Be present, O merciful God, and protect us through the hours of this night, so that we who are wearied by the changes and chances of this life may rest in your eternal changelessness; through Jesus Christ our Lord. Amen.[9]

A rule redeems the time. A fourth benefit of developing a rule of life based on our vows, taken before God, is that we then place our life on a spiritual footing. Following such a rule of life "redeems the time." At the outset of this chapter I quoted from Ephesians: "See then that you walk circumspectly, not as fools but as wise, redeeming the time" (NKJV).

To redeem the time is to set all of our living in the context of the holy; it is to relate all of our living to God. I first encountered the phrase when I was shadowing one of those small-town priests as I prepared for ordination. He explained to me that the phrase has been used to describe the Anglican way of life, that the Anglican tradition is one of daily, weekly, and yearly habits.

These include daily prayer, through the structured services of Morning and Evening Prayer; weekly Eucharist; and the seasons of the church year.[10]

Daily prayer orients our day to God, by offering to God in the morning our activities of the day, and at day's end reflecting before God on the events of the day and giving thanks to God for the day that has passed. Weekly Eucharist allows us to recall Christ's giving of himself for us and to receive his presence and strength in Communion. Observing the church's seasons helps us to follow Jesus, to take upon ourselves his birth, ministry, death, and resurrection, so that these events affect our everyday lives. To have such habits as part of the structure of our life lifts our life from the mundane and meaningless and instead puts our life in the context of something eternal and holy: it "redeems the time."

We must put such habits into practice intentionally, however. They do not develop by themselves. Especially in the ordained ministry, with its varied demands and time pressures, clergy need a structure, a pattern of life, so that we might keep our attention focused on God and God's ways, on Christ and how he gave his life for us, on the Holy Spirit and the guidance the Spirit offers for our daily living and acting and deciding. Such a pattern works toward keeping us humble, for it focuses attention away from ourselves and toward God.

Chapter 2

Don't Hurry:

The Pace of Time

"Be still, and know that I am God."
—Psalm 46:10

YEARS BEFORE I SET OUT for myself guidelines to live by, years before I ever even thought in terms of having a "rule of life," I did make one rule for myself. I have had to keep remaking it time after time, to keep reminding myself of its wisdom. It is this: Don't hurry.

I first made this rule in desperation. It was summertime. I was ordained, working in a position in which I had a large portion of the summer off, part of it for vacation, part of it for study and continuing education. During the rest of the year I worked six days a week, in charge of a growing congregation. I was diligent about taking Monday as a day off, but on that one day each week I never fully recharged before launching back into work on Tuesday. There were so many things I wanted to do on that one day, things for which I did not have time the rest of the week. I especially began to ache for time to read.

In the second or third summer of this annual scenario, I realized how much better my life was in general during the summer months. It was not the absence from work that made the difference: I truly enjoyed my work and loved my congregation. The difference was that in the summer I was not racing from one activity to another. The volume of activity or responsibility was not the problem; the problem was that I anticipated the next activity before I had completed the current one. More specifically, I noticed a tendency to have in my mind the volume of things that needed to be accomplished, the desire to race through one in order to get to the next, and the general debilitating effect this habit had on me. It left me feeling frantic and stressed. If, however, I simply completed the task before me and then calmly moved to the next one, I remained more serene, was more effective in the task, and retained a greater awareness of God's presence and assistance in the activity.

And so one summer I told myself that when I returned to work, I was to live by the command "Don't hurry."

A professor in seminary had tried to teach this to us students. He was a pastoral counseling professor at Boston University. One day he told us, as we sat in the lecture hall, to close our eyes and then to imagine God's presence with us. I closed my eyes and experienced what at that point in my life felt like God's presence: a sense of comfort and reassurance enveloping me. "Now," the professor said, "imagine yourself running around trying to get things done." After a pause, he asked, "What has happened to that sense of God's presence?" It had completely disappeared. God was gone.

More than thirty years later, I still remember this lesson more than anything else that professor taught. Have I always lived by it? Not at all. If I had, I would not have been creating my "Don't hurry" rule a few years into ordained ministry. And over the years since then, I have had to keep rebuilding this rule for myself.

What Makes Us Hurry?

WHY DO I HAVE TO KEEP RELEARNING this lesson not to hurry? I am not alone. Life, the world, employers, the media, all assume that we will hurry. The general pace of life throughout the world is fast. Many facets of our common life encourage people to hurry. Fast food restaurants are a good, and obvious, example. They have drive-through windows where one can get one's meal even more quickly than if one were to park, get out of the car, and go inside—and then one can eat while driving to one's next destination.

Another obvious example of something that makes us hurry is our wired life. We are tied to electronic devices that work in nanoseconds. A particularly annoying series of television advertisements for a cell-phone carrier several years ago asserted that a message coming through on *their* phones will arrive x number of seconds sooner than on the phones of their competitors. Waiting for a silicon chip to accomplish some task tends to make something inside us hurry: we are anticipating the completion of the task, so we can move on to whatever comes next, and we tend to become impatient.

In addition, our electronic devices give us a never-ending number of things we can do or are supposed to do: answer text messages and emails, post to social media, search for and update apps, surf the Internet, play games, read the news, check the weather. I enjoy using my computer, and I think my tablet is useful and fun, and people consider me to be fairly "tech savvy," especially for someone in middle age, but I still recognize, and remind myself, that my electronic devices can change how I experience and live my life. Specifically, they can create an internal experience and an external reality that I do not have enough time in the day and so I need to hurry.

The Internet and especially email has changed the practice of ordained ministry. When I was first ordained, email did not yet exist for the general public. If I needed to contact chairs of church committees, or if I wanted to check on people for pastoral reasons, I had to phone or visit them. If they did not work in a place at which they could accept personal phone calls, then I had to wait until the evening. I might spend some evenings making phone calls. Now ministers can make many contacts electronically. On the one hand, it is much easier, and more efficient, simply to send someone an email or text message than to keep trying to reach them by telephone. On the other hand, one's ministry runs the risk of becoming an endless stream of electronic contacts. When I worked in a diocesan office, I spent a substantial part of my workday writing email messages. An endless stream of emails adds to the sense of needing to hurry, unless one develops habits that keep one less focused on one's email inbox. And, I might note, checking on someone pastorally by email or text is not especially pastoral. The contact allows people to know that you are thinking about them, but it does not allow for any kind of true pastoral interaction.

Another feature of contemporary life that makes us hurry is multitasking: doing several things at once. We routinely hear that young people can multitask easily: that theoretically they can complete their homework while listening to music and watching television and talking on the phone. Dave Crenshaw, who teaches time management, says that multitasking is really "switch-tasking": one is constantly switching one's attention back and forth between the tasks, with the result that trying to accomplish two tasks at once takes twice as long as it would have if one had completed each one separately.[1]

Some years ago, I noticed that a number of retreats for youth or young adults began with the demand that the participants turn in all their electronic devices. They were to spend the retreat without text messages, phone calls, social networking sites, emails, earbuds, video games, and all the other digital means that distracted them from the tasks at hand: focusing on God and on one another. If multitasking were so natural and easy for young people, there would be no reason to take away everyone's electronic devices when they go on retreat.

Lest I be accused of being an old fogey who detests electronic devices, and that I do not understand that multitasking is normal to some people, let me say that it was a very unelectronic task that first made me notice the detrimental effects of multitasking: I was filling my dog's water bowl.

My husband and I have divided household tasks so that he does the laundry and I wash the dishes. We came to this division because I dislike doing laundry and he dislikes washing dishes. So each evening after dinner, I wash the dishes. I also try to tidy the kitchen in general, an effort that at one point included filling our dog's water bowl. It was a large metal water bowl, which I could easily balance on the divider between the two halves of the kitchen sink while I ran water into it from the faucet. The temptation was to put the bowl on the divider while I accomplished some other small task in the ten seconds or so that it took to fill the bowl. When I did this, however, I noticed that a part of my mind was distracted. Would the bowl overflow? Would it become unbalanced, there on the divider, and fall into one of the sinks, splashing the water about? Neither of these results, if they happened, would be a catastrophe.

I do not love washing the dishes and cleaning the kitchen so much that I wish to spend a substantial part of my evening on these tasks. I would rather spend the time with my husband. I was therefore trying to complete the various kitchen tasks as quickly as possible so that I could get on with more pleasant pursuits. But I noticed that this effort to hurry, especially trying to do something else while filling the dog's water bowl, was making my mind feel distracted and rushed. At a subtle level, it was enervating me. I decided the preferable route was simply to wait while the bowl filled, return it to its place on the floor, and then proceed with whatever else remained to be done.

I have tried to apply this lesson from this simple and everyday task to the larger and more momentous tasks of my life. I need to focus on whatever it is I am doing without anticipating whatever task is coming next. After all, that was the experience that had led originally to my rule of "Don't hurry."

Living far from where we work is another feature of life that adds to the sense of hurrying. Commute time is basically time wasted, time taken away from real life, no matter how much we may try to make our commute time "productive" with audiobooks, reading (if we are using public transportation), or making business calls on our cell phone (never mind that talking on a cell phone while driving—even hands free—is unsafe). I can think of no activity we can do while commuting that could not be better done somewhere else at some other time.

A study in the United Kingdom found that adding twenty minutes to one's round-trip commute time per day "has the same negative effect on job satisfaction as receiving a 19 percent pay cut." The average daily commute time in the United States at the time of the study was fifty minutes and in the United Kingdom, sixty minutes. "Researchers found that each extra minute of commuting time reduces both job and leisure time satisfaction—though not overall life satisfaction—and increases strain and worsens mental health for workers."[2]

I believe the reason that commuting raises stress is that it essentially makes us hurry. Commuting is such a waste of time that one wants to get through it quickly, yet one is bound, a captive to the car, train, subway, or bus. Hurrying then becomes an inner experience rather than something one can do externally; it becomes a spiritual state.

All these features of life that prompt us to hurry, all the expectations from the world, employers, the media, essentially boil down to one thing: we are expected to be endlessly productive. We are always supposed to be accomplishing *something*. An idle second becomes a second that is not devoted to getting something done. If we are sitting watching our child play in a soccer game, we could be using our smartphones to text or send emails to our colleagues, parishioners, or business associates. If our spouse is telling us of a particularly challenging event at work, we could listen with one ear while we also make spaghetti for dinner and set the table. If we are waiting for the dog's water bowl to fill, we could also bag the kitchen trash. Far be it from us to let a second go by without getting something done.

At one point in ministry, I worked in an office of eight people. Every year we held a day-long staff retreat. At one such retreat, we examined our respective personalities and strengths so that we could organize our office and our work tasks to take advantage of what each of us did best. To analyze our strengths, we used a tool called the Clifton Strengths Finder published by the

Gallup Organization in a book called *Now, Discover Your Strengths.* After a half-hour test on a computer, one receives one's top five strengths from a list of thirty-four.

Of the eight of us, five people had the strength "Achiever." This is how the Clifton Strengths Finder characterizes this strength:

> . . . You feel as if every day starts at zero. By the end of the day you must achieve something tangible in order to feel good about yourself. And by "every day" you mean every single day—workdays, weekends, vacations. No matter how much you may feel you deserve a day of rest, if the day passes without some form of achievement, no matter how small, you will feel dissatisfied. You have an internal fire burning inside you. . . . After each accomplishment is reached, the fire dwindles for a moment, but very soon it rekindles itself, forcing you toward the next accomplishment. Your relentless need for achievement might not be logical. It might not even be focused. But it will always be with you. As an Achiever you must learn to live with this whisper of discontent. It does have its benefits. It brings you the energy you need to work long hours without burning out. It is the jolt you can always count on to get you started on new tasks, new challenges. It is the power supply that causes you to set the pace and define the levels of productivity for your work group. It is the theme that keeps you moving.[3]

In our staff retreat, our discussion of this strength was illuminating. One of the three of us who did not have this strength commented that the language used to describe it was negative, such as the term "relentless," she said. The "Achievers" looked at her as though they did not understand what she was saying. There is nothing negative about the description, they said. She tried again to say it was negative; they replied that they found it quite affirming, that this is who they are.

For myself, I suddenly understood why in this office I constantly felt that no matter how much work I accomplished, I was perceived as never doing enough. The tasks of ministry never do "get done"; there is always more that one could be doing. But one must learn to live with this reality. I knew this truth, but I still experienced in that workplace a constant pressure that one could always be "accomplishing more."

I believe that the theme of "Achiever" has become the expected norm for contemporary society in general. Note the description: The "relentless need for achievement . . . is the power supply that causes you to set the pace and define the levels of productivity for your work group." In other words, the Achievers set the standard for everyone else. All of us are supposed always to be accomplishing something.

Exercise: Do you find yourself hurrying through your day, whether in actual fact or by constantly anticipating what you must do next? Is there anything in your life that makes you especially inclined to hurry?

What Are We Accomplishing?

WHAT, THEN, ARE WE SUPPOSED to be accomplishing? The modern criterion is that we accomplish something concrete and measurable, something we can check off on a to-do list and show to someone who demands evidence that we are working, whether that be a bishop or a governing board, or our own internal monitor.

These days the Church seems fixated on achieving something. I have noticed that churches, and especially their governing boards, are enamored of two approaches to ministry that are based on efficiency and accomplishment: prepackaged programs and strategic plans. On numerous occasions I have sat with governing boards or pastoral search committees who asked me what *program* they could institute that would welcome newcomers, appeal to young people, grow people's faith, or accomplish whatever other aim they had. In other words, they wanted a prepackaged and time-tested program that would fix their church in some way: repair it from whatever they felt its problems were. The underlying motivation was usually that the church leaders wanted money from newcomers to help support their church.

I responded, first, that if the underlying motivation for wanting new people is that the current members want newcomers' money, new people will sense this and stay away. Second, I have said that some programs are better constructed than others and some would suit a particular congregation better than others would. Next I emphasized, however, that no matter what the program, what truly matters is the spirit behind its implementation. What will truly make a church appealing to anyone, what will cause faith to grow, is the presence of the Holy Spirit. If the Holy Spirit is not present, then no program will have any true long-term effect. If the Holy Spirit is present, then the particular program used does not particularly matter. But the effects of the Holy Spirit are not truly measurable; they just *are*.

So, the Church requires measurable results these days. This demand leads to another fixation: strategic plans. I have participated far too many times in the development of strategic plans, whether for a congregation or a diocese. Only once did I feel that any good came from the experience. In that particular case, the congregation had become fractured and was demoralized. The resulting good from the strategic planning was that the process itself made people talk to one another about what had been positive in their experience during their time in that congregation. The process boosted morale and produced cohesion. Was the strategic plan of any use afterward? Not particularly. Did we have specific goals with measurable outcomes? No. Did this matter? I do not believe it did.

Eugene Peterson points out that churches and pastors are enamored with programs and strategic plans because they are not mysterious, as God is, or messy, as human beings are. And so churches

> avoid both mystery and mess by devising programs and hiring pastors to manage them. A program provides a defined structure with an achievable goal. Mystery and mess are eliminated at a stroke. This is appealing. In the midst of the mysteries of grace and the complexities of human sin, it is nice to have something that you can evaluate every month or so and find out where you stand. We don't have to deal with ourselves or with God, but can use the vocabulary of religion and work in an environment that acknowledges God, and so be assured that we are doing something significant.[4]

The goals of ministry are not so easily measured.

I remember an event in which I had a sense of having truly accomplished something in ministry. I had just preached about how I had come to the Christian faith. As people greeted me after the church service that day, two different people said to me with eyes glowing, "That's what I want to believe. That's it!"

To my surprise, the thought I immediately had in response was, "If two people have came to faith during my time here, then I have done my job." Two people, in five years in that church: not much of an accomplishment, in the world's eyes. We had also built a new building, the attendance had grown by 50 percent, and we had a burgeoning Sunday school and youth group. Those accomplishments, however, are according to the world's measurements. The true sense of satisfaction for me came from two people being set on fire for the Christian faith.

In another sense, however, I had done nothing. One of these two people was a complete surprise to me; I had never imagined or sensed that he desired to have faith. God is the only one who "accomplishes" things in ministry; all we leaders do is set the stage. As the Apostle Paul wrote, "I planted, Apollos watered, but God gave the growth" (1 Cor. 3:6). Yes, we can set the stage badly or well, we can give the plant nourishment or not, what we do and how we spend our time in ministry matters, but we do not determine the outcomes. The outcomes are up to God.

The question of what we are accomplishing gets to the heart of the matter: the purpose of ordained ministry. For several decades clergy have heard that our true purpose is to help people find their calling, that we are to enable them to do the work of ministry themselves, in whatever way God has called them to do so. For example, Lyle Schaller describes six "paradigm shifts" he considers to be necessary for the Church in the twenty-first century, the "most radical" of which is "greater expectations of lay volunteers." He says, "Instead of doing ministry, the clergy are being asked to identify, enlist, nurture, disciple, train, place,

44

support, and resource teams of lay volunteers who will do the work."[5] Another book on ministry in the twenty-first century says, "the only real role of clergy is to just get out of the way and let lay leaders lead." The author amplifies this statement by saying that the role of priests is "helping lay people recognize their gifts and then nurturing their development."[6]

Ministry in a church definitely benefits when lay leaders discover how they can use their God-given talents in the service of Christ, both within and outside the Church. This book assumes that lay people are intimately involved in ministry. I have been awed by and grateful for the varying gifts possessed by laypeople in a congregation, both in everyday ministry and when the congregation undertakes a major project of some sort.

But is enabling people to find and use their gifts all there is to ministry? What about faith? If pastors enable people to spend their time and energy in doing lots of church work, or lots of work outside the church in the name of Christ or of the Church, but they have not faith, have we truly accomplished our purpose? Or have we yet again capitulated to society's expectations that all of us, both ourselves and our parishioners, are always to be getting something *done*? William H. Willimon says that when he entered the ministry, "much was being said of the pastor as 'enabler'—the one who humbly stands in the wings, coaxing the laity out onto the stage of ministry, giving them the tools that they need to be in ministry."[7] Willimon says he was initially attracted to this model, but eventually discovered that the role of the pastor as enabler of ministry assumes a well-formed laity:

> a church full of people who knew what they were to do
> as disciples if only they had the leaders to provide them
> proper motivation and encouragement. The churches

45

that I served seemed to me anything but that. They were full of people hanging on for dear life, tentative, unsteady; needing, I thought, a pastor to step out and model for them the moves of ministry. They needed more than reticent "servant leadership" (a more contemporary variation of this theme).[8]

Exercise: What do you consider to be the purpose of the ministry you do? What tasks or demands do you feel are placed upon you that you believe are extraneous to the role of a pastor? Does the source of the demand make a difference (e.g., governing board member, trusted church member, colleague, person in the community)?

Consider this quotation from William Law: "This is the only measure of our application to any worldly business, let it be what it will, where it will, it must have no more of our hands, our hearts, or our time than is consistent with a hearty, daily, careful preparation of ourselves for another life."[9]

If you apply this criterion to your ministry, how does it change where you place your attention?

The Use of Time

HOW, THEN, DO WE USE OUR TIME? I can recall asking this question of myself, or of the Lord, at times when I had reached a point of frustration and exhaustion in ministry, but knew that there was another way to live. I also knew that a large part of the problem was that I was not spending my time wisely or well. The use of time in ministry involves a paradox. On the one hand, we have to set a basic schedule for ourselves so that we are not spending our time running around merely reacting to the latest need that has arisen. On the other hand, we have to dispel the notion that "my time is my own."

The first side of the paradox is that we have to establish norms and expectations for ourselves as to how we will use our time so that we are not endlessly responding to each and every perceived need that arises, whether they be pastoral calls, community events, or committee meetings. Willimon quotes Henri Nouwen as saying to a group of pastors, "If you do not know what is absolutely essential in ministry, then you will do the merely important." Willimon continues, "Because so much of what a pastor could do is important, it is easy to become bogged down, sidetracked by the merely important to the neglect of the absolutely essential, unless one keeps ever before oneself the essential theological rationale for ministry."[10]

Many people offering advice about time management suggest that we mark out times on a calendar not only for appointments with others in our work, but also for personal time and for activities that are not actual appointments. We mark out such times in advance before our schedule fills up. It is remarkable in ministry how quickly our schedule can go from being empty of appointments to being saturated. For those in ministry, therefore, we should mark out times for family, friends, prayer, and reading; these are the activities that we easily shunt to the sidelines when people start pressuring us to do something that they consider to be important. Peterson says that he "mark[s] out the times for prayer, for reading, for leisure, for the silence and solitude out of which creative work—prayer, preaching, and listening—can issue."[11]

Peterson also suggests what to do when people invite us to an event or meeting that conflicts with an item in our calendar that others would consider expendable, such as time for prayer or time spent with our spouse or other family members. Instead of telling people the specific commitment with which their request conflicts (this is none of their business anyway), he simply says, "My appointment calendar will not permit it."[12] They cannot argue with this statement.

Each place I have served in ministry, I have set a day as a day off (actually, a Sabbath day) and another day as a study day, and I have publicized this schedule. On the study day, I am at home working on a sermon. I have found that being at home keeps me out of the general busy-ness of some of the church or diocesan offices in which I have worked and thus less likely to be interrupted. I am still accessible by telephone in cases of emergency or pastoral need.

I also have set a mental list of what types of activities take priority over others. When invited to take part in a community event, for example, I weigh how important my attendance is to the ministry in the place where I serve. Am I promoting my parish or enhancing community relations (I might go), or is it merely an opportunity to promote myself (I will not go)? I came to realize that if I attend every event and every committee meeting that someone wants me to attend, then I am not available—physically, emotionally, or spiritually—when a pastoral need arises.

Setting a basic schedule helps us pastors to rid ourselves of "busy-ness," which is, essentially, hurrying through our tasks. To hurry through our tasks is to approach them with that mindset I noticed in myself early on in my ministry: that as I worked on one task, I had in mind all the remaining tasks I still had to accomplish. During those years, someone read to me a quotation from Peterson's *The Contemplative Pastor*. The passage kept rumbling around in my head. Mind you, I did not actually read the book for another ten years, which may be a comment on how "busy" I was, how much I was trying to accomplish things.

> But the word *busy* is the symptom not of commitment but of betrayal. It is not devotion but defection. The adjective *busy* set as a modifier to *pastor* should sound to our ears like *adulterous* to characterize a wife or *embezzling* to describe a banker. It is an outrageous scandal, a blasphemous affront.[13]

Peterson acknowledges that sometimes pastors are busy. What he objects to is how the adjective is used "to flatter and express sympathy."[14] When pastors are busy, he says, it is usually for two "ignoble" reasons: One is that we are vain and "want to appear important." The second is that we are lazy: "I indolently let others decide what I will do instead of resolutely deciding myself. I let people who do not understand the work of the pastor write the agenda for my day's work because I am too slipshod to write it myself."[15]

> **Exercise:** How do you prioritize events in ministry, especially when they might compete with one another? How do you respond when asked to attend an event that conflicts with a personal appointment?

Our Time Is Not Our Own

IF ENDLESSLY AND EFFICIENTLY accomplishing some goal is not a suitable aim or measure for ministry, then what is? This question applies to the other side of the paradox outlined above: that our time is not our own. The alternative measure, more suitable to the nature of being a pastor and priest, is simply waiting on God. So much of ministry involves waiting on God—and, indeed, on human beings—that hurrying is antithetical to the nature of ministry. Neither God nor people are predictable or controllable. As Willimon points out, "the pastoral ministry can appear hopelessly inefficient and archaic. By standards external to the church, so much of a pastor's time can appear wasted. The afternoon spent visiting in a nursing home or the hours spent in preparation for Sunday's sermon may not be an efficient use of time as the world judges these matters."[16]

The use of our time cannot be measured according to societal norms and expectations of efficiency. Little is efficient in ministry except for simple administration. Willimon suggests that pastors need to learn to do their administrative tasks quickly so that they can get on to the real work of ministry, or as he says, "more invigorating activities such as reading books, preparing sermons, visiting the sick, counseling the troubled, and being in prayer."[17] These activities, however, are inefficient in society's estimation. All of them take time, none of them can be predicted or controlled, none of them truly have a measurable outcome. Purging oneself of expectations of efficiency and never-ending accomplishment is difficult. To do so requires rethinking one's attitude about time.

Behind many of the expectations of efficiency in ministry lies the belief that we "own" our time. I noticed early in ministry that I could not go into a church office with a preconceived notion of what I was going to accomplish while there. Let's put it this way: I could go into the office with a preconceived notion, but I had to hold that notion lightly and be ready to cast it aside at any moment. A parishioner might walk in or call me on the phone, troubled about something and needing to talk. Someone could die, or an emergency could arise that required me to jump in the car and drive to the hospital (and in such cases as these, I needed to hurry).[18] When one is dealing with people, anything can happen that requires one to adjust one's conception of what one is going to accomplish that day. As Willimon comments,

> I have always been grateful for the delightful diversions that occur in the Gospels as Jesus is on the way some-where and gets sidetracked, diverted by someone in need, or by some odd occurrence. These digressions remind me that much of my best ministry is when I am open to surprise and interruption, and willing to submit my plans to God's plans or to people's needs.[19]

C. S. Lewis addresses this notion that our time is not our own in *The Screwtape Letters*, a series of epistles from a master devil to a junior devil with lessons on how to "convert" (*ensnare* might be the better term) a human being to whom he has been assigned. Through these epistles, Lewis comments on human sinfulness: in this case, he is showing how a person can feel injured "to find a tract of time which he reckoned on having at his own disposal unexpectedly taken from him." The person in question was looking forward to spending his time in one way, but someone shows up and disrupts his plans, and he is thrown "out of gear." These events anger the person, Lewis comments, "because he regards his time as his own and feels that it is being stolen."[20] Lewis says that there is no argument we can offer to support the notion that our time is our own. Our time belongs wholly to God.

Ministry is full of people showing up who disrupt our plans, such as the person who phones or visits right when we had been planning to do something else, or the sudden death that requires us to drop everything for pastoral and liturgical duties. If we regard these occasions as intrusions on "our time," the resentment will show through in how we treat the people involved.

Again, ministry is not efficient and cannot be reduced to measurable outcomes. Yes, we can count the number of sick people we have visited, but checking them off a to-do list is not the heart of what ministry is about. The purpose of visiting the sick is so that they might be consoled, prayed for, and listened to, and so that they might know the presence of God in the midst of their illness and travail.

Even though some of us are better pastoral caregivers than others, however, and even though how we approach a pastoral visit is under our control—whether we approach it prayerfully or nonchalantly or irritably—we cannot possibly control whether the people we visit experience God's presence or whether they are healed or consoled. The effect of our visit is in God's hands. We cannot control or predict the outcomes of our visits to the sick, nor are the outcomes truly measurable. Anyone who has visited sick people knows that some visits *seem* to go better than others. But do they? By what measure? We cannot truly know the effect of our visit on someone, and we must leave the persons and the visits in God's hands.

We also must remember that to a sick or dying person, we represent someone or something far greater than ourselves, even if unconsciously. We are simply obeying a call from God to visit someone. I can recall sick people I have visited who greatly appreciated my visits, but the reason for their gratitude was a complete mystery to me. For other people, my showing up in their hospital room made them afraid that they were dying, so they or their families shied away from having me visit. ("The priest is here! I'm dying!" seems to have been the thought.)

Death, indeed, is the event that takes precedence over anything else and that also illustrates how much our time is not our own. I have several times dropped everything I was doing or had planned to do when I received a phone call that someone was close to death or had just died. I consider that death is an event so fraught with spiritual and emotional quagmires that I will be available. When a death occurs, I must assume that God calls me to be with this dying person and his or her loved ones. If there are no loved ones, then the dying person may well need my presence even more.

Exercise: How do you respond when something or someone disrupts plans you have made? Does your response depend on who or what disrupts your plans?

Our Time Belongs to God

I RECOGNIZE THAT BY HAVING URGED those in ministry to set a schedule, I am suggesting that "our time is our own," which it is not. We set a schedule that permits us to try to handle the responsibilities of ministry, while recognizing that any of it might change at any time. Our time does not belong to ourselves, nor does it belong to other people; our time belongs to God. As one who far too often has accepted other people's expectations for how I spend my time, I can attest that taking this attitude toward time is not easy.

In the end, in ministry, we are always waiting on God. We can cultivate "best practices," we can develop a rule of life, we can be efficient in our administrative tasks and prayerful and faithful in everything else, but we still cannot predict or control the results of ministry. There is no magic formula. We wait upon the people among whom we serve, for we do not know when or why they might respond to some venture we have undertaken or to some pastoral effort on our part. Ultimately, we are always waiting upon God. Hurrying through our tasks will only tire us and distract us from being able to hear and respond to God's guidance.

How do we spend our time? The Lord is, of course, the appropriate target of the question. If all our time belongs to God, and if the one we are serving in ministry is God, then we need to ask God how we should use our time. Indeed, God is the resolution of the paradox: our time is not our own, because it belongs to God, yet we cannot let others set the agenda for our lives and for ministry, because we must do what best serves God. To discern what fulfills this criterion we must spend a significant portion of our time in prayer. After a brief introduction to the next section, we turn to the topic of prayer.

Part 2
The Basics

Chapter 3

GOD AND PEOPLE:

Navigating Two Worlds

Standing in that fateful intersection between God's people and God, at that risky transaction between Christ and his Body, the church, stands the priest. It is no small thing to be in mediation between God and humanity, to offer the gifts of God's people, to intercede for the suffering of the world in prayer, rightly to divide the Word of God. With trembling and with joy, the pastor works that fateful space between here and the throne of God.

—William H. Willimon, *Pastor*

ONE OF THE TASKS that clergy have is to officiate at weddings. Whenever I officiate at a wedding, one word comes to my mind for what my role is. Not *priest* or *officiant*, although I certainly am both of these. The word is *rock*. I am meant to be a rock for the couple, the wedding party, and the family. In other words, I am meant to be solid and steady, in the middle of all the change that weddings represent and in the midst of sometimes awkward family dynamics and even occasional turmoil. I am meant to have the answers—which usually have to do with who stands where and who does what when. I am meant to give directions, usually whispered to the couple, such as, "Now we're going to have the vows. Face one another, take right hands, and repeat after me." I am meant to be steady, reliable, and trustworthy.

Of course, I myself am not the rock. God is the rock. God is the rock as the couple takes vows of marriage before God. As a priest and as the officiant, I am representing God, and God is the rock. In many cases, the couple does not realize this truth about God, but I always hope and pray that over the course of their married life they might come to learn it: they might come to know that God is the rock on whom they and their marriage stand.

Of course, wedding couples are not the only ones who fail to realize that God is the rock on which we stand. Clergy must depend on God and turn to God in all things, for God is the foundation of what we do and how we live. Psalm 62 warns us against putting our trust and dependence anywhere else:

> Put your trust in him always, my people;
> pour out your hearts before him, for God is our refuge.
> The peoples are but a breath,
> the whole human race a deceit;
> on the scales they are altogether lighter than air.
> …though wealth increase, set not your heart upon it.[1]

God must be the rock because the task of a priest, the task of clergy, is to stand in a vortex between God and the people and to navigate both worlds. All the tasks of the ordained ministry have two foci: God and the people among whom we serve. They together are the reason that we undertake this work we do. Clergy stand at the intersection between the two, the intersection between God and the people. It is not an intersection easily negotiated, however, like a simple crossroads in a flat, deserted plain. It is a vortex: a whirling mass, like a whirlwind maybe.

From one direction we navigate the world of people's everyday lives: work and school and family; ethical questions and questions about life's meaning; life and death and birth and marriage. We navigate this world simply by being with people, maybe at parties or football games or in church or talking about a movie they have seen or a book they have read. To some extent, we navigate this world not only with our own parishioners, but also with anyone with whom we are in contact who knows we are a pastor, such as the bank teller or the shop clerk.

From another direction, we also navigate the world of God, the world of the Spirit. We have learned how God has moved in people's lives in the past, as recorded in Scripture and history and the traditions of the Church. We navigate the world of God by standing at the altar and consecrating the bread and the wine to be the spiritual food and drink of the people, so they can taste Christ in their very being. We navigate the world of God by telling someone that God has set aside the horrible deed they committed. We tell them that their sins are forgiven, wiped clean. We navigate the world of God by learning the sometimes subtle and always insidious ways that evil works so that we can discern what is of God and what is not. We stand at a junction point in which we must communicate theological and biblical truths to people. In other words, we talk to them about God and we try to communicate, in word and deed, who God is. The late Archbishop of

Canterbury Michael Ramsey put it this way, and for me it is the best description of being a priest: "*to be with God with the people on our heart.*"[2]

The most direct way to navigate the world of God is with prayer, with whatever kind of sincere prayer best allows us to be in touch with God. We stay in touch with God in prayer while we navigate the world of people's lives, so that we bring God into all their quandaries and concerns and celebrations, and so that we meanwhile remain firmly rooted to the rock of God. Standing in the vortex between God and the people is a risky place to be, after all. It demands of us all that we can give. Specifically, it demands that we not fall into any of the occupational hazards of being a priest: thinking we already know it all, and we have seen it all; doing our tasks by rote, and speaking to people with stock phrases; or getting caught up in some trendy new flashy approach. Rather, we must go among people with God in our hearts, and go to God with the people in our hearts.

This knowledge that we stand in a vortex between God and the people must lie behind all that we do, no matter the form of ministry in which we serve. For example, we might run a church. But we are not professional bureaucrats, and God forbid that we should end up thinking of ourselves as such. Ministry involves a fair amount of administration. I worked for seven years full-time in a bishop's office, but God forgive me for the times I ended up focusing on administrative tasks as though *they* were what was important. Some clergy work in hospitals or social service agencies. But a pastor is not simply a social service caregiver, because other people can do the tasks needed there better than many clergy can.

Instead, we are always standing in the vortex between God and the people, so that the people might be touched by the holiness of God and their lives might be transformed. Such transformation is not under our control, however, but God's. Another challenge of standing in the vortex is that we must acknowledge that we are not in control. We may not even be aware of how God is working through us in someone's life, but we are there, nevertheless.

Because this position of standing in the vortex between God and the people is a demanding task, we might easily desire to focus more on one of the two foci of ministry—God or the people—to the neglect of the other. Saint Gregory the Great, in his sixth-century treatise on the pastoral life *The Book of Pastoral Rule*, warns against a priest neglecting the flock because one is enthralled with the spiritual life, and he also warns that one cannot neglect prayer for the sake of tending to the flock. Gregory "describes the inherent tension between action and contemplation as a healthy pastoral balance, and he rejects as unqualified those who are unable to balance these diverse conditions. Essentially, the spiritual director [pastor] must commit himself to the administrative obligations of office without sacrificing his own contemplation."[3] Standing between God and the people feels like a vortex in part because one is always trying to find the balance between the two.

THE CHAPTERS IN THIS SECTION concentrate on the central foci of God and the people. The chapter on God is specifically about prayer, for prayer is our means of communicating with God: not only in speaking (aloud or silently), but also in listening. Prayer is the central task of ordained ministry—one may even say the central task of a baptized Christian—but a task that is often neglected in favor of tasks that are more visible and, frankly, easier. The chapter on prayer will include sections on different kinds of prayer and on how to build a prayer life.

It is difficult to say which constitutes the thornier relationship: God or the people? In the ministry, we are involved with people in intimate details of their lives: their relationships with others, their relationships with and feelings about God, their preparation for death. All of these concerns permeate their living, whether they recognize this or not.

Being involved with people intimately, however, always raises ethical concerns. We have to recognize and navigate certain boundaries in our relationships with them, even while we simultaneously recognize that ministry occasionally may involve stepping beyond boundaries, while retaining ethical integrity and remaining faithful to both God and the people. We have to know when to step over some boundaries and when not to; to develop such discernment requires a solid prayer life, so that one is guided by God instead of by one's own delusions or the needs of others. Legal constructs do not always fit with the circumstances of ministry, yet the ethical standards by which clergy must live are higher than many lawyers could contemplate.

The topic of relationships with people also includes discussion of a parson's approach to one's family and friends. Another difficult task of ministry is to learn to balance the demands of people in one's parishes (or wherever one serves in ministry) with those of one's family. A pastor must figure out when, where, and how to have friends who are outside the parish and how to negotiate relationships within the parish that evolve into friendships. The chapter on boundaries will cover these and other issues that arise when one serves in ministry.

Chapter 4

PRAYER:

The Essential Task

Many times while I was at prayer, I would keep asking for what seemed good to me. I kept insisting on my own request, unreasonably putting pressure on the will of God. I simply would not leave it up to his Providence to arrange what he knew would turn out for my profit. Finally, when I obtained my request I became greatly chagrined at having been so stubborn about getting my own way, for in the end the matter did not turn out to be what I had fancied it would.
— Evagrius, *Chapters on Prayer*, #32

PRAYER IS THE MOST IMPORTANT ACTIVITY in a minister's life. If ministry is about God and people, if clergy are in some sense a mediator between the two, then prayer is vital because it is the means of communication with God. Without prayer, the God side of that whole equation is missing; we are left simply (and inadequately) with the people. Once we are relying

63

solely upon ourselves, gone is God as the help, the strength, the sustenance, and the guide in our communications and dealings with people. We have become the arbiter of all; we have opened ourselves to the vagaries of our own minds and those of the people with whom we work. Prayer reminds us that all we do is about God. Prayer reminds us what we do is dependent on God.

The basis of ministry is doing the work of God, under God's direction. It is not our work; it is God's work. We are merely a tool, a vehicle of communication between God and the people among whom we live and work. But to do this work, we need to listen to God. God is our boss. We may say that we work for a vestry or governing board, or for the people of our congregation, or for a bishop. Most clergy I have encountered do say that they are working for God. But in day-to-day life, when we are being pressured by a bishop or a congregation to do such-and-so, it might be easier to acquiesce and do what they wish rather than remember that they are not in charge and that quite possibly what God wants of us is much different from what the congregation or the bishop or anyone else wants of us.

And so we pray, to keep focused on God, that we can receive direction from our true boss. As Walter C. Klein says,

> [The priest] need not be more "advanced" in prayer than any other person in the parish, but he should persevere when others give up, endure when others collapse, trust when others suspect, and be instant [*sic*] and persistent with God when others relax. For the priest, in a distinctive way, prayer is something to be done—an assignment, a commission, a charge, a task that is at once a worry and a joy, an onerous and yet precious responsibility.[1]

64

Why Do We Pray?

To use Klein's words, our task and responsibility is to develop a prayer life—regular habits of prayer—so that we cultivate an ability to listen to God and keep returning our attention to God, through all the distractions and noise that would forever pull our attention away from God.

Think of piloting a boat from location A to location B on a river. Location A is a life lived with little to no regular communication with God. Location B is a life in which all is taken to God in prayer, and we live aware of God's infinite grace and mercy, able to withstand the vicissitudes of life and ministry. Do we ever fully reach location B? Perhaps not. I have met a few people who seemed to be at that point, but they were advanced in years and had survived a variety of interesting and difficult circumstances. And sometimes we seem to approach location B, and then get tossed back again. The currents of life push us back downstream.

A regular prayer life allows us to go meandering up the river that leads from location A to location B. We develop practice steering the boat, we become accustomed to the river and its currents, we learn how to pilot the boat in all sorts of conditions. If we have no prayer life, and suddenly in the midst of some tragedy or crisis want to pray, it is as though we are asking suddenly to be beamed up, as in *Star Trek*, to location B, with no experience of navigating the waters.

Now someone could easily respond, "Oh, I'm praying all the time. As Paul says, 'Pray without ceasing.'[2] I toss up little prayers during the day, such as when I'm driving in the car."

I understand this. A number of times I have prayed as I approached pastoral situations that I felt inadequate to handle. As I drove to the locations, I prayed that God might help the person

I was going to see and that God help me know what to say and how to respond to the person. The meetings always seemed to go better and to be more suffused by God's grace if I prayed beforehand. This is basic pastoral practice, to pray before entering into a pastoral situation.

But "car prayers," and other little prayers we toss up during the day, do not a full and complete prayer life make. These little prayers must be grounded in a more substantial life of prayer. Times intentionally and specifically set aside for prayer form the basis of the practice of prayer; such times are the meals, and the little prayers we toss up are the snacks. We need to have a pattern of times of unambiguous prayer, to return us to a state of mind and being so that we *can* pray without ceasing. As Eugene H. Peterson says,

> I know it takes time to develop a life of prayer: set-aside, disciplined, deliberate time. It isn't accomplished on the run, nor by offering prayers from a pulpit or at a hospital bedside. I know I can't be busy and pray at the same time. I can be active and pray; I can work and pray; but I cannot be busy and pray. I cannot be inwardly rushed, distracted, or dispersed. In order to pray I have to be paying more attention to God than to what people are saying to me; to God than to my clamoring ego. Usually, for that to happen there must be a deliberate withdrawal from the noise of the day, a disciplined detachment from the insatiable self.[3]

Exercise: Why do you pray?

Why Don't We Pray?

IF WE NEED PRAYER SO MUCH, why don't we pray? If prayer is so essential to the pastoral life (and to the life of any Christian, quite frankly), why is prayer one of the first activities that one neglects? Several factors could contribute to an inclination to neglect or even avoid prayer.

The first reason we so easily neglect prayer is that we may feel that we are not actually *doing* anything when we pray; we are not performing some outward action that could be checked off a to-do list or observed by others. We are not visiting the sick, writing a sermon, preparing for a board meeting, teaching a confirmation class—the list of tasks that we could be doing at any given moment is endless. And one of the realities of the ministry is that we never, ever complete the full list of tasks that we could be doing. More tasks than can be done always await us.

We even might experience pressure from others who do not understand the importance of prayer and who believe that it is a waste of our time: we are supposed to get on with *doing* something. I once heard a colleague tell a group of clergy that one morning he was in his church saying Morning Prayer. A parishioner came to the church office looking for him. When told by the church secretary where the priest was, the parishioner said angrily, "We don't pay him to pray!" This tale is representative of others I have heard. Pastors may avoid standing up to such pressures and even internalize the message that when we are praying, we are not doing what we are supposed to be doing.

Another reason we might neglect prayer is that we may feel as though we are reaching out to God and often receiving little or nothing in return. Prayer is not just our talking to God, in whatever fashion; it is communication between God and ourselves.

Going further, one could say that prayer mostly consists in listening to what God has to say to us. But the ways in which God communicates with us may not be as straightforward and obvious as are our interactions with the people whom we encounter in life and ministry. We can easily, therefore, ignore communicating with God in favor of doing something else in which the results, or at least the pressures, are more obvious. One of the advantages of developing a regular prayer life is that one becomes more accustomed to the subtle ways in which God might communicate with us. One also learns that, as someone has said to me, God has three answers to prayer: "Yes," "No," and "Later."

Because prayer consists mostly in listening, we also might avoid prayer because we cannot tolerate silence. Silence is a two-edged sword: it can feel life-giving and blissful; it also can feel threatening, even terrifying. Feelings, impressions, and thoughts might arise in the silence that we do not wish to face. Some people might even be overwhelmed emotionally by a sense of God's infinite love and forgiveness, coming to them in prayer; they do not know how to handle such an experience.

An additional reason we might avoid prayer is that we expect it will make us feel better. Prayer, however, does not always lead to feelings of peace and ease. We will address this issue in some detail.

> **Exercise:** Is there anything that keeps you from praying, even when you might want to? Also, when have you experienced "Yes," "No," or "Later" as an answer to your prayers?

Feeling Better

WE MIGHT BE TEMPTED TO BELIEVE that prayer will make us feel better. We may not say this, but wanting to feel better might be the underlying motivation for our prayer. It can be very easy to go along through life blithely, completely ignoring any impetus or inclination, or even command, to pray, until something happens to upset us; then we decide that the way we will regain our equilibrium and cope with events is to pray.

Such a motivation, however urgent, unfortunately makes prayer about ourselves. It is difficult to go from praying very little or offering perfunctory prayers on an irregular basis, to expecting to get some kind of assurance or answer when pouring out one's heart and soul in prayer in an attempt to regain our equilibrium. Such assurance might indeed come, as all such matters depend on God's grace. We could, however, cultivate a regular prayer life so that our spirits are tuned to the ways of God and so that prayer is not an activity foreign to our pattern of life.

Our motivation for praying cannot be that we want to feel better immediately, because prayer may not make us feel better at all, and for several reasons. The first reason is that prayer can be difficult. At different times, a person at prayer might be restless, distracted, bored, or afflicted with a variety of uncomfortable or unsettling thoughts and feelings. The temptation to give up at such times may be strong, but generally one should persevere.

In intercessory prayer, as another example, praying for some people is easy. The prayer flows freely and one has a feeling of peace. Praying for some others can be incredibly difficult. I have had the experience of feeling as though I am pushing against a brick wall when I attempt to pray for some people. One might never know why. The possible reasons are several: I may not like

69

the person (but this is no reason to cease offering prayer on the person's behalf); I may not be the proper person to pray for this individual, and therefore I should not attempt in-depth prayers; or there might be an evil force trying to prevent prayers for this person. Determining which course to take is a matter for discernment; the point is that the prayer is difficult, and the person praying does not feel better.

What to do in the case of spiritual interference is beyond the scope of this book, but I offer a few basic courses of action. One can enlist the help of other people to pray for the person (protecting confidentiality, of course). One can take measures to protect oneself spiritually. (I have found praying Ephesians 6:10–20 to be one effective means.) And sometimes one can simply open a window, literally. Opening a window is a simple, practical, and often very effective action when besieged by negativity and evil, whether in the midst of praying or in conversation with another. There is nothing like fresh air; it invites in the Holy Spirit.

Another reason that feeling better cannot be our motivation for praying regularly is that prayer can put us in touch with God, but if we are on the wrong track, then being in touch with God might make us feel lousy. Saint Ignatius of Loyola, a master of discernment in the Christian tradition, emphasizes the importance of the general trajectory of our life as he describes the phenomena of spiritual consolation and desolation.

Consolation is a state of peacefulness, inspiration, tranquility, courage, and strength. Desolation is characterized by anxiety, restlessness, sadness, loss of hope, and a sense of confronting obstacles. If we are on the right road in general, if the general trajectory of our life is toward God—if God is our basic orientation or what we might call our "fundamental option"[4]—then when we make a good decision or move toward God, we will experience consolation. If we take steps or make decisions contrary to God, then we experience desolation.

If, however, we are on the wrong road in general, if our fundamental option is for that which works against God, then we will experience what seems like consolation when we continue to make decisions that move us away from God, and we will feel justified in our actions. We will experience what feels like desolation when we make decisions that move us toward God, because the evil spirit is trying to keep us from God.[5]

Most people are not solely on God's side or solely against God. Instead, we have areas of our life in which we are moving toward God and areas that we secretly desire to keep hidden from God. Prayer becomes the way over time that our entire life is laid before God. All might go smoothly in some areas and at some times. But eventually, if we pray honestly and faithfully as best we can, with God's help, we will find that areas of our lives and our selves are being reordered according to God's gracious will.

If we pray solely in order to gain peace or equanimity, or for any other good reason, we may find ourselves frustrated in any event. Rather, let us pray in order to offer praise to God and to learn God's ways. Knowledge and understanding gained through such prayer will eventually lead to an increasing ability to practice discernment in all things. Clergy confront numerous difficult situations on a regular basis. In order to face these situations, we must have good faculties of discernment, developed and nurtured through prayer.

Exercise: Do you, or have you, prayed in order to feel better? Can you recall a time when this attempt did not work? Do you know why? When have you experienced the consolation and desolation that Saint Ignatius describes?

Developing a Prayer Life

EACH OF US HAS TO WORK OUT the pattern of prayer that best suits our lives, our personalities, and our situations. Working out a pattern is what it means to develop a rule of life, after all. Let us, however, make sure that we do not omit some form of prayer simply because it is uncomfortable to us. Prayer is hard work, after all; it has little to do with easily sitting down and making ourselves feel comfortable. Prayer is communication with the Almighty. Sometimes it is not easy to hear what God might have to say to us. Sometimes other forces alien to God would want to prevent our praying or hearing, such as when we seek to discern God's will or when we intercede for others.

Thus, in praying, we can easily fall into what is comfortable and familiar and forget several movements of prayer that are essential to a well-rounded life with God. For example, if we struggle with the Christian doctrine of sin—as some people do—we may be uncomfortable with including prayers of confession in our prayer life. If we are of an activist nature, then times of silent prayer may be too unsettling. Within the Christian tradition are a variety of forms of prayer, and the tradition has had various ways of categorizing prayer.

One of the ways to categorize prayer uses the acronym ACTS: prayer should involve, in this order, acts or prayers of Adoration, Confession, Thanksgiving, and Supplication, with supplication involving intercessions for others and petitions for ourselves. The basis for this practice is to provide the discipline of focusing on God first and focusing on the self last. Otherwise, it is very tempting to pray first for oneself and one's needs and wants, maybe then move to prayer for others, and only then— maybe!—to offer praise to God. Prayers of thanksgiving prompt us to remember those details of our life for which we are grateful. Cultivating gratitude has a powerful effect on the condition of our spirits in general. Thus, using the ACTS formula, or something similar, requires us to include in our prayer life kinds of prayers that we could otherwise easily omit.

The other advantage of starting one's prayers with adoration, confession, and thanksgiving is it takes us out of ourselves and directs our attention at the beginning of our prayers to God. Imagine that something is weighing on us, and we wish to pray about it. We immediately launch into petitioning God about it, or complaining to God about it, or in some way approaching the Lord preoccupied with this problem or concern. This is not to say that we have to go through elaborate prayers of praise, confession, and thanksgiving every single time we pray to God, but if we start with some kind of prayer of praise and adoration, before bringing our petition to God, our attention and focus might be drawn away from the concern we bring and directed more toward God. In other words, if we have a tendency to become obsessed about a prayer concern, or if it tends to raise anxiety, anger, or some other strong emotion within us, we might well be more able to listen to God about the matter if we start off with prayers of praise rather than prayers of petition.

I will now describe the practices that have become my life of prayer. I offer them as a way of describing what has helped me to establish a balanced life of prayer—one that could always use some tweaking—in the hopes that this description might spark your reflections about your own prayer life. At one time or another, one or another of these practices has had or will gain more importance, but in general, these are what constitute my prayer life. I notice the difference—something seems to be lacking—when I neglect any of them. They return my attention and my focus to

God and help me to remember that all that I do is by God's grace. These practices are silent prayer and the Daily Office, with intercessory prayer included in the latter. Strictly speaking, the Daily Office is an act of public worship, but it serves also as individual devotion and as a form of prayer for communicating with God. Within the elements that make up the Daily Office, one offers a variety of prayers.

> **Exercise:** What forms of prayer make up your life of prayer? How do you communicate with God? How do you experience God communicating with you?

Silent Prayer

I START EACH DAY with about thirty minutes of silent prayer. Such prayer goes by a variety of names: meditation, centering prayer, contemplation—the name depends on the particular tradition from which one comes. The primary point is to shed the thoughts and concerns of everyday life so that one can be in communion with God. Of course, as one sits in silence, all those thoughts and concerns keep arising in one's mind. One does not focus on them; instead one sets them aside—in centering prayer, for example, by returning to the word or phrase that one allows to repeat in one's mind over and over again.

I find silent prayer indispensable. I devote about thirty minutes to it at least once a day, in the morning, and preferably also in the late afternoon. If I go without practicing it, I find my mind keeps trying to hold on to things, such as worries, schedules, perceived insults, or the effect of dealing with people's problems. It is as if people and events "stick" to me. Thoughts about all these things might arise as I sit there in silence, but through the prayer and a short rest afterward, they dissipate. It is as though I am shedding them.

Shedding all these thoughts clears away stress more efficaciously, I find, than, for example, exercise. While exercise is necessary and is stress-relieving (more about that in chapter 14 on the body), it is not intended to direct us toward God. Silent prayer allows me to enter a deep silence in which I can hear and listen to God more easily because all the "noise" of the day and of life is at least partially cleared away. Silent prayer—immersing oneself in silence—reconnects us to the Source of all that is. As Klein comments,

> we have to go back to the original silence for the word that makes us one. Revelation emerges from the silence out of which creation emerged. The word of revelation is not shouted at men. The heavens declare the glory of God, but only attentive and obedient ears can hear what the heavens are saying, and by itself it is unintelligible. Silence is the non-existence of speech, but it is also the possibility of speech, the not-yet-existence of speech. In silence there is an infinite potentiality. For this reason, the prophet, in order to be a speaker, must first be a listener.[6]

Such deep silence can of course be experienced in the midst of worship. I was not always an Anglican. One of the experiences that converted me to the Anglican tradition, and indeed to the Christian faith, was attendance at Eucharist services in the Episcopal Church, where I regularly experienced a deep silence in the midst of the liturgy. The priest and congregation were speaking words, we were perhaps hearing music or singing hymns, but coursing throughout the service, like a subterranean current, was a profound silence that seemed to be of eternity.

Such deep silence might also be experienced in a holy place. Another way that I practice silent prayer is to sit in a quiet, empty church and just listen. This is not sitting and using a word or phrase, as in centering prayer. Instead, it feels as though the silence I am entering in these experiences is outside of myself, rather than inside. I am immersing myself in holiness, by being in a holy space.

At one time in my life, I utterly depended on such silent prayer in an empty church. It was the same time of my life as when I began attending Eucharist services. I felt that God in Christ was beginning to get a hold of me and lead me onto a path toward the Christian faith. I happened to live in an old working class neighborhood, and about two blocks from my apartment was a fairly new and large Roman Catholic church. The church was left open during the day, for which I am forever grateful. I would go into the church, usually in the late afternoon, and just sit. I might mull over whatever dilemma I was facing at the time, but eventually such thoughts would fade away. I might look at the stained glass windows, which were numerous, and see if I knew the story being told in each. The stained glass windows served the purpose with me that such windows have often served through history: they teach people the faith.

All in all, sitting in that church, I felt as though I was soaking up holiness. The experience had a converting effect on me. I can identify no particular thought or belief that came from sitting there, several days each week, for several years. I can only say that sitting there in the silence allowed me to hear God.

The Daily Office

THE DAILY OFFICE IS A STRUCTURED WAY to read Scripture and to offer prayers on a daily basis; it consists most basically of Morning and Evening Prayer. (The word *Office* means a worship service.) It can be filled out with a Noonday office and Compline, a prayer service said before going to bed at night. The Daily Office is a bedrock of the Anglican tradition, especially in England, where before the industrial revolution daily worship "was surprisingly well-attended" in the parish churches.[7] I had always heard, long before I became an Anglican priest, that Anglican clergy were bound by their ordination vows to say the Daily Office each day. This is true in the Church of England,[8] but not in the Episcopal Church. Morning and Evening Prayer are intended as forms of public worship, but in the United States, "private or family prayers became an increasingly common substitute for daily public worship."[9] The ordination vows in the Episcopal Church simply require that each day one reads Scripture and prays. The Daily Office provides a structured way to fulfill these vows.

When I have offered public observance of Morning Prayer in whatever parish I was serving, only a few people joined me in its observance. I also ended up wavering for a time in my practice of the Daily Office. I have found, however, that when I have omitted observing some form of the Daily Office—whether the full office or a shortened form—I notice the difference. Something is missing from my life. Something is missing from my relationship with God.

Some form of prayer in the morning and the evening forces one to start and end the bulk of the day with God. In the morning, one is beginning the day by orienting oneself and one's activities toward God. As Klein says, "Every morning [the priest] invites God to speak to him, and if this is a sincere invitation, he clears his mind of preoccupations and quietly awaits a reply."[10] At the end of the day, or at least at the beginning of the evening, one is looking back on the day, asking forgiveness where needed, and giving thanks for grace received. In either case, one is returning one's focus to God and diverting one's attention away from oneself.

Each of the offices has a theological meaning that returns one's attention to God. In the morning, "the rising sun is experienced not only as an image of God's creation, but also as a sign of the new creation initiated by Christ's redemptive activity . . . . Thus the celebration of light in the morning becomes a celebration of Christ's resurrection." Prayer in the evening, with the themes of penitence and thanksgiving, allows us to "approach . . . the day's end as an image of the end of human life," both personal and eschatological.[11]

The Daily Office, using the set forms given in the Book of Common Prayer, keeps one immersed in Scripture and prayer on a regular basis, and it provides a structure that encompasses the kinds of prayer included in the acronym ACTS. After opening lines in which one lifts one's voice to God, one says an "invitatory psalm": a psalm that invites one into God's presence. The invitatory psalms (based on Psalms 95 or 100) are a means of adoration. They force one to start by offering praise to God.

I discovered at one point the power of this practice even when one does not *feel* like offering praise to God. The experience occurred during a time of my life when things were not going well: there was significant illness in my family, I was adjusting to a new ministry, and finances were tight. I was praying relentlessly for a positive outcome in one circumstance, but this outcome was not forthcoming.

At the time, my husband and I would go into our church each morning for Morning Prayer, before he went to work. We said the opening lines and then launched into the Invitatory Psalm:

> Come, let us sing to the Lord.
> Let us shout for joy to the rock of our salvation.
> Let us come before his presence with thanksgiving,
> and raise a loud shout to him with psalms . . .
> [Ps. 95:1–2, BCP]

As I said these words aloud, inwardly I protested. I did not *want* to say these words. I was angry and did not understand what was happening in my life or why. But I said them anyway, standing in a pew, staring at a huge, backlit cross at the front of the church behind the altar. And inwardly my anger dissolved, and I recognized that the Lord God is, indeed, the rock of our salvation and worthy of all thanksgiving and praise. I felt as though God was both present and trustworthy, even though I did not understand the reasons for certain events in my life.

Following the Invitatory Psalm, one reads Scripture: a psalm or psalms, then one to three lessons from the Bible. The Daily Office provides a way to read the Bible "in course": to read through the books of the Bible in sequence, day by day. One advantage of such a practice is that it forces one to read the Bible, including books and passages that one might otherwise neglect. Following the Scripture, one says the Apostles' Creed, and then prays a variety of intercessory prayers, the topic to which we will turn next.

Intercessory Prayer

INTERCESSORY PRAYER—praying for others—is one form of prayer among many others, but for the priest, it is crucial. When I say that prayer is the most important thing that clergy do, I mean that statement in two respects: prayer is our means of communicating with God, and prayer is essential to our being a bridge between God and humanity. The late Archbishop of Canterbury Michael Ramsey says that a priest should be a person of prayer. He explains that the Greek word we typically translate as "intercede" "means literally not to make petitions or indeed to utter words at all but to *meet*, to *encounter*, to *be with* someone on behalf of or in relation to others."[12] Thus "as priestly intercessors," he says, "we are called, near to Jesus and with Jesus and in Jesus, *to be with God with the people on our heart.*"[13]

In order to be able to meet or be with God on a regular basis with the people on our heart, we have to cultivate a practice or a habit of being with God in general. Again, we need to make prayer a regular part of our everyday life so that we cultivate a habit of being with God. We cannot ignore prayer, ignore God, as we bustle about a busy day, then sit down for a few minutes and rattle off a laundry list of petitions: "Whew! God, I've got a few minutes now. Could you please bless John, and Bethany, and Simon's mother, and the Johnsons' marriage. I know there are some other people, but I forget them right now. I'll catch you later on those. Bye! Gotta run!"

I confess there have been times in my ministry when this is essentially what I have done. And then when someone asked me to pray for them, and I said I would, I realized that if I did not truly engage with God in prayer for them then I would be an absolute fraud: deceitful before both God and humanity. I would not be keeping my word in a matter of spiritual and eternal importance. Instead of periodically rattling off a laundry list of petitions, therefore, we have to cultivate enough stillness, in spending time with God, that we can truly *meet with* God with the people on our heart. We have to be still enough before God that we can listen to what God might say.

As pastors, we engage in intercessory prayer for several reasons. The most obvious is that we are bringing someone's problems, someone's life, to God, who alone is the One who has the power to do something about the situation. Some people might protest that this attitude is defeatist, because of course we can do more for someone than simply pray for them.

People might say that praying for someone is no solution. We need to get out and do something! Sometimes we do. Intercessory prayer is always part of the solution, however, because it works. It truly works. When we go to God with the people on our heart, we are calling on the Almighty to intercede in this person's life. We cannot predict the results of intercessory prayer, for we of course are not God, but in my experience, *something* happens. We cannot forecast what that change will be—it may be what we have prayed for, and then again, it might not.

The temptation, instead of simply praying for or with someone, is to try to fix the horrible situations that people face. Our modern society is an activist culture; we expect to *do* something. Sometimes we can fix a problem. Sometimes we can find people the help they need, if some kind of tangible help will fix whatever it is they face. Such help might simply be to refer people to a specialist whose job it is to provide actual tangible assistance, such as a social worker, a physician, a psychologist, or a plumber. Sometimes we can help people be reconciled with loved ones from whom they are estranged. Sometimes when a person is weighed down with guilt, we can hear a person's confession, give the person guidance as to how to amend his or her life, and assure the person of God's forgiveness.

Those last two examples, however, rely on God's grace to be accomplished. We cannot force a reconciliation between estranged family members, and providing guidance to a repentant sinner requires God's grace in addition to whatever knowledge we might possess about hearing confessions. Absolution of sins is by definition a bestowal of God's grace. Clergy are not really in the business of providing tangible help, although our activist culture likes to encourage us in that direction. Even in circumstances where we can help people by doing something, we still rely completely on God's grace for the thing to be successfully accomplished. We have no control over results.

Many times, however, we can do nothing concrete. The temptation in such circumstances is to force some kind of solution. How can we know that the solution we are trying to force is what the person actually needs? Are we merely satisfying our own need to be helpful?

Should situations not improve, a further temptation would be to succumb to depression and feelings of uselessness. This hardly seems like a temptation: who wants to be depressed and feel useless? If we expect to solve people's problems, but are unable to do so, we risk thinking that we are useless. Such a feeling runs counter to what many clergy expect of ourselves. We want to be "good pastors"; we want to be useful and appreciated. Note, however, that the focus is still on ourselves: *We* are supposed to be able to fix their problems. *We* are supposed to be able to withstand hour after hour, day after day, the immersion in people's emotional and spiritual troubles.

And that is *when* and *why* we need prayer. How can we fix

people's problems by ourselves without the help of the Lord Almighty? How can we live day in and day out with the sadnesses, the tragedies, and even the joys of other people's lives? One of the great privileges of ministry is to be with people in what are some of the most intimate moments of life: birth, death, marriage, illness, making difficult decisions, facing loneliness—the list goes on. Through ministry, we become a part of another person's relationship with God. When I returned to parish ministry after a gap of seven years, I was struck anew by the immensity and frequency of tragedy in people's lives. In those seven years away, I had forgotten how many tragedies one witnesses in parish ministry; I thought again that when one stands in a pulpit looking out on a congregation, one knows only a smidgen of what the people sitting there have to deal with. Over so many years of ministry among the same group of people, one *might* begin to learn the details of their inner lives, if one is paying attention to God and the people *and* if one has the compassion and the courage to listen. If the pastor has not learned such details, for at least some people in the congregation, then one has had a rather limited ministry.

And here is the trouble with such an education. To be exposed to all the details of people's lives can make one feel as though one has been immersed in an emotional and spiritual blender. It is as though we are tossed down the river with them, swirling in the eddies and the rapids, rather than being able to navigate all these tumults with grace from the shore. It is quite possible to have a wedding, a funeral, and a baptism all in one week or even in one weekend. In any given week, one easily can encounter people in all sorts of life situations: one might visit a lonely elderly person in a nursing home, visit someone enduring chemotherapy, lead a confirmation class with teenagers, and meet with a couple planning to be married. Each of these situations involves the navigation of emotional and spiritual minefields.

We as pastors have to walk the knife's edge of being with people in all the situations of their lives, without becoming embroiled in these situations emotionally and spiritually ourselves. We must be compassionate—literally, *feel with* them—without succumbing to the feelings ourselves or being weighed down by such feelings. In addition, clergy become a lightning rod for people's attitudes toward God and for people's emotional issues. We stand at the junction between God and humanity, and it is a tumultuous vortex in which to stand.

The only way to stand in this vortex and thrive is to go to God with the people on one's heart. It is to yield to God the people and their situations. We must be a pure channel for God's grace—as pure as our imperfect nervous systems and personalities will allow!—and recognize that none of what is going on is about us *and* that we cannot fix everything.

I remember the first time that I noticed a pastor's dependence on God and the concomitant inability to fix people's problems, although it has slipped from my mind many times since then. As a seminarian serving an internship, I often visited an elderly woman who had a difficult marriage, a chronic illness, and financial troubles. I could visit with her, talk with her, and pray with her, but the circumstances in which she lived were beyond my ability to fix. I remember as I left her house one day, I looked up at the sky (not that God is in the sky) and I offered the woman and all her problems to God. I prayed that I could not fix her situation, and by myself, I could not carry it in my heart. I do not remember now the exact prayer I said, but I essentially asked God to take her problems, to bring grace into her life, and to help me be a pastor to her in whatever way I could.

Exercise: Do you have a pattern by which you regularly offer intercessory prayer for people? When have you experienced the need to "fix" a situation for someone, or to offer concrete help? Do you have criteria by which you distinguish when offering concrete help is appropriate and when it is not?

Chapter 5

PASTORAL CARE:

"Talk Story"

*I exhort the elders among you to tend the flock of God that is
in your charge, exercising the oversight, not under compulsion
but willingly, as God would have you do it—not for sordid
gain but eagerly. Do not lord it over those in your charge, but
be examples to the flock.*

—1 Peter 5:1c–3

I ONCE SAID TO A LAY EMPLOYEE in the Church, "This work
would be great if it weren't for the people." Some crisis was
occurring, and she and I were attempting to deal with it. I
paused, reconsidered, and then said, "Of course, the people are
what the work is all about."

Christian ministry is for the sake of the people, in the name
of God. The trick in this ministry, however, is to realize that the
work we do may be for the sake of the people, but in ways that
they may not easily recognize as being for their benefit. One

temptation in ministry is to respond to people's demands and meet what they consider to be their needs, out of our desire to be liked or to be successful. Our true role, however, is to be concerned for their eternal souls and to treat them in such a way and to conduct our ministry in such a way that our actions accord with what God desires. That is why prayer is so crucial: we remain focused on God in the midst of all the other demands and pressures placed upon us, so that we have the clarity of mind and spirit to be able to discern God's leading.

Nevertheless, the key principle in the focus on people in ministry is "relationship." We must form relationships with people. This is true whether we are in a small church, in which case we most likely will have some sort of relationship with everyone in the congregation, or whether we serve in a larger church, what has been called a "program-size" or, even larger, "corporate" or "resource-size" congregation. The prevailing wisdom for clergy serving in large congregations is that they cannot possibly know everyone in the congregation.[1] Even in these larger churches, however, the minister forms relationships with and interacts with associate pastors and the key lay leaders in the congregation. Ministry is still about relationship.

Ministry involves relationships with other people as well, in addition to the people among whom one serves. We form relationships with colleagues, church officials, and bishops, if any. The most important relationships of all, but the most easily neglected in the midst of ministry, are those with family, and also friends. An ordained person must navigate all of these different relationships and negotiate the potential conflicts that arise among them. In the next chapter we will discuss a variety of potential conflicts.

One key to relationships is that they take time to develop.

We cannot hurry them. I often have heard from experienced colleagues that authentic ministry in any setting does not begin until the ordained leader has been present for about five years. Before that, according to the received wisdom, the pastor and the congregation are negotiating power dynamics, and the congregation is coming to know and learning to trust the pastor. Trust has not truly developed until about five years have passed. People have to learn that the pastor is trustworthy and dependable; such knowledge does not come quickly, wiser heads taught me.

Two particular places I have lived taught me that relationships take time to develop. Each is a place in which the pace of life is slower than that in much of the United States. These are places that emphasize relationship.

Let's talk about Ireland. I lived in Dublin for three years in the early 1980s, when Dublin was still basically a large "small town." I was not much of a drinker, but I came to enjoy the practice of sitting in the pub with one's friends and neighbors and talking. As I remember, we joked we were "solving the problems of the world," for our topics of discussion were often anything but frivolous. Back in the States, it would be called "shooting the breeze" or "chewing the fat": just sitting with people and talking about anything at all. Decades later, serving in ministry in the midwest of Ireland, in a rural farming community near a city, I learned that visiting with parishioners is the primary measure of one's ministry; visiting is what matters most to people.

The other place that taught me that relationships take time is Hawaii. In Hawaii the term for that practice of just sitting and talking is "talk story." My husband and I lived in Hawaii for nearly twenty years. For most of that time, we lived on Oahu, the most populous island, but we lived in what is called "the country," meaning outside of the city of Honolulu. We lived near a beach.

89

On any given weekend, and especially on holiday weekends, families came and camped on the beach, perhaps for the day, perhaps for the weekend. They would swim, play horseshoes, cook and eat food, and "talk story." There was no attempt to get anything "done": no need to accomplish anything that was measurable and could be checked off a "to-do" list.

Maybe one thing is being accomplished: people are building relationships. This is the basis of life in Hawaii, and this has been the basis of life in Ireland in the time that I have been there. In the last church position I held in Hawaii, one of my responsibilities was to work with congregations to find priests to fill open positions. I learned that we needed to recruit priests who could "talk story": who could build relationships with the people in their congregations. This does not mean building friendships. It means being relaxed enough to sit and chat with people and listen to them, with no agenda, no program, no desire to get something done. Such chatting often leads to delving into issues of greater depth, and that, after all, is what ministry is about.

The lack of an agenda or a timetable means that such relationship-building happens in all sorts of times and places—often when one least expects it. I might go to the grocery store in the village where I live and in the space of half an hour be offering care, of some sort, to several different people. I might chat with one person about her mother's health, and with another about how his business is doing, and with another about the state of the weather. Yes, these are just basic human interactions, but in a world that is increasingly fast-paced and impersonal, such interactions provide human connection. And because I am a pastor, and people know it, I have a bit of latitude to engage in such conversations, and the conversations allow me to model divine care for the people. The interactions are not about me. Instead, these little engagements with people are opportunities in which God provides an opportunity to be a vehicle of God's grace, as much as I am capable of doing that.

In time, such interactions build good things. I said in chapter 1 that when I was in the ordination process, I learned the value of such regular interactions from shadowing two priests. Such interactions do not depend on living in a small village. Wherever we are, even if we are not ordained, we can be a baptized Christian modeling Christ's care for people. A priest I knew who served in a growing suburb spoke of offering pastoral care to the bank clerk, among others. When we travel, my husband and I have begun to chat with wait staff, clerks, taxi drivers, and anyone else we encounter. Some people look at us as if we were crazy, or they seem suspicious of why we would speak with them. Most seem genuinely grateful for basic human interaction, which does not have a set purpose to it.

Exercise: How do you cultivate relationships in your ministry setting?

Pastoral Care

THE GENERIC TERM FOR OUR RELATIONSHIPS with the people among whom we serve is *pastoral care*. This term must be distinguished from *pastoral counseling*. Counseling requires specific training, which the vast majority of clergy do not receive during their education. Pastoral counseling also typically takes place in specific venues or contexts. A pastor in charge of a congregation should not offer counseling to parishioners for a whole host of reasons.

Instead, we offer pastoral care—which perhaps is much harder to define! We bring to people the word of God and the presence of God (as much as grace allows) in all sorts of life situations. When we engage with people, including in all those little interactions I mentioned earlier, and especially in more extended conversations, our purpose is more than to be merely kind and palliative. Our purpose is not simply to meet their needs or to tell them what they think they want to hear, as much as they might wish this. Our purpose should be to care for them in light of the gospel of Christ; in other words, their spiritual well-being is the goal. The phrase traditionally used to describe such work is "the cure of souls" or "the care of souls." As William H. Willimon says, "The gospel is not simply about meeting people's needs. The gospel is also a critique of our needs, an attempt to give us needs worth having. . . . Our care must form people into the sort of people who have had their needs rearranged in the light of Christ."[2]

The first church leader to make pastoral care of this sort part of the work of clergy was Saint Gregory the Great late in the sixth century. Before Gregory, church leaders writing on the duties of a priest, such as Ambrose and Augustine of Hippo, described the primary responsibilities as "the instruction of elementary doctrinal beliefs, the distribution of the sacraments, and the supervision of charity."[3] These responsibilities all can be accomplished in a fairly hands-off way, if one desires. A cleric's duties did not include the development of a relationship with congregants in which the priest or bishop "monitored [their] gradual spiritual growth."[4] Gregory, however, regards the priest or bishop as essentially a monastic *abba*—one who looks out for the spiritual well-being of the people.

Gregory's book, *The Book of Pastoral Rule*, describes how to deal with all sorts of people in chapters in which he discusses two extremes of the human continuum. He starts with simple and obvious differences—for example, the rich and the poor, the patient and the impatient, and the humble and the proud. He then proceeds to contrasting differences that are less obvious and that require an ability to perceive subtle differences and motivations in people's behavior, such as "those who are successful in worldly pursuits and those who desire the things of the world but are unsuccessful," "those who deplore sins of action and those who deplore sins of thought," and "those who do not begin good works, and those who begin but complete few of them."[5] His perceptiveness of human nature is profound.

He acknowledges that the cleric tending to such spiritual development also has to be concerned for people's external welfare, or the people will not listen. "Therefore, if a spiritual director is to instill a concern for the internal life, he must blamelessly provide for external necessities as well. Let all pastors devote themselves to the internal matters of the laity, but let them not fail to provide for their external life as well."[6] He does warn, however, that clerics can become too busy in concern for the laity's external needs and "forget that they have undertaken the care of souls. Therefore, it is necessary that the attention that is given to the external concerns of the laity must be kept to a certain limit."[7]

Responsibility for the People

THE PHRASE "THE CARE OF SOULS" implies responsibility for the people, as does Gregory's descriptions of how to treat people with different character traits in order to help them toward greater spiritual growth. Once again, Gregory's advice provides a balance between extremes as he describes the work:

spiritual directors should have compassion for the laity
that is justly considerate and discipline that is affection-
ately severe. . . . Indeed, it is necessary that whoever directs the healing of wounds must administer with wine
the bite of pain and with oil the caress of kindness, so
that what is rotten may be purged by the wine and what
is curable may be soothed by the oil.

In short, gentleness is to be mixed with severity—a
combination that will prevent the laity from becoming
exasperated by excessive harshness or relaxed by undue
kindness.[8]

The Anglican tradition originally included in ordination rites
to the priesthood an Exhortation that clearly specified a priest's
responsibility for the people in one's care. The source for the first
Anglican ordination rites was the work of sixteenth-century German Reformer Martin Bucer. Included in the Exhortation is the
following statement: "If by any fault of yours the church suffers
injury or harm, you know how great an offence you have committed and what dreadful punishment will be visited upon you."[9]
Obviously the injury or harm to the church to which Bucer referred was not harm to the physical building, but rather spiritual
harm to the laity.

Bucer also states the responsibility in more positive terms
when he says that the priest is not to rest until he has brought
all those in his care "to such a unity and perfection of faith and
knowledge of the Son of God and to such a measure of the full
grown life of Christ, that they give no room at all for error or
offence in their manner of life."[10]

I have attended workshops about the church in contemporary times in which presenters suggested that the role of clergy is

to be like an *abba* in a monastery, in that we guide people in their spiritual development. At the same time, however, both clergy and laity can find distasteful the suggestion that the clergy, or anyone trained in the spiritual disciplines, might be able to offer any kind of admonition or critique about how people live their lives. People complain that such an attitude is "clericalism"—the attitude that clergy think they know best and can be too dictatorial.

As an example, some writers have objected to the Anglican exhortation because, they say, it makes the laity passive and dependent on the clergy.[11] They say it diminishes the ministry of all the baptized by emphasizing the role of the clergy. But to downplay the ministry of the clergy does not, in the end, elevate the ministry of the laity.[12]

One could also protest that it is highly unlikely that *all* the laity in one's care will come to a full unity and perfection of faith that they give no room at all for error or offense in their manner of life. After all, it is a very idealistic goal to expect that all the members of a church will grow into the full stature of Christ. One can respond to this objection by turning to Ezekiel. The prophet speaks first about a sentinel who does or does not warn the people of coming danger; if the sentinel warns the people, and they do not heed the warning, their blood is on their own heads. But if the sentinel does not warn the people, then their blood is on his head (Ezek. 33:1-6). The passage continues with words from the Lord:

> So you, mortal, I have made a sentinel for the house of Israel; whenever you hear a word from my mouth, you shall give them warning from me. If I say to the wicked, "O wicked ones, you shall surely die," and you do not speak to warn the wicked to turn from their ways,

> the wicked shall die in their iniquity, but their blood I
> will require at your hand. But if you warn the wicked to
> turn from their ways, and they do not turn from their
> ways, the wicked shall die in their iniquity, but you will
> have saved your life. [Ezek. 33:7-9]

This is an uncomfortable passage. It makes me wince every time I hear or read it, for it strikes fear in my heart as to whether I am holding true to my calling. No doubt its message is unpopular, in part because of the emphasis on death and punishment, but also because it places responsibility for "the people" in the hands of the sentinel.

To use an analogy from medicine, lay persons in the realm of medicine are expected these days to take some responsibility for their health and their medical care. Gone are the days of "doctor knows best," in which patients asked no questions and acquiesced to whatever their physician prescribed. But patients still expect their physicians to be knowledgeable in their respective fields and to bear responsibility for the patient's care. If the patient chooses to ignore the physician's best advice—for example, to exercise more regularly or to stop smoking—then the results are on the patient's head (although some would deny that); if the physician does not follow through responsibly in the patient's care and offer the best advice and guidance possible, then the results are on the physician's head.[13]

The passage from Ezekiel insists that I have a sacred responsibility for those in my charge—my parishioners, if I am serving as a parish minister. I must concern myself with the condition of people's souls and not be overly distracted by all the administrative duties of the church. Nor should I be overimpressed by the exciting new prepackaged "programs" that promise a quick fix to this or that problem, nor focused on personal concerns for career advancement or worries over power politics. My primary responsibility is to focus on making God real to the people through everything I do: in preaching, pastoring, teaching, living, and even the administration of the church.

Clergy abdicate our responsibility when we deny our power, authority, and knowledge as leaders in Christ's church. The responsibility to represent Christ in a leadership position and to concern ourselves with the spiritual welfare of the people among whom we are charged to minister is a serious matter.

But what if the people are not interested in growing into the full stature of Christ (or even some small bit of it)? Saint John Chrysostom points out that the priest or pastor is in a different position than a physician or a secular judge. A pastor in charge of the care of souls might well see just where people are straying from the path that would take them to greater faith and greater life, but the people may not wish to listen to the insights or advice of the clergy. A person must submit to a secular judge, but in the case of religious instruction and guidance, the "patient" is in charge of accepting the proffered treatment. "For this reason," Chrysostom says, "a lot of tact is needed, so that the sick may be persuaded of their own accord to submit to the treatment of the priests, and not only that, but be grateful to them for their cure."[14]

This diplomatic advice of persuasion over coercion comes from one whose name means "golden-tongued" because he was such an eloquent and skillful preacher. Even if we had the power to "restrain sinners," he says, we should not use it, because following God should be someone's own choice: "God gives the crown to those who are kept from evil, not by force, but by choice."[15] We have the responsibility of offering "treatment" to people in our charge, and woe be it to us if we ignore this responsibility, but the people are perfectly free not to listen to us.

The paradox here is that the pastor must be authoritative without being authoritarian. In attempts to avoid clericalism and to emphasize the ministry of the laity, we have essentially thrown out the baby with the bathwater. We have tried to make clergy "equal" with the laity by refusing to acknowledge that clergy have, or should have, a special body of knowledge—namely, spiritual realities and dynamics. We are supposed to recognize that we do have such knowledge, while remaining humble before God.

Instead, clergy (and seminaries and denominations), in an effort to avoid dealing in spiritual realities (which we are never taught to begin with), default to employing methods and knowledge from other fields. We resort to psychological theories or business models as guiding principles, rather than to rely on the spiritual laws and dynamics that underlie human behavior. Far better would be to learn these spiritual laws and realities—such as, if one messes around in the occult, one will be burned—and recognize that included within these laws is the necessity of recognizing that God is in charge, and not we ourselves. Saint Gregory the Great describes how the one in charge of the care of souls can hold authority without becoming authoritarian ("he" in the first sentence refers to Saul in the stories in 1 Samuel):

> In a wonderful way, when he was small to himself, he was great to the Lord; but when he thought of himself as great, he became small to the Lord. For often when the soul is inflated because of the authority it holds over the laity, it becomes corrupted and moved to pride by the allure of power. In truth, one controls this power well if he knows how both to temper and to assert it. For he controls this power well if he knows

how to use it to gain a mastery over sin and also knows how to mingle with others as equals.[16]

Gregory cautions that the one who rises high in rank within the church needs to take special care not to despise the laity: "And those whom he surpasses by the accident of power, he believes himself to have transcended by the merits of his life." Because of one's position, a person with spiritual authority can "sin without penalty before humans" and therefore needs to be especially careful in one's relationship with God and with other people.[17]

> **Exercise:** What do you feel is your responsibility for the people among whom you serve? How do you respond or react to the passage from Ezekiel?

Being Liked, and Liking and Loving Others

PROVIDING PROPER PASTORAL CARE may make us unpopular with others. People generally do not like examining their lives and making changes; no matter how much we might talk about God's love and care for us, spiritual growth is difficult. And then where are we? How can we possibly do the work given to us if the people do not like us?

One of the occupational hazards of being a leader in the church, especially an ordained leader, is the desire to have people like us. This desire, perhaps more than anything else, feeds the notion that "it's all about me." We become so focused on how we are doing in other people's eyes that we focus unduly on ourselves. It is better, quite frankly, to listen to feedback for whatever we might glean from it for the future but to remain unattached to what anyone says, positive or negative.

Gregory, with his uncanny insight into human nature, encapsulates the paradox involved in seeking approval from parishioners. He says that we have to be likable without caring whether we are liked.

> It should also be known that good spiritual directors desire to please others, but this is to lead their neighbors by the sweetness of their own character to an affection for the Truth. It is not because they desire to be loved, but instead because they use affection for themselves as a sort of road to introduce the hearts of their audience to the love of the Creator. For it is certainly difficult for a preacher who is not loved, regardless of how well he speaks, to be heard. The one, then, who is set over others should study how to be endearing so that he may be heard, but not so that he can be loved for its own sake.[18]

At issue in ministry is not only how others view the clergy, but also how the clergy view the people. When I was ordained, a bishop and several other people passed on the advice that I should love the people. It is advice that I have often heard delivered to those newly ordained, that what is most essential in ministry is to love the people.

The question arises as to what this advice means: exactly how do we love the people? Obviously we will like some people in a congregation, or any other ministry setting, more than others. We may even feel that we love some of them, but depending on what we mean by "love" this could land us into trouble (see the section on negotiating boundaries in the next chapter). And of course there will be some people whom we do not like at all, whose presence annoys us, or with whom we disagree on matters vital to our theology and worldview. Are we still required to "love" these people, and again, what does that mean?

I had a clue to the answer to these questions one day when I had lunch with a parishioner. I had not seen her for some time, because she had been away on a trip. As she told me about her adventures, and about various events taking place in her life, I realized that I disagreed with her about almost every view she was expressing. Whether she was talking about the place she had visited, or about her theology, or about her personal life, she was voicing attitudes that I regarded as arrogant or offensive.

Nevertheless as I talked with her, I felt that I loved her. But it was not my love, for though I had had many dealings with her during my time in that church, and she had been a helpful parishioner in many ways, I had never loved or even liked her. Instead, as I sat listening to her over lunch, I felt as though I was regarding her with God's love—a love that recognized exactly who she was and had compassion for her. I remembered the rich man who asks Jesus what he must do to inherit eternal life. Jesus recites to him the commandments. The rich man responds by saying to Jesus, "Teacher, I have kept all these since my youth." And in Mark's Gospel we then hear what happens next: "Jesus, looking at him, loved him . . ." and then told the rich man that his love of possessions was getting in the way of his knowing the kingdom of heaven (Mark 10:17-22).

"Jesus, looking at him, loved him." Jesus sees the man for exactly who he is, has compassion for him, and offers to him the means to find fuller, even eternal, life.

When ministers are told to "love the people," this is the type of love that is required. It is not our love with which we must love the people, for that is not always possible, and when it is

101

possible, it may well be unwise. Instead, we are asked to love with God's love. We are an imperfect conduit for the divine love that recognizes someone for who they are, through and through, has compassion for them, and is able to guide them toward the means for a more grace-filled and holy life. To have such a love for people requires that we are not caught in our own personal reactions to who they are and thus are more able to maintain a godly perspective on them. We must remain grounded in God ourselves.

A similar dynamic is required when we hear a person's confession: we must remember that we are pronouncing God's absolution and forgiveness, not our own. Of course, not every Christian denomination has the tradition of sacramental confession. Penance is a sacrament in the Roman Catholic tradition; in the Anglican tradition, to make an individual confession to a priest and receive absolution is an option. The Anglican saying about such confession is, "All can; some should; none must." In other words, it is an option for anyone, but no one is required to do it.

While the dynamics of hearing confessions is beyond the scope of this book, I mention it because the priest is not pronouncing one's own forgiveness. The priest is not the one wronged; instead, the priest is dispensing God's forgiveness. It is a similar dynamic when we talk about "loving the people." We regard the people with God's love, not our own. as much as we can and with God's help.

> **Exercise:** Are you attached to how people react or respond to you? How do you understand the advice to "love the people"?

Chapter 6

RELATIONSHIPS:

Boundaries, Friendships, and Other Thorny Issues

*It is your duty to visit the sick, to know people's homes, . . .
and to be trusted with the secrets of the great. Count it your
duty, therefore, to keep your tongue chaste as well as your eyes.
Never discuss a woman's looks nor let one house know what
is going on in another.*

—Jerome, Letter 52, #15

NEGOTIATING BOUNDARIES in relationships may be the trickiest role of being a pastor. Pastors are allowed to overstep many of the boundaries that would otherwise exist in relationships in society. For example, I have asked people questions that would have been invasive or even insulting coming from someone other than a pastor, but coming from me, in my role, they were quite permissible. On the other hand, pastors have to be very careful to maintain certain boundaries, lest they wander into all sorts of minefields, including developing inappropriate

103

sexual relationships, using parishioners to meet their own emotional needs, using parishioners to meet their financial needs, or becoming beneficiaries in the wills of elderly parishioners.

Clergy are allowed into a variety of intimate situations. We are present at the key transition points in people's lives, especially birth, marriage, and death; these times of transition are steeped in people's hopes and fears, not to mention the confluence of a number of family dynamics. We have to know how to be genuinely present in these situations (instead of, for example, grinding out yet one more wedding homily). We have to be genuinely present, however, without becoming caught up in the situation to such an extent that we become enmeshed and cease being a link to God. In other words, we must remain present to both God and the people so that we are truly a mediator between the two.

As we stay longer in a place of ministry, and relationships deepen, we become more and more part of people's lives, not only in these formal times of transition but also in ongoing daily life. As I stated at the onset of the previous chapter, through my years of being ordained, I heard many times from older and wiser colleagues that true ministry does not begin until you have been in a place for at least five years. Each of the first five years involves negotiating various power dynamics, and after the fifth year, if the ministry is going well, people settle in with the pastor and trust begins to develop. They will then tell you things or include you in their lives in ways that would not have happened to such an extent in the previous years.

In fact, sometimes I have seen people leave a parish just as they reach this five-year point. (I have done it myself.) Was the ministry beginning to demand too much of one? Perhaps one was having to exercise too much discipline to maintain the requisite boundaries? Or was one too fearful of getting too close, of caring too much? Had one been defining the ministry by external goals one was trying to accomplish—such as to raise a building, increase giving, or establish a youth ministry—and once those aims have been accomplished, one felt that one's role as pastor in people's lives did not matter so much?

This discussion raises the topic—often debated among clergy—of whether one can be friends with people in one's parish. I was taught "don't do it." I entered my first pastorate with this instruction in mind. I discovered there, however, and in each place that I have served since then, that the reality is more nuanced than that warning indicates. I found in each place I have served that there have been maybe two or three people in a congregation with whom I was automatically "friends." I liked these people, and I found it easy to be around and to converse with them. The experience has made me reflect on the nature of friendship and attraction: not sexual attraction, but what it is that makes us like someone and able to get along with them as friends. I believe friendship is indefinable. It just is.

At the same time, I also recognized that I could not be friends with these parishioners in the same way that I might be with someone who was not part of the congregation. I identify five differences. One is dependence: I cannot depend on these people for friendship. Yes, I can appreciate their friendship, but I cannot count on it. If they walk away, if they decide they no longer wish to associate with me or to maintain contact once we no longer live in the same town or region, it cannot matter to me. I have to let go of them.

A second difference is self-disclosure: specifically, how much I reveal about myself to them. With people in the church, I always have to be aware what constitutes "too much information." More specifically, I have to remember that I am first and foremost a pastor to them and that they need me to be a "rock": I must continue to model the faithfulness, the steadfast love, and the trustworthiness of God. I cannot be a rock if I am pouring out to them my deepest spiritual anguish or my financial woes or details of a family relationship. If I do reveal some private information, I have to do so for a good pastoral reason and I have to be conscious about what I am doing.

The third difference is that in the end I cannot treat these people any differently than I treat other people in the congregation. I have to be equally available to all parishioners as pastor and priest. When I left the first church I served, a woman thanked me for not having favorites. The truth was that I definitely preferred some people in the congregation to others, but in my role I could not treat people differently. In the congregations I have served since then, I cannot be sure that I have done so well at not treating people differently.

There is an additional reason that we cannot be friends with parishioners in the same way that we might be with others outside of the congregation. The reasons mentioned so far have been emotional, pastoral, or organizational. There is also a spiritual reason: as their pastor I have a responsibility for their spiritual welfare, as described in the last chapter. I have to remain aware of what is best for them spiritually and not allow that concern to be swayed by my own personal feelings.

Finally, I observe a difficulty with becoming friends with parishioners: one runs the risk of losing one's mystique. A priest has a certain air of mystery, a mystery that arises because we simultaneously deal with profound situations and topics while also maintaining a certain reserve or dignity. Clergy need to have *gravitas*. If, however, we become friends with a parishioner to the extent that our faults become too clear to them—quite frankly, if they see us sin in word, attitude, or deed a bit too often—then we lose that mystique and gravitas. One can lose one's mystique with parishioners not only by becoming friends with them. Becoming irate with a parishioner will have the same effect, as will complaining to one parishioner about another.

One can understand how such a loss might occur by reflecting on a dynamic that might happen with some clergy spouses. A clergy spouse lives with the pastor and sees the pastor with all one's warts, sins, and imperfections. I have spoken with spouses who have lost all respect for the ordained person because the person they see and hear in the pulpit and in church settings seems inconsistent with the personality they see at home. They hear sermons preaching love and forgiveness, for example, but do not experience such in their marriage. They come to believe that the parson to whom they are married is a fraud. Becoming friends with parishioners can risk a similar outcome, although not to the same extent.

As with most dynamics in ministry, however, a paradox is involved in these observations about becoming friends with parishioners. We cannot depend on our parishioners to meet our own emotional needs, but we must remain vulnerable. We cannot appear as a stiff "professional." There is a fine line between maintaining proper boundaries and closing oneself off so much that one appears stiff.

I remember experiencing this paradox during my first year in seminary. I worked a field education placement in a psychiatric halfway house. My role was to go to the halfway house two evenings a week and on some Saturdays, eat dinner with the residents, talk with them, and arrange outside activities with some of them. For the first four months or so, things went along well enough, but I had no real connection with the residents.

Then in February, I suddenly underwent emergency surgery. I was in the hospital and then the school infirmary for two weeks. When I finally returned to the halfway house, the residents were more comfortable with me, as though they trusted me more. For the rest of the school year, my relationships with them were deeper and more relaxed. My supervisor suggested that my having to undergo surgery made me more of a real person to the residents. I was more like them, even though my hospitalization had been for physical reasons, and theirs for mental. I was no longer just a seminarian, on my way to being a "professional." I became a parson, a representative person.

> **Exercise:** Do you consider any of your parishioners to be friends? Are they friends in a different way (or not) than people with whom you are not in ministry? What guidelines have you adopted for how you will conduct these friendships? How do you walk the line between being vulnerable and a "real person" while refraining from using your parishioners to fill your own emotional needs?

"Forsaking All Others"

THE PHRASE "FORSAKING ALL OTHERS" comes, of course, from traditional marriage vows. This phrase encapsulates the challenges that arise as the married pastor develops relationships with others, including parishioners, colleagues, and superiors. In the marriage vows, the phrase likely means that one is promising to refrain from having romantic or sexual attachments with persons other than one's own spouse. However, I have come to think that the phrase has a wider application.

It is very easy for a pastor to develop strong attachments to

Participant Observer

One of the most useful classes I took in seminary was not in theology, the Bible, pastoral care, or any other traditional topic for a seminary. It was an ethnography class. The seminary offered it in order to teach us students that in ministry we are participant observers: we must enter a community and be fully a part of it, while also remaining separate from it.

Within the community in which one serves, the parson must walk a fine line between being part of the community, yet remaining separate from it. If one becomes too immersed in the community, one is not able to have sufficient distance to be able to bring the gospel of Christ to bear on any situation in which the community finds itself. One must always be able to stand back and discern God's presence or God's call in the midst of everyday life, especially during tragedy or conflict.

I am reminded of watching expert surfers standing on the shore for a good length of time, watching the waves to study what is happening at that moment before venturing into the water, even though the surf break might be one they had surfed hundreds of times. They must recognize the conditions of the ocean, the waves, the wind, and any other circumstances before they themselves head into a potentially dangerous situation. The parson must be able to step back and survey what is happening in order to be able to assess what to do in any situation, while remaining firmly rooted in prayer.

If the pastor is too aloof and has no connection with the people, there is little relationship on which to build the trust necessary for the people to accept the pastor's words and actions as authentic. In other words, if pastors are either too distant or too enmeshed with the people, they will lose their authority. Pastors must be able to relate always to both the people and to God.

and relationships with parishioners. As said above, we deal with intense and intimate situations and topics. We are permitted to overstep certain boundaries that others have to maintain. The needs of one's parishioners are truly never-ending; one could spend all of one's time visiting people, or one could continually drop everything to attend to yet one more person. I have heard parishioners speak glowingly of pastors who have visited a dying family member every day of the week, for example. In some cases, this might be necessary. But then pastors have to choose carefully just how many people they have the time to treat this way.

More important here, one has to be aware when such care for one's parishioners impinges on one's own marriage or family. Thus, the vow of "forsaking all others" suggests that one's spouse has to remain the most important person in one's life, and all others come far down the line in importance. In ministry, it is very easy to rationalize to oneself—and attempt to convince the spouse—that time spent away from one's spouse or family, or skipping yet one more family dinner or family vacation, is necessary and, indeed, one's godly duty, when in fact one might just need to be needed.

Of course, this conflict between the time and attention devoted to parishioners versus one's spouse is one reason that the Roman Catholic Church maintains the policy of clerical celibacy. The priest is to remain celibate and single in part so that no other relationships compete for his attention and attachment. I feel it is not my place to comment on Roman Catholic doctrine, but I will say that as I serve as a priest I appreciate having a husband, for a whole variety of reasons. Many of these reasons help me to be a better pastor and priest than I would have been otherwise. But I have had to learn that my husband comes first in time and attention. I am thankful that he understands the pastoral demands of ministry; and I am equally thankful that he will occasionally tell me if I am devoting too much time and attention to parishioners, or to my "job" in general, to the detriment of our marriage as well as to my ability to pay attention to God.

For my part, I have come to believe that my marriage vows come before my ordination vows, for a variety of reasons. For one, they came first in time; I was married before I was ordained an Episcopal priest. But even if that were not the case, the marriage vows still are primary. In marriage, I have made vows before God to one particular person. In ordination, I have made vows to God to live and to conduct my ministry in a particular way, but the people come and go. Either I leave a particular ministry setting, or within one setting, people move away, die, or become more or less intensely involved in parish life. I do not have the same level of sustained commitment to them and their welfare, nor the same level of attachment, as I do with my husband.

The third reason that my marriage vows come before my ordination vows is that I hope my marriage will endure long past the point that I retire from active ministry, if God so decrees that we both are still alive past that point. A marriage is meant to be more enduring—until death, as traditional marriage vows say—than one's relationship with people among whom one serves in ministry.

I have often said that I would much rather be a member of the clergy than a clergy spouse. Spouses, and clergy families in general, endure a number of pressures and stresses. A full exposition of them is beyond the scope of this book. Suffice it to say that ministry necessitates strong commitment in a marriage. Ministry demands intense training, a change in one's way of life, and expectations for behavior that the spouse might not be interested in following. This is true to some extent for lay ministry as well.

111

The Basics

I have observed that people in a congregation expect even lay ministers—those with pastoral or liturgical responsibilities—to exhibit high standards of faith and ethical behavior.

"Forsaking all others" also has implications for how the pastor will interact with others, both parishioners and colleagues, in some concrete situations. In one's rule of life, the pastor has to establish guidelines before encountering some potentially thorny situations. I offer two examples. Where I currently serve, the parish office is in the church-owned house in which my husband and I live. It is a big old house on a fair expanse of land. In other words, it is isolated. I also visit parishioners in their own homes. My husband and I have established a rule that neither one of us will be alone in the Rectory with a member of the opposite sex, nor will I visit alone in a house with a male parishioner (other than perhaps one of an advanced age, but I am increasingly closer to such an age!). This practice may seem extreme, but it is in keeping with advice of the past several decades that pastors should not meet in offices with closed doors, even in a multi-staffed church office, unless the door has a window in it. The practice is to protect my husband, myself, and, frankly, the parishioners from gossip, temptations to misconduct, and suspicion.

The second example applies to colleagues. Long ago, I made a rule for myself that I would not have lunch with male colleagues. The only times I have broken this rule have been when there was a clear power difference between the colleague and me: when a bishop took me to lunch on my first day in a new job, for example, or when I was a parish priest and had a pastoral lunch meeting with a parishioner. When a male colleague invited me to lunch, however, "to get to know one another better," I declined. The invitation seemed innocuous enough, but I saw no particular reason that I had to "get to know" this colleague any better than

I already did or why I needed to meet with him in a more private, personal context. I later discovered that this particular colleague had a pattern of going to lunch with the female priests in the diocese.

Naturally the married pastor should have healthy friendships with people other than with one's spouse. In one's rule of life, however, one has to consider how often and in what ways one will interact with these friends, as well as how one will be connected with others on social media.

> **Exercise:** How do you balance relationships with your family and parishioners or others with whom you are in ministry? If you are married, do you and your spouse have any guidelines or agreements about how often and in what ways you will, or will not, interact with those in your care? How do you choose those with whom you will connect on social media?

Confidentiality, Privacy, and Secrecy

THOSE IN MINISTRY HAVE ACCESS to so much confidential information! And people will try their best to pry it out of us. For example: A parishioner is sick or goes through surgery, and others will try to find out from the pastor how the person is faring. To tell them may be tempting, in part because members of the church are meant to care for one another and therefore we may think that others can help tend to the sick person. Or perhaps we are tempted to divulge what we know in order to show just how "on top of things" we are and to demonstrate that we have, in fact, been looking after our parishioners.

No matter the underlying reason for the desire to divulge

information about others, it is seldom wise to do so. I routinely have told a vestry (governing board) that I will not tell them or anyone else in the parish the state of someone's health. I had to do this when a person well-respected in the church was ill but did not want anyone to know. Some people had the information, some did not, but I knew that if I was the source of any updates on the person's health that I would be violating confidentiality.

This issue becomes particularly sticky when a church has any kind of healing ministry, as has been the case in several of the congregations in which I have served. A Christian healing ministry could involve people actively praying in person for those who are sick. (Might I note that people undertaking such a ministry need to be trained, for perhaps no ministry is so rife for people coming to think "it's all about me" than the healing ministry. But that is another topic.) A ministry of Christian healing might also simply involve the church keeping a prayer list that is read during worship services. One has to be very careful that any ministry of healing does not become fodder for gossip in the name of compassion and Christian charity.

Keeping confidentiality is a matter of trust. Pastors have access to people's private lives. Occasionally we also have access to secrets, especially if we are a priest hearing sacramental confessions. I adhere to the instruction in my own religious tradition that says, "The secrecy of a confession is morally absolute for the confessor, and must under no circumstances be broken." By the way, the priest also does not later discuss the content with the one making confession: "The content of a confession is not normally a matter of subsequent discussion."[1] If the sin has been laid aside and absolution given, the matter should not need to be revisited.

The topics of confidentiality, privacy, and secrecy also apply to the life of the pastor. We might keep a number of issues and feelings private from those among whom we serve because to do otherwise would be inappropriate: we would be using the people to fill our own emotional needs, and they might well feel uncomfortable by knowing the information.

Secrets, on the other hand, are those pieces of information that we fear would have negative consequences on ourselves, our lives, our ministry, or the lives of our families if revealed. A pastor might have a number of private matters, but to have secrets is unwise, although probably unavoidable. Of course this means that as much as possible, we should avoid behaviors and situations that might require a secret! One also has to beware of keeping secrets in one's personal relationships because like all secrets, these, too, take an emotional and spiritual toll. It might be something as seemingly innocuous as sending off a few more work-related emails on the sly when your spouse thinks you have finally laid your work aside.

> **Exercise:** How do you maintain the confidentiality required in your ministry, especially when confronted with curious or well-meaning queries from others? How do you deal with other people's secrets?

RELATIONSHIPS WITH OTHER PEOPLE bring both joy to ministry and yet involve the pastor in some of the thorniest situations one might encounter. To weather the difficulties, and at the same time to continue to enjoy ministry, one again has to keep one's focus on God. The way I have come to think of it is that we need to be faithful to God in how we treat others. To say we have to "love the people," or respond to their needs, or use any other such phrases, could still leave us mired in severe difficulties. Whether I am dealing with parishioners, colleagues, a bishop, my husband, or my family and friends, I have realized that I must remain faithful to God in how I treat them all.

Part 3
Central Tasks of Ministry

Introduction to Central Tasks of Ministry

ORDINATION VOWS OUTLINE how clergy are to live, and they define the basic responsibilities of ministry. One's responsibilities are categorized by word and sacrament, but the vows themselves mention particular tasks: pastoral care, which we addressed in a previous chapter; leading worship, including the administration of sacraments; preaching the word of God; and one task that some people may not consider to be so central and necessary to the practice of ministry: reading and study. The chapters in this section address these particular responsibilities.

No doubt clergy could think of other tasks that they would consider central to their ministry. Social action or advocacy come to mind as one possible example; involvement in community affairs is another. I have not included these. The United Methodist Church specifically mentions them in the General Examination for all candidates: "Will you, in the exercise of your ministry, ... participate in the life and work of the community, and ... seek peace, justice, and freedom for all people?"[1] In the Episcopal Church, the ordination of a Deacon speaks of the ministry of this office as being one of service in the community.[2]

Such activities are, indeed, expressions of the vows to care for people, or to live as an example to others, or to model our life according to the gospel of Christ. As individual clergy forge a rule of life, they may choose activities not specifically mentioned in the chapters that follow. I have included here those general tasks that historically have been included in ordination vows, and still are, especially the vows of those being ordained as ministers of word and sacrament.

Having said that, however, I will add two additional comments. First, lay people commissioned for a liturgical or pastoral role in the church will also need to include in their own rule of life an attention to worship, to reading and study, and perhaps to sermon preparation and preaching, depending on whether they are authorized for such a ministry.

Second, all baptized Christians are certainly expected to include in their own lives worship and reading the Bible. These activities are not restricted to those who are ordained!

Chapter 7

WORSHIP:

Opening a Lens on the Realm of God

Though it is not always apparent, the worship of the church is a dramatic enactment of a great and cosmic trial in which the justice of God is poised against all the powers that spoil creation and enslave human life. In this trial Christ is the one true and faithful witness. "For this I was born, and for this I have come into the world, to bear witness to the truth" (John 18:37). All human testimony is authentic only to the extent that it remains faithful to the witness of Christ.
—Thomas G. Long, "Preaching as Bearing Witness"

When my husband and I are on vacation, we try to go to church wherever we happen to be. If I do not attend church, I feel as though something is missing, despite my daily practice of prayer. Faith, God, and the basic story of the Christian faith form a background to my life, like music playing

121

somewhere in the background of my consciousness. And when I do not go to church, the music becomes fainter.

I remember once we were on vacation for three weeks. We went to church the first and third weeks but not the second. On that Sunday, we were in a rural area, visiting friends. The friends lived in the back of beyond, as the saying goes, but there was a little Methodist church down the road that I considered attending. As it turns out, I confess, we did not go. We sat outside and chatted with our friends.

The time we spent talking was a blessed time. We sat under tall trees to the side of their house on a little hill looking out over the fields of Kentucky. A fine breeze blew on that hilltop, and the July sun was not yet too hot. We talked about serious things: children and grandchildren, the purpose of our lives, and our hopes. It was good to be with them, and I was reminded that friendship is a blessed thing. But it was not the same as worship. Perhaps it would have been different had we been talking about God, for talking about faith can feed faith, can turn up the volume on that background music, but even talking about God is not the same as worshipping God.

In the days that followed, I noticed that something was missing. The following Sunday when I did go to church, I felt as though I was soaking up God because I was very thirsty. I had the feeling of, Oh yes, this is what it's all about. Even though it was one of those Sundays that churches sometimes have that are like a liturgical comedy of errors, being in a church and worshipping was still a relief. It was as though the background music had become faint enough that I had a hard time hearing it, and worshipping made the volume go back up again.

But it was not just that the music of faith had become faint. It was as though some other mindset started to become more prominent, what you might call the noise of the world. Without the regular disciplines of worship, prayer, and reading Scripture, life becomes more humdrum, boring, ordinary. One's life lacks verve and vitality. It is as though my mind remembers, but somehow I fail to experience, the basic story of the Christian faith: that new life and hope arise out of death and despair, that God is faithful, that in the midst of ordinary moments there is the potential of holiness and grace.

It matters to be in the company of the people of God, to hear God's word together, to receive the Sacraments, to keep tuned to the music of faith. Worship is the fundamental act of the Church; without worship, if the Church fails to be the central time and place that people can gather to turn their attention to God, the Church ceases to fulfill its true purpose.

So what is the place of corporate worship (meaning the worship of the Church, the worship of a congregation) in an individual pastor's rule of life? Are there traps and pitfalls of which one must be aware? Because leading worship is a primary activity in a clergy person's life, one can succumb to the temptation to treat it as a performance or simply another task, rather than as a time of coming before God.

This topic, perhaps more than any other in this book, applies also to the Christian lay leader. More and more, in many denominations, laypeople are being trained and commissioned to lead worship in an individual congregation or in a group of congregations. Such leaders might think that they are simply standing before a group of people and conducting the service, according to a pattern that they have been taught. Instead, they are being called upon to represent the Church and to serve God. The congregation will expect more from these leaders, in terms of high standards of faith and behavior, even in their everyday lives, whether or not the leaders like or realize that they are subject to such expectations.

Worship Is About God

Worship has no utilitarian material purpose. Its sole purpose is to turn the attention of a group of people to God, their Creator, Redeemer, and Sanctifier, and to give praise and thanksgiving to God. Worship does indeed have practical *effects*, such as growing the church, or bringing together a group of people in fellowship with one another, or helping individuals to feel better, or giving people a time and place to relax, but these effects are not the *purpose* of the worship service.

Nor is worship meant to be a vehicle whereby the worship leader can demonstrate one's dramatic capabilities. When I was in seminary, we students commented to one another that we who were training for ministry had come to seminary primarily from three different backgrounds: politics, psychology, and drama. Leading worship can be an exhilarating experience for someone who likes to stand before a group of people and put on a show. One is serving amid (one hopes) the power of the Spirit of the Lord God Almighty.

Worship is a response to God's grace; we worship in gratitude for the grace and salvation given to us in Jesus Christ. Worship also, as said above, reminds us of a different reality—a reality that is more real than the one that surrounds us in the world, because it is of eternity and truth. "Prayer is not so much an 'activity,'" William H. Willimon says, "as a way of life for the church. We worship God, not for utilitarian or pragmatic purposes, but rather because we have been loved."[1]

"A way of life for the church": worship also must be a way of life for the clergy or lay leader who regularly leads worship. I often recall the Dean of a seminary saying at the beginning of a new school year that those in the second year would notice that one of their classmates was no longer present. The reason was that the Dean had discovered that the student and his wife were not attending church on Sundays because, they reasoned, "we will be attending Sunday worship for the rest of our lives," and so they were taking time off from Sunday worship while they had the chance. The student was asked to leave the seminary. Worship must be an automatic activity for those who do or will lead worship in the church; regular attendance at worship, even if we are not leading it, must be part of our own rule of life.

Different traditions and denominations have many styles of worship according to their history, and different styles of worship suit people of different temperaments. The discussion of the relative values of different styles of worship has become controversial, and such a discussion is beyond the scope of this book. No matter what the style of worship in one's church, however, the person in charge of planning worship might keep the following two points in mind: Worship is not meant to be a spectator activity. And, worship is "supposed to be boring," as my mentor in my church internship used to say. Both these points help the person leading worship, and the worshippers, to remember that worship is about God and not about themselves.

The first point is that worship is not meant to be a spectator activity. There are many churches these days in which a worship service is basically an elaborate show. Often these "shows" are very well-done, professionally speaking, in terms of lighting, sound, speaking, and the flow of the event. But the assembled congregation is passive; they are not required to participate by speaking, praying, or singing. It is true that sometimes, when attending church, one just wants to sit there and "let it wash over you," but such is generally the case in specific circumstances (a person in deep grief comes to mind). Normally, if one is attending worship, one should be required to respond *in some way*, so that the worshipper is making a personal response and commitment to God.

Elaborate and flashy shows are not the only form of worship that turns the congregation into spectators. In my own tradition, worship in a cathedral (or other church) with a good choir can have the same effect, if the congregation sits and listens to the choir sing various pieces of the service that normally the congregation would say or sing, such as the Lord's Prayer. The service can be beautiful, but the congregation has little opportunity to express their own faith demonstratively.[2]

Services that do not require a response from the worshipper *possibly* could have a converting effect, whether the worship is of the flashy show or the traditional choral variety (or anything else). By sitting in the congregation and letting the service "wash over them," the attendees might be moved to want to respond. God can work through many things, and as I have often observed, God can use our own, less-than-holy motivations to bring us to faith. I know that personally, before I ever followed a Christian path or considered myself a Christian, attending worship in one of the great English cathedrals spurred my heart and soul to want more. In conclusion, then, a church might offer several types of worship services: some for the uninitiated (what have been called "seeker services") and some for those wanting to delve deeper.

The second point offered above might appear antithetical to the first. "Worship is *supposed* to be boring," I heard repeatedly from my mentor when I served as a seminarian intern in a church.

He would say this to those who objected to the service—a typical Protestant one of readings, hymns, prayers, and a sermon—being "boring." Allowing people to avoid such boredom is exactly the reason for the kinds of worship services mentioned in the previous paragraphs: a service that is a well-done "show" with lots of stimulation. The prevailing argument for such services is that people these days have short attention spans and are used to constant stimulation; they will not sit still, or appreciate, a more traditional kind of service, with a fair amount of silence and with elements that might feel alien to their sensibilities, not to mention a message that is completely alien to anything they know.

The point my internship mentor was making with his provocative statement is that worship is supposed to be different from forms of entertainment. It is supposed to show us a different way of being; it is meant to open a lens on the realm of God, where shows of expertise pale in comparison with the power of God. Worship is meant to offer us a fair amount of silence, even the silence that can run within the liturgy itself. As Willimon says, "The church withdraws from what the world calls 'real' in order to better discern the world as God intends—the new heaven and new earth (Rev. 21:1) of which the church is a foretaste, a world more 'real' than what the world calls reality."[3]

Establishing a Customary

A USEFUL TASK FOR A CLERGY PERSON in charge of a congregation is to write what is called a "customary" for the church. Because a customary is essentially the congregation's "rule of life" for its worship, it becomes part of the parish minister's own rule of life as well. A customary addresses topics such as scheduling, format, and responsibilities. Some questions that could be addressed in a customary are as follows:

- Is the main service of the church on a Sunday morning, or is there some reason that another day or time would work better?

- How many services will there be, and at what time(s)?

- Will there be any weekday services?

- Will the clergy in charge lead all the worship services, or are there others (assistant clergy, lay leaders) who will lead any of the services, and if so, on what rotation schedule? Will these other leaders assist in services led by the clergy in charge?

- Who will choose the music, and especially the hymns or songs, for the worship services? Is there any list of hymns from which one chooses, or any criteria for choosing them? Does the church's denomination have "authorized" hymnals, or can any source be used for the music?

- Will the Sunday lessons come from a lectionary? If so, which one? If the Revised Common Lectionary is used, will the readings during Ordinary Time come from the "Paired" or "Continuous" track?

- Will the preacher base sermons on readings from a lectionary?

- How often will Eucharist services be offered?

- If this is a liturgical church with a tradition of honoring saints, will there be services for the saints' days?

- How will Christmas, Holy Week, and Easter be observed?

- Does the congregation have any other special days of

observance? Are there civic holidays that the church customarily observes?

- Does the church take part in any ecumenical services?
- Is there a rotation of lay people taking part in the worship services—for example, as readers, musicians, or those who set up the church—and if so, who sets the rota?

This is a sampling of questions that one might address in writing a customary. Even if the pastor does not formally write a document and call it a "customary," one still has to answer such questions to establish the worship practices of a congregation. Some factors that the pastor needs to take into consideration are

- the tradition in which one serves,
- the congregation's historical practices and customs,
- one's own schedule and commitments, and
- whether one has assistance in leading worship.

In fact, an individual congregation might feel very strongly about the answers to certain of these questions and resist mightily any attempt on the part of the clergy to change them.

Exercise: Consider the above questions for your own ministry setting. How much have you "inherited" and how much have you set? What additional questions might you add to these in establishing a customary for worship?

Authority

MOST PEOPLE LEADING WORSHIP are under the authority of someone else. Accepting that authority can be difficult. In the tradition to which I belong, a bishop has the ultimate say over liturgy that may be used in the diocese, and clergy are bound to follow the bishop's direction. Bishops, however, are subject to another authority: namely, the tradition in which they serve. In the Anglican tradition, the rubrics (i.e., the instructions, which appear in italics) in the Book of Common Prayer are as authoritative as the church canons (i.e., the church laws). Even if one bristles at some of the instructions and requirements, one is still supposed to obey them.

If a clergy person's denomination does not employ bishops, the congregation and clergy are still responsible to the tradition of which they are a part. This statement is true even in a church with congregational polity, in which each congregation calls its own minister, governs itself, and makes its own decisions. The churches of such a denomination might be bound by some form of covenant, or agreement with one another, about how they will operate. Two very different American denominations with congregational polity—the Unitarian Universalist Association and the Southern Baptist Convention—both have some form of covenantal agreement that bind them together. While they might argue that the covenant is organizational, and not liturgical or theological, one can reasonably assume that if a minister from one were to lead worship in a congregation belonging to the other, the liturgical forms used and theological views expressed would likely be foreign or alien to the congregation. Each has a tradition to which the worship adheres.[4] If those leading worship are not accountable to a particular tradition, then they are determining how a congregation should worship God based solely on their own desires and predilections. While in an individualistic society one may believe this is appropriate, such an attitude might be arrogant and spiritually dangerous for the worship leader.

Laypeople in a congregation who assist in leading worship also have to accept the leadership of the clergy in charge, who in most Christian traditions have the responsibility for overseeing the spiritual and liturgical life of the congregation. The clergy person has the responsibility of being true to the tradition, and also of leading the lay assistants.

The above discussion of authority pertains primarily to the liturgy of the church's worship services. Chapter 9 will address how the issue of authority applies to preaching.

> **Exercise:** To what tradition do you belong? What are the requirements, if any, for the conducting of worship? To whose authority are you subject?

Perfection and Relevance

I REFERRED BEFORE TO ATTENDING A CHURCH that was experiencing a "liturgical comedy of errors" on a Sunday that I was present. Sometimes it happens: lectors stumble through the lessons, a bird flies around the church, the pages of a book one is using seem suddenly to be stuck when one tries to turn them, things fall over, candles go out, the sound system crackles, severe weather distracts everyone in the church. Sometimes, no matter the extent and seriousness of the preparation, things simply do not go well. Then one needs a sense of humor, especially about oneself. No worship service will ever be perfect, for only God is perfect.

A person sitting in the congregation also needs to remember that no worship service is perfect. Laypeople can adopt the attitude of "church-shopping": looking for a church that "meets my needs." C. S. Lewis, in *The Screwtape Letters*, comments on those who are church-shopping (the book consists of letters from a senior devil to a junior devil; therefore "the Enemy" and "He" refer to God):

The search for a "suitable" church makes the man a critic where the Enemy wants him to be a pupil. What He wants of the layman in church is an attitude which may, indeed, be critical in the sense of rejecting what is false or unhelpful, but which is wholly uncritical in the sense that it does not appraise—does not waste time in thinking about what it rejects, but lays itself open in uncommenting, humble receptivity to any nourishment that is going.[5]

Even though most clergy have encountered such church-shopping and the inevitable criticism of the worship service, we clergy still can be terrible "pew-sitters." Unless we are so grateful for the chance to worship without being in charge—unless we are desperate to have the worship "wash over us"—we are likely to critique the worship service *and* the person leading it. Clergy, too, must seek simply to worship God in church—to lay ourselves "open in uncommenting, humble receptivity to any nourishment that is going."

I often have thought of the words of a seminary Dean during student orientation. He told us to remember that "no one can ruin worship for you." The Dean probably had come to this recognition through hard experience. He had strict guidelines for how the students were to conduct our daily required worship, and some students liked to defy him. Perhaps I am projecting how I might have felt in his shoes, but I imagine him sitting through the student-led worship services, realizing that this was still a worship service in which he was present as a worshipper, not strictly as a seminary Dean with the responsibility of evaluating the students.

One critical evaluation that worshippers might make of a worship service is whether it is "relevant." For as long as I have been in ministry, I have felt the pressure placed on clergy to make sure that the worship service and the preaching are relevant to those who attend, or who might attend. The pressure comes from numerous sources: popular media, denominational structures, church members, and those who might be considering attending church. All of them might evaluate church worship and activities according to mostly unstated criteria of what will reach people in the current age.

It is a conundrum for clergy. Yes, we have to reach people somehow. As we adapt and adjust our worship words and forms, however, we must be careful not to water them down or rob them of their power in order to appeal to people who have no understanding of Christian faith. One way might be to introduce the Christian faith in a way that is nonthreatening and genuine. Quite frankly, the best way to do this is simply to live one's faith. This is the challenge for clergy and all those who have some role of Christian leadership.

This concern with relevance is a persistent matter, for Walter C. Klein commented on it in the 1960s:

> We have heard the word *relevance* often enough to be completely tired of it and unconsciously to resist it. In the vocabularies of some theological writers it is scarcely more than a fancy name for convenience and usefulness. Under the cover it provides we adjust all religious teaching to human limitations. Only by an abuse of language can we pretend that our technique is biblical. If the God for whose "pleasure [all things] are and were created" (Rev. 4:11) is not relevant to our deepest fear and bewilderment, there is nowhere in the universe any relevance to anything.[6]

133

I realize that these words will be antithetical for some people. Note, however, Klein's words "deepest fear and bewilderment." People of all eras and places yearn to have their deepest fears assuaged and bewilderments addressed. Our worship, our prayers, our preaching must touch people in the depths of their beings, while we also remember, yet again, that we are not perfect and nor is anything we present in a worship service. God is capable of taking our imperfect attempts and using them to bring about transformation in someone.

The Use of Set Prayers

ONE OF THE QUESTIONS clergy and worship leaders face (both for leading public worship and for private prayers) is whether to use "set prayers"—in other words, prayers and liturgical forms that are previously written. The decision depends in part, at least in public worship, on one's tradition or denomination; as mentioned above, clergy are accountable to the tradition to which they belong. The decision is also, in a sense, connected to the issue of relevance because people might assume that if a prayer or liturgical form has been previously set down, it cannot be "relevant" to a current circumstance.

The Anglican tradition of which I am a part uses almost nothing but set prayers; a book of authorized services is one of the distinguishing features of Anglicanism in any of its constituent parts around the globe. Within a particular service, some parts are given (for example, the wording of a creed and of the Eucharist), while the priest or other person so designated may write the prayers of intercession, or use suggested forms from the Book of Common Prayer.

Other denominations might offer a loose structure for their services, perhaps with suggested, but not required, forms for the various parts of the service. A clergy person putting together a worship service has to choose the pieces from those offered, or borrow the parts of the service from various sources, or compose the service.

A compelling argument for the value of set prayers appears in the Hawaiian Book of Common Prayer, which King Kamehameha IV translated from English into the Hawaiian language in 1862–63 in preparation for receiving the first Anglican bishop in the Islands, sent by the Church of England. The King wrote a Preface for the Prayer Book in June 1863 in order to introduce and explain the Anglican form of worship, which the King himself had experienced in a visit to London in 1849 when he was fifteen years old. One of my former liturgy professors said that the King's Preface to the Prayer Book is the best argument and explanation for the use of a set liturgy.[7]

The King's explanation states that the people cannot truly pray unless everyone knows the liturgy by heart, nor can they truly pray together. If the leader is praying, but the worshippers do not know what the minister will say next, then they will be anticipating what will come rather than truly immersing themselves in the prayer:

> No man's prayer can avail much, while his attention is bent on following the line taken by the person praying. His thoughts digest the words which fall from the mouth of the minister, but his heart does not offer up those same words in supplication to God; no sooner has he made them his own and is about to discharge his heart of them understandingly, than, following all

135

the time the voice of him who prays aloud, some new thought enters his mind; or otherwise absorbed with what his mind has taken hold of, he misses the thread of the spoken prayer, and hurrying to find it again, he forgets God for the moment, and by the time his thoughts have once more settled upon Him, he hears the "Amen."[8]

Memorized prayers have an advantage for an individual worshipper also, including in one's own personal devotions: the memorized prayer becomes part of us. If we know the prayer "by heart," then we can pray it with all our heart. Klein says, "A memorized prayer is eventually absorbed into the life of the person who memorizes it and is charged with his own devotional impulses. This is as far removed as possible from praying by rote. Prayers that we can repeat without hesitation free us for worship and guide us in worship."[9]

I discovered how true this can be after four months attending a required daily Morning Prayer service in an Episcopal Church seminary, where I heard the same rotation of prayers each week. In January as I sat in a classroom preparing to take the first in a weeklong set of denominational ordination exams, one of the collects (short prayers) from the Morning Prayer service arose unbidden into my heart and mind. It calmed my anxiety, assured me of God's presence, and oriented me toward the task at hand. I would not have been able to compose, on the spot, such a suitable prayer—although, as I have often taught confirmation classes, "God, help me!" may be a short prayer but still can be quite an appropriate one!

Exercise: Do you use any "set prayers" in worship services or in your own private prayers? Or do you prefer to compose them beforehand or extemporaneously during the worship service?

Online Worship

THE COVID-19 PANDEMIC brought to the forefront an issue that had already been circulating: Does one have to attend church in person in order truly to worship? Is an online service, whether on television, via a videoconferencing service, or as a prerecorded service, as good as attending a worship service in person? Even before COVID-19 appeared, worship services already were available on television, but the lockdowns brought about by the pandemic made acute the need for some kind of worship that did not require people to gather in person.

Certainly a person can worship God anywhere, whether it be in church, at home, on a bus, or in a foxhole. What matters is the individual's intention. Being with the assembled body can increase the intensity of the worship service. Perhaps you have had the experience of engaging in silent prayer in a group and finding that it is more intense than praying silently by oneself. There is something about the Body of Christ gathering together that increases the power of the experience. Being in a holy place also can increase the power or intensity of the worship experience.

Perhaps the difference between online worship, of whatever variety, and in-person worship is similar to the difference between a meeting via videoconference and an in-person meeting. During the pandemic, meetings went online. But many people found that, while convenient, much is lost in an online meeting. It is not the same as being in people's presence. Back-and-forth conversation is more difficult, if not impossible; one cannot read nonverbal cues, such as body language, as easily; one cannot quite grasp the "feel of the room."

Perhaps we might conclude that online worship offers people an alternative to in-person worship, which at times is helpful or even, as during the pandemic, necessary. But the experience of worship, in many cases, is diminished or reduced. One just does not quite get the full experience—not only of worshipping God, but also of being part of the Body of Christ. Of course, one challenge of worshipping in the presence of other people is that the worshipper can experience the personal foibles, irritations, impatience, conflicts, and the like that human nature can provide in an assembled group! This challenge, too, can be part of our spiritual development.

> **Exercise:** How did you worship during the COVID-19 pandemic? What differences did you experience between how you worshipped then and worship in a church with others?

Coffee Hour

On the matter of fellowship in church, clergy and other church leaders should recognize that some people attending church are present only for worship. They find fellowship—such as the typical "coffee hour"—utterly distracting from and damaging to their worship experience. Christians should not be considered lacking in virtue because they want to worship and leave. Whenever I attend church as a congregant, I rarely ever stay for coffee hour.

Is the Leader Worshipping?

IS THE PERSON LEADING WORSHIP, the officiant, actually worshipping?

Yes and no.

Officiants must be worshipping at some level, or else they are just leading a show. On the other hand, worshipping includes an element of relinquishing control. Officiants are in charge and simply cannot completely let go and immerse themselves in the worship service; they must remain aware of what is happening.

In chapter 3, I said clergy are standing in a vortex between God and the people and navigating the worlds of both. Here is the task of an officiant in a worship service: to stand between God and the people and to communicate, in word and action, God's presence, word, and power.

Annie Dillard has spoken of the power in worship and implies the danger of serving as the officiant:

> I often think of the set pieces of liturgy as certain words which people have successfully addressed to God without their getting killed. In the high churches they saunter through the liturgy like Mohawks along a strand of scaffolding who have long since forgotten their danger. If God were to blast such a service to bits, the congregation would be, I believe, genuinely shocked. But in the low churches you expect it any minute. This is the beginning of wisdom.[10]

One has to be prepared for standing between God and the people and saying the words of the liturgy. One prepares by praying before the service, and by refraining from business or all but the lightest pastoral conversations before the service, so that one can approach God with one's mind, heart, and spirit prepared to encounter the power of the Holy Spirit (as if we can ever be fully prepared for such an encounter). I feel that I prepare myself as well as I can to lead worship, and then I place myself in God's hands and experience the Holy Spirit at work, in myself and in the congregation.

Ideally, and as hard as this may be, the officiant has to be prepared for worship morally and ethically as well, seeking forgiveness for one's own sins and coming before God with a clean and forgiving heart. Jesus's words in the Sermon on the Mount are instructive:

> So when you are offering your gift at the altar, if you remember that your brother or sister has something against you, leave your gift there before the altar and go; first be reconciled to your brother or sister, and then come and offer your gift. [Matt. 5:23–24]

Clergy and lay officiants alike generally discover that leading worship is exhausting. During the worship service itself, the experience can be energizing, even exhilarating. And then later, perhaps after a few hours, one needs maybe a good meal and often a nap. Being in that spiritual vortex between God and the people means that not only is one experiencing the power of the Holy Spirit—an experience that can jolt our imperfect nervous systems and our not-completely-clean spirits. The officiant (and the preacher) experiences, and even absorbs, the emotions, pains, and hopes of the people in the congregation. Prayers of preparation before the service(s) and cleansing prayers afterward help to dispel these influences. But the officiant still might well find that some form of physical sustenance is necessary in the hours after the service, be that sustenance in the form of food, sleep, or mild exercise.

Yes, therefore, the officiant is actually worshipping. The officiant is immersed in the service and is subject to the unpredictable movement of the Holy Spirit. But to be "in charge" of the service means that the officiant must remain aware of what is happening: Are the lectors coming forward to read at the appropriate times? Are the musicians ready and are they playing the right pieces of music? Are all the accoutrements of worship set up (for example, needed worship books, elements of Communion, candles)? A worship service consists of many different elements. The church might have teams of laypeople who help with these various responsibilities, but the officiant still has to retain some awareness of whether all is in place, both before and during the service. I also notice the condition and reactions of people in the congregation, as well as whether or not newcomers seem to be familiar with the flow of the worship service, and whether anyone is helping them.

Anyone participating in a visible role in the worship service also must remain aware that they are visible and responsible; they cannot fully relax into the service. I still remember one Christmas Eve service in which I realized that two acolytes were suddenly, but very quietly, raising their feet from the floor in front of them and placing them on the bench on which they were sitting. A large cockroach (this was in the tropics) was crawling on the floor. I remain impressed that the acolytes protected themselves while not shrieking or jumping up; in other words, they knew the congregation could see them, and the flow of the worship proceeded without a hitch.

Because of the need to remain aware, anyone with a visible role in the service cannot freely worship. A church, therefore, might refrain from regularly assigning a particular layperson a visible role, because then the person is always working in the service.

And what about the clergy? When do they "not work"? Clergy occasionally want to "sit in the pew"; they might attend a weekday service at a colleague's church, or worship at a retreat center. That the clergy are always working when leading worship has implications for what constitutes Sabbath for clergy; we will address this topic in the Sabbath chapters.

> **Exercise:** Do you feel as though you yourself are worshipping when you lead worship? Do you ever have the opportunity to attend worship somewhere else, and do you wish to do so?

This discussion implies that one crucial element of the nature of worship is that the worshipper is not in control of events. Certainly someone who is letting the worship "wash over me" is a seemingly passive recipient of the worship service. But the worshipper who is actively participating by singing, saying prayers and other elements of the service, sharing the Peace with other congregants, receiving Communion, and such like, is still not in charge and, indeed, by such participation may be opening oneself to the possibility of being transformed by the worship service. One is there to open oneself to the Almighty, to hear God's word, to receive God's blessing, to turn up the volume on the music of faith, to be reminded of the different reality—the new heaven and the new earth—that God offers to us in Christ. In order to receive, in order to be transformed, worshippers have to let go of their expectations and their demands in order for God to work in them. I offer this provocative statement from Klein: "Neither in the Apostles' Creed nor in the Nicene Creed is there any mention of the specific needs of those who assemble in God's house."[11]

These comments lead to three further implications: First, those who lead worship on a regular basis need a time and place to worship where they are not in charge, preferably also on a regular basis. Second, it matters what we worship. If, in worship, we are opening ourselves to the worldview and influence of a particular reality, then we had better make sure that this reality is real and true—in other words, that it is truly of God. And the third implication is that those who put together worship services should be careful that what they offer truly reflects the gospel of Christ. As quoted at the beginning of this chapter, "All human testimony is authentic only to the extent that it remains faithful to the witness of Christ."[12]

Chapter 8

READING AND STUDY:

Read, Mark, Learn, and Inwardly Digest

Blessed Lord, who caused all holy Scriptures to be written for our learning: Grant us so to hear them, read, mark, learn, and inwardly digest them, that we may embrace and ever hold fast the blessed hope of everlasting life, which you have given us in our Savior Jesus Christ; who lives and reigns with you and the Holy Spirit, one God, for ever and ever. Amen.
—Collect for Proper 28, *Book of Common Prayer*

MY HUSBAND AND I JOKE that whenever we move house, we have to pack up and move sixty boxes of books. We have moved back and forth across the Pacific several times and across the Atlantic once, as well as moving a fair distance on the United States mainland. We have sacrificed furniture we have liked—sold it off or given it away—in order to decrease the load in the moving container. But no matter how much I might cull the book stash, we still seem to end up moving about sixty boxes of books each time we change residence.

Most clergy I have ever met love books. We yearn for them the way a carpenter might yearn for tools or a knitter for yarn. In my first days in seminary, the Dean of Students worked through a sample budget for us students. His recommended book budget represented a sizable amount of money, and as the seminarians looked a bit stricken, he told us not to skimp on our book budget. These are your professional tools, he told us.

His advice stuck in my mind. It is odd to think that books are tools that clergy need. What is it about study and reading books that help us fulfill our responsibilities?

In considering this question, I will address it in four ways:

- Why do we need to read and study?
- What is the special place of Scripture in our reading and study?
- Of all the many things that we could read, from all the possible books and magazines, how do we discern what we should read?
- How might we systematically undertake reading and study?

We need to read and study for a number of reasons:

- that we might be well-rounded
- to help us develop what is called a "pastoral imagination," which also prevents us from becoming stale
- so that we can teach

First, we need to be well-rounded. That same Dean of Students pointed out to us students that clergy are the last generalists. In a world and a society that values and encourages increased specialization, clergy are generalists precisely because we need to be able to interact with people from many different walks of life. As Walter C. Klein says, "In the present world, [the priest] is the sole universal interpreter."[1] I have served as a parish minister in six different locations in the course of ministry, and each of those locations has been quite different because of the subcultures that the people in the congregations represented. Two were congregations in thriving suburbs of major American cities hundreds of miles apart; another church consisted of active-duty military members; a fourth was primarily Japanese American; another emphasized a Hawaiian ethos. In yet another location, it helped to be able to talk about the price of milk and to know the differences in farming various kinds of cattle.

This variety means that clergy must be constantly learning. We have to have the enthusiasm, and the time, for reading and study. True, not all our learning is from books. I will learn better about farming different types of cattle by talking with parishioners or by scanning a farming journal than by reading a textbook. But clergy must have an enthusiasm for learning and an ability to see connections between what we learn and the lives of the people among whom we serve. As Klein says of what we could discover when we leave formal theological training and enter active ministry, "every day's ministry is replete with theological problems that clamor for responsible investigation." Clergy are "charged with the total interpretation of human existence, a task that does not consist solely in the repetition and exposition of authoritative formularies,"[2] such as we might learn in seminary.

Developing the ability to interpret human existence in the light of the gospel is called having a "pastoral imagination," a term described by Craig Dykstra in a book chapter entitled "Pastoral and Ecclesial Imagination." It means being able to see the connections between the ways of God and regular, ordinary, everyday life (including the price of milk) amid all the varied and complex demands of ministry. Dykstra lists several requirements as contributing to the development of a pastoral imagination and "indispensable to good ministry":

- "a deep, sustained, and thoroughgoing engagement with the Scriptures and with a sound theological tradition"
- an understanding of human behavior fostered by extensive personal experience and gleaned from novels, poetry, history, psychology, the Bible, and theology
- "a disciplined spiritual life through which one enters into the deeper levels of one's own self, encounters one's own deepest hopes and fears, and, placing them in God's hands through sacrifice and prayer, learns to trust the spiritual *terra firma* that enables one to live a faithful and generous life"[3]

A pastoral imagination should develop over the course of years of ministry, as a pastor is trained and transformed. Its development will proceed more easily if we leave time and space for reading and study. Such abilities are not served well by rushing from one appointment or activity to another. Reading and study require that we stop the mad dash; they encourage thinking and reflecting; they help us consider how to respond to the many different situations we encounter, rather than just reacting to them. As Dykstra says, "Extensive reading and serious observation, along with a great deal of accumulated personal experience, is essential to the emergence of a mature pastoral imagination."[4]

Put another way, reading and study help prevent us from becoming stale. It is very easy to go through one's training for ministry, to feel that one has "made it" once one has a ministerial position, and then to ignore the need for any further learning. One has to keep learning in order to keep alive one's ability to respond to the situations one encounters and to see how God is working anew in each of them. If we are satisfied with what we initially learned, then we risk the possibility that our responses to people and to situations will become hackneyed and trite.

Ministry demands that we keep changing and adapting; in other words, ministry demands the most from us that we can possibly give. As Dykstra says, pastoral ministry requires from pastors "their best thought, their full energy, their deepest engagement. ... pastoral ministry requires real strength of every kind."[5] Reading and study provide a way to gain perspective on ministry, on the people among whom one serves, and on God's call. I have found that reading and study (writing this book, for example) provide a means of learning just how God is demanding that I change and grow in greater faith and love of God in response to the situations I encounter in ministry. In other words, reading and study help to provide necessary perspective on the situations and people I encounter and force me to consider my own responses in ministry and where I might do better.

Reading and study help a pastoral imagination to develop, but it is not and never can be a cut-and-dried or predictable process. As with all ministry, one is always responding to God. As Dykstra points out, "But the pastoral imagination is not something to be achieved or attained. It comes as a gift. At the very heart of pastoral ministry there lies the good news of a power that is not our own, a labor that ultimately is not our work, a grace that is not of our own doing."[6] Ministry is not about us.

A third reason that ministers must undertake reading and study is so that we might teach others. Teaching is one of the basic tasks of ministry. Some teaching might take place in sermons, but sermons are increasingly shortened these days, and sermons have a different purpose than simply teaching the assembled congregation. Graham Neville comments that what Saint John Chrysostom says about preaching would these days apply better to teaching. Teaching is necessary so that the people in one's charge might grow in the faith; such training is part of the responsibility toward the people described in chapter 5 on pastoral care. "For, as Chrysostom says, in dealing with spiritual ailments we have only one technique and method of healing, beside the example of a good life, and that is teaching by word of mouth. . . . there must be good teaching, if the priest is to promote the spiritual health of the congregation. Words are his weapons and he must know how to use them."[7]

The world in which we live is essentially alien to the Christian gospel. William H. Willimon predicts that "more of a pastor's time will be spent in the education, formation, and enculturation of the members of the congregation to be people who know how to analyze the corrosive acids within the surrounding and essentially indifferent—at times openly hostile—dominant culture."[8] In order to have such discernment, people need training in Scripture, prayer, how to live a Christian life, and more. Essentially, the teacher is providing, especially through teaching Scripture, a lens through which people learn to refocus their lives from what the world values to the true values of a life of faith.[9] Through teaching, we also help people learn a different vocabulary for understanding the world and life:

> From Scripture, the church is given more than directives, rules, codes for contemporary Christian behavior. The main gift of Scripture is a world, a culture, a

reality constructed (as all worlds, cultures, and reality are fabricated) through words. . . . Christians are those who, through Scripture, are taught to name the world, not merely as "nature," but rather as "Creation." We learn to name our lives not as under the grip of fate, or luck, but as guided and cared for by providence. We do not make "mistakes." We sin. We do not want to be improved. We hope for salvation.[10]

To make a point, one might consider how one's teaching would change if it were cast in specifically Christian or scriptural terms. For example, many in the Church today are developing programs for teaching about climate change in order to encourage and emphasize our environmental responsibility. In a Christian context, such teaching should be cast in terms of God's Creation, rather than simply "Nature" or "the environment." A Christian context brings changes in how we view the whole enterprise.

Exercise: How do you, or how could you, develop a regular pattern for making reading and study part of your life? Are there particular topics to study that would be helpful in your place of ministry? What would help you perceive connections between the Christian gospel and the context in which you work?

The Primacy of Scripture

WE ARE SHAPED by what we read. Education in the church these days is called Christian *formation* because what we learn *forms* us; it shapes who we are and who we will become. We can be shaped by anything that we read, the movies or television programs that

151

we watch, the music and podcasts that we listen to, and anything else in which we immerse ourselves. We need therefore to choose carefully what we will read, study, watch, or listen to; we base our choices on what enables us to be most faithful to God.

The primary arena of study is Scripture. Willimon says,

> I am not free to rummage about in other texts before I have submitted to the biblical text. I am not at liberty to acknowledge as source of ultimate truth those contemporary, culturally sanctioned sources such as psychology, sociology, economics, and so forth before I have done service to the historic faith of the church. It is fair to have a lover's quarrel with the tradition of the church, to wrestle with and to question which tradition is sanctioned by God and which is spurious irrelevancy. Yet it is not fair to place oneself or one's culture above the story of Jesus of Nazareth as represented in the creeds, councils, and faith of the church.[11]

A pastor and preacher must be steeped in the words of the Bible, because the Bible must undergird our entire way of thinking about life. As said above, it becomes the lens through which we view life. Klein comments, "We should live with it, breathe it, think it, reproduce it."[12]

I first had an inkling of how much Scripture should form our thinking when I was in the ordination process for the Episcopal priesthood. I attended a workshop on preaching led by Herbert O'Driscoll, an Anglican priest who was originally from Ireland but who had moved to Canada in the mid-1950s. What I most remember from that workshop was a simple story. When he was growing up, he lived near a cottage inhabited by two sisters and a brother, named Jim, Mary, and Maggie Byrne. O'Driscoll describes the experience in his book *A Doorway in Time*: "To a child, those three were already mythic, living in at least two levels of my awareness since they were the living figures in which I thought of the biblical family of Lazarus, Mary, and Martha in the house in Bethany."[13]

When I attended the workshop, I was amazed that someone would see their neighbors as characters from the Bible. Now I understand that we want to be so steeped in the Scriptures that we see life's events in biblical terms. My husband and I now routinely see events in biblical terms, meaning that events and people remind us of episodes and characters in the Bible. For example, a standing joke between us is that when we are driving somewhere unfamiliar, when a convenient sign would help us to find our way, one of us will say, "But we're not looking for a sign, of course, because it's a vain and perverse generation that seeks for a sign," paraphrasing Jesus speaking to the Pharisees and Saduccees in Matthew 16.[14] We are joking, of course, but the joke also serves as a subtle reminder to us that we are not to be seeking for a sign, but instead we are to live by faith.

I began the practice of reading the Bible daily several years before I ever adhered to the Christian faith; I thought I should know more about the Bible and, to be honest, I felt the need for some kind of weighty spiritual sustenance. I chose to use the daily lectionary in the Episcopal Church's Book of Common Prayer to read the Bible each night. As I read, I felt that I was reading truth—not necessarily that every event happened precisely as described, but that the book itself told of a deep and underlying truth at the heart of all existence. I had this experience especially when reading the Gospels.

The Bible puts life into an eternal perspective. Reading and studying Scripture immerse us in a profound way of seeing the world and in another way of living than that which we normally encounter in the world in which we are immersed day to day. It might seem odd that this would be so, since the Bible is full of violence, betrayal, deceit, and any other kind of sin one can imagine. In other words, it presents so clearly the worst possibilities of human nature. If we wanted to observe the nature of human beings, all we would have to do is look around us in this world, read the news, or deal with our neighbors (or, often, our families).

This observation is exactly the point, however: the Bible shows us what people are like, but in relationship with God. The behavior of the characters in the Bible does not occur in a vacuum but in the context of one's life with God—or in the context of an attempt to avoid dealing with God. God is the main character of the Bible.

The Bible is a difficult book because of the events it relates, and because the culture in which these events take place is so different in many ways from the one in which we live. One can especially feel how strange and difficult the Bible might seem if one looks at it from the point of view of the people in the pews, or those who are not in the pews at all. Every so often as I sit in church listening to a church member read one of the lectionary lessons for the day from the Bible, I ponder if anyone in the congregation is wondering why we read these stories, teachings, and history of a people who lived thousands of years ago in a land far, far away. When leading Bible study classes, I also have found, especially when reading from Genesis, that participants wonder why on earth these stories are in the *Bible*. They think of the Bible as a rule book and assume that most of the characters in it are people of stellar behavior whom we are supposed to emulate. During one Bible study on Genesis, as we read about the adventures and lives of our patriarchs and matriarchs in the faith, one young woman asked in shock if we are supposed to take these people as examples of how to live.

I have answered such questions by saying that the Old Testament is descriptive, not prescriptive. In other words, it describes how people of a certain place and time behaved, not how they or any of us are supposed to behave. It does contain passages that are prescriptive—the Ten Commandments and passages from the prophets come to mind. But the main sweep of the story through the Old Testament describes a people living in relationship with God—a God of infinite patience and mercy who constantly calls people to the Almighty so that they might find forgiveness, joy, and new life.

An excellent way to communicate the infinite lovingkindness of God as told in the sweep of the Old Testament stories is through the lessons suggested for the Easter Vigil, the most important service of the Christian year in Anglican churches. One reads in this service a selection of up to nine readings, one of which is always the story of the Exodus, each followed by a psalm or canticle in response and a prayer.[15] A person attending the service experiences these readings while sitting in a candlelit church on Easter Eve (or preferably, I believe, before sunup on Easter morning). A tall white candle represents the light of Christ, and individual small candles are lit from this central candle.

The readings of the Easter Vigil tell the story of "salvation history": how God worked through events to bring salvation, healing, and new life to God's people. When I was confirmed in the Episcopal Church, the priest teaching the confirmation class used these nine readings from the Easter Vigil to teach us this salvation history, so that we could grasp the basics of the Christian faith.

Back to the Vigil service itself: after hearing salvation history from the Old Testament, the worship continues with a proclamation that Christ is risen from the dead, the renewal of baptismal vows, a Gospel account of the Resurrection, and Eucharist.

This service tells the story of how God has worked in the lives of people, through history. It is the story of our faith, and for those who are followers of Christ, it is our story. It is the story of a people who struggled with flood, slavery, oppression, famine, war, exile, and sin. But it is also the story of a people who found themselves delivered miraculously from their enemies, who were fed in the wilderness, who were guided and directed and protected through many trials, and who were released from exile and allowed to return home and rebuild their lives. Through all of these events, there was one constant, and that was the hand of God. Through all these events, the people experienced—or the prophets reminded them—that God was always there, with steadfast love and care, sometimes cajoling them, sometimes pushing them, sometimes chastising them (through the prophets), but always ready to forgive, always showing mercy, always bringing forth life. The ultimate expressions of such care from God are the incarnation of God in Jesus Christ and his resurrection from the dead.

The New Testament is a different kind of book from the Old. We need to read and study both Testaments because each contributes to faith and to the knowledge and worship of God. I appreciate the Old Testament because of how well it relates human nature and our relationship to God in the midst of everyday events and history. The stories of King David show us both great faith and also the dangers of arrogance and sin, not to mention complex family dynamics. The rants of the prophet Amos are as equally true today as they were in ancient Israel. My husband

and I occasionally undertake the exercise of reading through the entire Bible in a year. The most recent time we did this, I felt that one way to describe the exercise was simply, "There is nothing new under the sun" (Eccles. 1:9). The context, culture, and details of the biblical accounts may be different from our own experience, but comparable circumstances, behaviors, and desires exist in our own day.

The New Testament is full of stories of human sin: Peter's denial of Jesus, Judas's betrayal, Ananias and Sapphira's lying in order to keep their money (Acts 5:1–11)—the list is endless. But when I read the New Testament, I sense a different reality from the surface of this one in which we live. Something in me breathes a sigh of relief when I read the New Testament, whether the Gospels or the Epistles. It is as if I am being reminded of God's presence in the midst of all the hoopla of the world, and I am being shown the hope and joy that run behind and beneath the surface of the world. Our responsibility as pastors is to communicate this alternative reality—which is the reality that is truly real—to our people. Willimon says we keep returning to Scripture because "We trust the Bible because it keeps making sense of, as well as disrupting, the world in which we live."[16]

The longer I serve in churches, the more I value reading and studying the Epistles of the Apostle Paul. The Gospels tell us the story of Jesus—his life, death, and resurrection—and by so doing lay the groundwork for the Christian life. The Epistles help us to interpret the life, death, and resurrection of Christ and apply these events to our life. Because Paul was confronting persecutions, dissensions, strife, false teachings, arrogance, and despondency in the churches to which he wrote, studying the Epistles can help a pastor facing difficulties in a church appreciate that such troubles are nothing new. And as they are nothing new, one can begin to understand how to approach dealing with them. At various points in my ministry, one passage or another from Paul's epistles has been the fodder for my prayers and has provided a guide by which I tried to live.

One has to be careful when studying the Scriptures. They must remain the bedrock of our faith instead of their study becoming a dry academic exercise that keeps us aloof from God. One reads Scripture to immerse oneself in God's presence and to hear God speaking in the midst of one's life. As Thomas Long says, "We go to scripture, then, not to glean a set of facts about God or the faith that can then be announced whenever and wherever, but to encounter a Presence, to hear God's voice speaking to us ever anew, calling us in the midst of the situations in which we find ourselves to be God's faithful people."[17]

The interpretation of Scripture is guided by the Holy Spirit; without the Spirit, who can understand what Scripture is saying? In addition, the interpretation of Scripture is not intended to be an individualistic exercise; it is meant to be undertaken by the Church. The Reformation led to the belief that an individual sitting in a closet, as one of my professors used to say, is perfectly free and able to interpret Scripture according to one's own personal predilections. The Holy Spirit may speak to one individually through Scripture, but interpretation requires the testimony of the Church. Willimon says that a pastor "listens to the [biblical] text for the whole church" and "interprets Scripture in light of the reading of the whole church down through the ages."[18]

Words become the Word by the empowering presence and activity of the Holy Spirit. Modernity taught that most rational human beings, regardless of background, training, or character, were perfectly capable

158

of unaided understanding, perfectly able to grasp and comprehend everything in the world simply by the use of reason. Scripture frustrates such limited knowing. Scripture opens itself up to us through the work of the Holy Spirit, whom we cannot rationalize or control, and modernity is high on control and rationalization.[19]

C. S. Lewis speaks to the dangers of studies of the "historical Jesus"—that aim to find and describe just exactly who Jesus was, separate from the testimony of the Gospels. Lewis says that the construction by each generation of an "historical Jesus" "destroy[s] the devotional life." These observations come from Lewis's book *The Screwtape Letters*, letters from a senior devil to a junior devil given the charge of "converting" a man to the devil's ways; thus God is described in the passage below as "the Enemy":

> For the real presence of the Enemy, otherwise experienced by men in prayer and sacrament, we substitute a merely probable, remote, shadowy, and uncouth figure, one who spoke a strange language and died a long time ago. Such an object cannot in fact be worshipped. Instead of the Creator adored by its creature, you soon have merely a leader acclaimed by a partisan, and finally a distinguished character approved by a judicious historian.[20]

We must not restrict the study of Scripture to sermon preparation alone. To do so confines our study to something of use to us; it becomes study with the purpose of generating a product, usually under the pressure of an impending deadline. Instead, reading and studying Scripture are meant to be a means of encountering God's presence and hearing God's word, free of any self-serving requirement of the preacher or the congregation. Think of this. The number of passages on which we will be called to preach is fairly small compared with the entirety of the Bible. We should be steeped in the whole book, so that we return to it over and over again in our ministry.

> **Exercise:** How do you, or how will you, structure in your life a systematic reading and study of Scripture? For example, do you use a daily lectionary, read through the Bible from start to finish, or use one of the systems that exists for reading the Bible in a year? What sources do you use to study the Bible: a commentary series, a journal, or individual works on different books of the Bible? Some commentaries are more academic in nature; some are aimed at preachers and pastors, by providing theological reflection upon the passages; some are a combination of the two. How might you see life's events in biblical terms? In other words, how might people and events in the world, or in your own life, remind you of people and events in the Bible?

What Else Do We Study?

SCRIPTURE COMES FIRST in our reading, but we also can learn from a variety of sources. The decision of what else we will read applies both to works related to religion, as a broad topic, and to works that seem totally unconnected to the work we do. As said above, we are the last generalists. Still, we need to exercise discernment and wisdom about what we will read, among all the possibilities that exist. As Neville says in his introduction to Chrysostom's *Six Books on the Priesthood*,

The Christian's voyage [today] is through seas unchart-
ed by the definitions of ecumenical councils. His pilot
must discover a channel between the perils of popular-
ized science, materialistic social philosophies, half-un-
derstood psychology, and plain selfishness disguised as
a noble protest against the "establishment." It is quite
an assignment for the preacher of fifteen-minute sermons.[21]

In other words, we should choose sources of merit and seriousness. As mentioned above, Dykstra names several topics in
his list of criteria crucial for good ministry: "novels and poetry,
history and psychology, and again, of course, the Bible and theology."[22] One could add science and technology to the list. These
fields help to give us a wide basis of knowledge, all of which aid
in reflection upon the situations encountered in ministry.

Of particular note are fiction and poetry. Fiction might
seem to be "fluff" reading. Works of fiction, however, can give us
deep insight into human nature and into the nature of life itself.
Poetry presents deep insights in a more fluid structure. Both can
provide relaxing reading, while at the same time giving us deep
understanding that can be of benefit to preaching and to ministry
in general.

Religious publishing also presents the Christian leader with
any number of books to read and conferences to attend. At various points in my ministry, I have made an effort to keep up
with contemporary books and magazines of religious thought.
As the years went by, however, I noticed that a church program
or an approach to theology would be popular for a year or two or
even three and then would fade away. Each of these programs or

approaches constituted a fad, one that promised a quick fix for church growth, or conversion, or church administration. But all fads and trends come and go. Why should we be formed by what is fleeting? If faith is about what is eternal, then those charged both with representing faithful living and also with teaching and communicating faith should be shaped by what has stood the test of time.

Recognizing my own limitations, I try to keep up as much as I can, through periodicals and recently published books, with the trends shaping the Church. Honestly, I examine some of these works in a cursory way; I am looking for the thread of current thought, while not wishing to be formed by it. Have I therefore already made a judgment call and dismissed such works out of hand without giving them a proper hearing? Perhaps in some cases. But when I read something and encounter one piece of jargon after another, or when one of the underlying messages of a work communicates "It's all about you," then I do not wish to be shaped by it because I know already that its words are not words of truth.

Instead, for my in-depth reading and study, I focus on the classics: those works that have stood the test of time and that have shaped the Church through the centuries.

Exercise: What do you read and study on a regular basis? What are your criteria for such choices?

How Do We Study?

IN ADDITION TO DETERMINING *what* we should study, we also must answer the question of *how* should we study. Because different people learn in different ways, it will be best if we choose the methods of study and learning that suit us as individuals. For years, I attempted to fulfill professional development require-ments by going to conferences. They enabled me to meet the diocesan requirements for continuing education. Several confer-ences I attended proved to be very helpful, but over time I dis-covered that I learn best by concentrating on reading about a par-ticular topic for a period of time. As I read, questions arise, my mind "turns on," and I start wrestling with how the topic applies to life and ministry.

I have encountered two different models for systematic study. One was from a former colleague, a man who was in his sixties at the time and serving a neighboring church. Over the years of his ministry, he had developed a study plan. He would choose a particular topic and then spend a year or so delving into it; when I knew him, he was in the midst of studying Shakespeare. Having this system gave discipline to his study: rather than spend-ing time flitting from one topic to another, by concentrating on one topic at a time, he was able to learn more about it and glean more insight from it.

I have occasionally done this myself on a much smaller scale. Several times in my ministry, usually at the instigation or request of my bishop, I have focused on one topic for a short period of time, in order to be able to produce a report for use in the church or diocese in which I was serving. I researched which resources I should use, then read them in a prescribed period of time. The intense focus on one topic enabled me to learn more about it and to see the interplay among the different resources I was using. I dare say I have retained more about these particular topics than I would have if I had spread out the study over a lon-ger period of time.

The second model for systematic study I have seen was a

study group composed of a number of clergy in one denomination who made a covenant with one another to spend a year studying a particular topic. The group consisted of about thirty clergy who met once a year for four days at a retreat center. They came from a fairly wide geographical area. Each year they would go through a specific process for choosing the topic of study for the coming year. Three members of the group then served as a program subcommittee whose responsibility was to do the following:

- conduct preliminary research on the topic in order to identify the best and most relevant resources, with a limit of 500 pages of reading
- assimilate a list of required and recommended reading
- formulate five paper topics and assign each one to a different member of the group
- assign the task of being the respondent for each of the five papers to an additional five members
- assign one group member to prepare an artistic way to approach the topic of study during the annual gathering, perhaps with a film or artwork
- choose a chaplain for the meeting, whose responsibility it was to conduct worship during their four-day gathering

Topics might be a theological doctrine, a book of the Bible, an ethical issue, or an individual author. I know of two different such study groups, and examples of topics I have seen them study have been War and Peace (during the time of the first Gulf War), William Blake, Redemption and Forgiveness, and the Letters of the Apostle Paul. The papers' authors are meant to deal with the topic in an academic way, but at the same time to keep in mind the ramifications of the topic for ministry.

The disadvantage of such a group is that one's study is essentially confined to the topics chosen by the group. It is difficult, especially if one is chosen as the author of a paper in a given year, to spend any significant amount of time on any other subject. The covenant of the group is such that the members agree to participate each year, barring some major difficulty, rather than picking and choosing which year they will attend based on whether they personally like the topic of study.

The advantages of such a study group are many and outweigh the disadvantages. As with the colleague who chose his own study topic for a year, being a member of a study group forces clergy to concentrate on a particular topic for an extended period of time. The requirement of writing an academic paper on a topic, or else the critical response to it, keeps alive the ability to think. Gathering with the same people each year while delving into and discussing topics in some depth develops significant collegial ties; my perception has been that these ties were of a deeper level than those I have witnessed in other clergy groups. Klein endorses the idea of clerical study groups as superior to clergy groups that meet together periodically. When clergy meet, say for an hour or two once a month, the clergy are not together for long enough, the clergy are too wary of one another (interactions often contain a significant degree of one-up-manship), and the group never delves into any real depth on a topic. The benefits of a study group such as described here "are virtually infinite, both for the hesitant mind and for the lonely spirit."[23]

I close this chapter with one caveat. A verse in the last chapter of Ecclesiastes always makes me laugh: "Of making many books there is no end, and much study is a weariness of the flesh"

(Eccles. 12:12). I would be remiss in addressing the subject of reading and study if I did not mention it! I think of it when I see the multitude of books being published. As essential as reading and study may be to ministry, and I believe they are, they are not to become the focus of ministry except in specific circumstances, such as teaching in a seminary. Even then, however, the main foci of ministry remain God and the people, not the study itself.

Chapter 9

PREACHING:

The Word

The preacher is a member of the community, set apart by them and sent to the scripture to search, to study, and to listen obediently on their behalf.
  —Thomas G. Long, "Preaching as Bearing Witness"

WHEN I WAS FIRST IN SEMINARY, I encountered a disagreement among some clergy about what constitutes the most important task of the ordained ministry. My mentor in the internship I served said that preaching is the most important task. He said preaching is where parish clergy have the greatest impact on a congregation, since the worship service is the central act of the congregation and it is where the greatest number of people are gathered together. (The same would hold true even if a church had multiple services.) A friend of mine, however, served an internship with a minister who declared that pastoral care is the most important task; he averred that if you are

167

with people in the trials and tribulations of their lives that your preaching will not matter as much.

In truth, each of these two ordained leaders was promoting the task with which he felt the most comfortable. The first time I heard my mentor preach, I remember critiquing his style according to criteria I had heard in a homiletics class: he did not have sufficient eye contact, he was not particularly dramatic or dynamic in his style. But by the end of his sermon, on sloth, I felt myself changed. Somehow his words had affected me.

Had I had my friend's mentor during my internship, perhaps I would now think about this differently, but I do believe that preaching is the most important task of the ordained ministry, at least for parochial clergy. My mentor's views agree with William H. Willimon:

> This emphasis upon preaching is not only, in many of its aspects, a historically and theologically defensible role for the pastor, but it is also a good use of the pastor's time. The pastor can be with many parishioners during the course of a week, in a variety of pastoral settings, and not be with as many people in as intentional a way as when the pastor ascends the pulpit to preach on Sunday. Focus on the preaching ministry is simply a wise use of the pastor's time.[1]

The ordination vows I took state, "As a priest, it will be your task to proclaim by word and deed the Gospel of Jesus Christ. . . . You are to preach. . . ."[2] To preach is to comment on, explicate, and interpret the Christian Scriptures in a way that makes those listening more able to receive the faith and more able to live their lives in communion with God.

Sermon preparation and preaching unite the central tasks of ministry: pastoral care, worship, and reading and study. Preaching occurs in the midst of a worship service. In the more Protestant, less sacramental denominations, the sermon is the central element of a worship service; everything else leads to the sermon. Preaching is a primary task of the ordained ministry in almost every Christian denomination (the Society of Friends—Quakers—are a notable exception).

One must read and study in order to be granted the authority to preach in many denominations. I learned that preaching is, indeed, the reason for the existence of seminaries. A seminarian does study other subjects in seminary—how to provide pastoral care, for example—but the chief reason for these Scripture, history, and theology classes is to provide the ordained person with the knowledge to expound upon the Scripture and, through sermons, to lead people to faith. Scripture, history, and theology constitute the core curriculum of many seminaries. I have witnessed several programs for training laypeople to lead nonsacramental worship services. The candidates must undergo extensive training in these subjects in order to be allowed to prepare and preach their own sermons.

Preaching is a central task of ministry for an additional reason: It is an activity in which the central foci of ministry—God and people—come together in a public way. Eugene H. Peterson says that the essential work of a pastor consists of three things: praying, preaching, and listening.[3] Praying builds our relationship with God; listening builds our relationships with people; and preaching unites the two.

This centrality, however, exposes the danger inherent in preaching. The visibility, regularity, and intensity of preaching can feed the feeling that "it's all about me." In preparing the sermon, one risks becoming enamored with one's own thoughts and ideas, instead of seeking to speak truth from God. In preaching, one stands before a body of people and delivers a sermon of one's own creation. The preacher must not become enamored with, dependent upon, or attached to the listeners' responses, whether positive, negative, or nonexistent.

So the preacher must remain aware that, in preparation and in delivery, one is standing before God, from whom one is to seek inspiration and guidance. I always say this prayer during sermon preparation to focus my spirit on the task facing me. While the intent is consistent, the words are not always the same:

> Almighty God, thank you for the privilege of preaching your word to your people. You know these people better than I do; you know them through and through, while I know them just a little (or maybe not at all). I pray that I may preach what you want them to hear. Help me as I prepare, as I write, and as I preach this sermon to preach your word and your truth. May your Holy Spirit guide me, and may I be true to the salvation granted us through your Son, our Savior Jesus Christ. Let me get out of the way so that your word might come to your people through what I say. Through Jesus Christ I pray. Amen.

The prayer may change, but it always includes: "you know these people better than I do" and "I pray that I may preach what you want your people to hear."

I pray this because preaching can provide a recipe for self-aggrandizement. It is a heady thing to stand before a group of people and expound on what is supposed to be (or what one hopes to be) eternal truth. I know that if I feel disinclined to pray this prayer, and especially if I feel I do not *need* to pray this prayer, then I am in danger of preaching something simply because I love my own ideas. Such an attitude is inappropriate. The congregation should not be coming to church to hear what I, personally, have to say; my task as a preacher is to preach the word of God and not my own philosophy.

> **Exercise:** How much time do you allot to sermon preparation? What level of importance do you place on preaching?

Authority

RELATIONSHIPS WITH PEOPLE are critical to the "success" of preaching. One cannot preach effectively unless one has been granted authority by those listening. One can attempt to preach, but if the people have not granted the preacher some authority and credibility, they are likely to listen with a jaundiced ear. I offer two examples: preaching in a homiletics class or to a group of one's colleagues. A homiletics class is an academic environment; it is not a worship service, which is the setting in which a sermon belongs, and the assembled body is listening with a critical attitude, often with evaluation form in hand.

One's colleagues are a tough crowd. They listen while comparing the preacher's message with the one that they are formulating simultaneously in their mind. What the preacher says is being contrasted instantaneously with what the professional audience would have said instead.

The concept of *authority* is a difficult one in our time because people are suspicious of authority figures. Jerrilee Lewallen, drawing on Fred B. Craddock's book *As One Without Authority*, speaks of inductive authority as opposed to deductive authority. Craddock's idea is that the traditional sermon with "three points and a poem" is deductive, in which the preacher tells the congregation what conclusions they should draw. Inductive preaching, on the other hand, "usually begins with something concrete, such as a part of the scripture, a story, an example, or a metaphor that engages the listeners' intellectual interests and emotional involvement. The sermon's route is charted toward allowing listeners to draw their own conclusions instead of leading from conclusions the preacher has drawn."[4]

Nevertheless, the congregation needs to grant some authority to the preacher in order truly to listen. Thomas Long says that the preacher is the person whom the faithful community has set apart to be a witness: to wrestle with the Scripture and to listen for God's voice and presence. The congregation may include people who surpass the preacher in faith, education, or knowledge of human nature. The preacher, however, "is the one whom the congregation sends on their behalf, week after week, to the scripture. The church knows that its life depends upon hearing the truth of God's promise and claim through the scripture, and it has set the preacher apart for the crucial activity of going to the scripture to listen for that truth."[5]

The preacher also must claim this authority, extended perhaps by virtue of training and ordination, but the preacher must claim it with humility. The preacher must recognize that being granted such authority is a privilege, not a right, and that one represents a long line of Christian tradition and, indeed, God Almighty.

The Particularity of the Sermon

ONE OF THE MYSTERIES OF PREACHING is that a sermon is bound to a particular time and place, with particular people. The preacher is explicating the word of God in a specific circumstance. Sometimes when I have been sweating over a sermon, especially if it has been a week filled with other job responsibilities, my husband will say to me, "Why don't you just toss one off?" or "Why don't you just pull one out of the barrel?"

I cannot do it.

I do on occasion pull one out of the barrel: my cache of sermons delivered at some point in the past. One can go back three years, or any multiple of three, to when the lectionary readings given for that particular Sunday in the year were the same, read through the sermon, update it a little for the current day and congregation, and—*voilà!*—one has a sermon.

Such efforts are not satisfying. The sermon does not seem to fit the current circumstances. I have even tried to recycle sermons that were well received when I first preached them, sermons that I thought were good sermons, and when I preach them in some new setting, I can tell while preaching them that they do not work. Either the sermon does not fit the congregation, or I do not feel inspired, or something is just *missing*.

The sensation that a sermon is falling flat is a horrible feeling. Preachers generally can tell when a congregation is listening to, or responding to, the sermon. It depends on the level of eye contact, the depth of the silence, the look on someone's face, and that indefinable sense that *it's working*. To stand and preach a sermon that is falling flat evokes that feeling of deadness, which is the antithesis of the gospel of Christ. Sometimes a sermon will not work, sometimes the preacher has a hard time pulling the sermon together, but to preach a sermon that falls flat because one has not done one's best to produce something worthwhile dishonors both God and the people who have come to worship and who have granted the preacher authority.

On a deeper level, one should avoid pulling a sermon out of the archives that is not suited to the occasion and the people, and one should avoid grinding out some sermon, because one never knows whether someone will show up who desperately needs to hear the word of God proclaimed. A colleague of mine long ago said that we are "hope peddlers": our task in preaching, and in fact in everything we do in ministry, is to bring people hope. People will venture into church when they are experiencing a crisis in their lives or going through a transition. They are seeking comfort, or truth, or hope. If I have been negligent in my preparation, if I have not tried to preach what God might want me to preach, if I have been arrogant in my attitude toward the task of preaching, then that person who needs a word of hope, who needs the truth of God, might not receive it from me that day, and I will have failed.

Some people would say, I know, that I am granting to preaching too great an importance. But from extensive experience in the search process in churches, both as a priest searching for a position in a church and as a deployment officer helping churches find the right pastor, I have seen the importance that congregations place on good, inspiring preaching. It is usually the number one requirement. They may not know or even agree on what they mean by such a statement, but they know they want it. They want the preaching they hear in church to make a difference in their own lives.

In truth, we never really do know what effect our preaching has on someone's life. They may not tell us. The effect may be incremental. The effect may be indefinable, as was the change in me wrought by my mentor's sermon on sloth. But as with so many activities in ministry, we fulfill the responsibility given to us and let God work the changes in people.

I still remember the first time that I realized a sermon that I had delivered had changed someone's behavior. I found the experience frightening. It was during that same internship, and I was preaching on the Sunday before the holiday commemorating Martin Luther King Jr. I do not remember what I preached, but the following Sunday a couple in the church came up to me and said that my sermon had made them go home, clean out their closets of clothing they were not wearing, and give the clothing to the poor. I remember being gripped by the realization that what I had spoken had changed their behavior. And therefore I had better be careful what I preach.

This is not to say that we are always responsible for what people do after we preach. People regularly hear something entirely different from the text of the sermon; perhaps they hear what they need to hear. But preaching is still an awesome responsibility, for it has tremendous power to affect people's lives. As Joyce H. Smith writes, "If you do not want to change people, don't preach. If you do preach, then be as responsible as possible for the changes you may make."[6]

> **Exercise:** Think back to a sermon you have heard that you especially remember or a preacher whom you particularly liked to hear. What was it about the sermon, or the preacher, that affected you?
>
> Have you ever pulled a sermon from the "archives"? What was your experience preaching it in a different circumstance than the one in which you originally delivered it?

Method of Sermon Preparation

SERMON PREPARATION is such a time-consuming enterprise that developing a method for such preparation must be a crucial part of the rule of life for a preacher. Many preachers learn this guideline: They need one hour of preparation for every minute of the completed sermon; thus, a ten-minute sermon should take about ten hours to prepare. Congregations typically are astounded by this guideline. Mind you, some of the preparation is in stewing over the readings: letting them percolate in the mind and heart as one goes about other tasks of ministry. Still, Graham Neville, in his introduction (originally published in 1964) to Saint John Chrysostom's *Six Books on the Priesthood*, comments, "It is unlikely that any priest to-day [*sic*] would devote a third of his working time to the preparation and delivery of his sermons, though it was not uncommon in the last century."[7] This is exactly the amount of time that many seminarians in the late twentieth century would have been taught was necessary and appropriate.

One must first decide whether to use a lectionary: a system that specifies Bible readings for a sequence of time, whether for Sunday worship or for daily Scripture reading and worship.[8] Perhaps this decision is dictated by one's denomination; perhaps the decision is up to the individual preacher. Even if one uses a lectionary, the preacher still has to decide which reading will be the sole or primary focus of the sermon. Some people preach almost exclusively on the Gospel passage;[9] others might find a connection among the readings and focus the sermon accordingly.

Preaching from the lectionary is a worthwhile discipline: it makes preachers wrestle with the whole of Scripture (although the lectionary still leaves out many uncomfortable bits), rather than focusing on those passages that they like. At one point early in ministry I chose a topic on which I wanted to preach and then found the readings to match. I became uncomfortable because this method left the whole enterprise of preaching far too much to my own whims. Better, I thought, to be subject to the Scripture and wrestle with what it might be saying to the congregation— and to me!—on any given day. In *The Screwtape Letters*, consisting of letters from a senior devil to a junior devil, C. S. Lewis describes two types of priests who are commendable from the devil's point of view. In the first, the preacher

> has been so long engaged in watering down the faith to make it easier for a supposedly incredulous and hard-headed congregation that it is now he who shocks his parishioners with his unbelief, not *vice versa*. He has undermined many a soul's Christianity.

The second type Lewis describes relates to the use of a lectionary:

> His conduct of the services is also admirable. In order to spare the laity all "difficulties" he has deserted both the lectionary and the appointed psalms and now, without noticing it, revolves endlessly round the little treadmill of his fifteen favourite psalms and twenty favourite lessons.[10]

Once preachers have addressed this question of whether to use a lectionary, they then have to move into preparing the sermon. Barbara Brown Taylor, in *The Preaching Life*, describes her method, which is similar to that used by many preachers.[11] Below is a general outline, drawing from Taylor, from conversations with clergy, and from instructions I have received over the years:

177

Read through the lessons. The best time to read them is not during the week before the sermon must be preached but weeks before. This extended time allows the readings to percolate in one's mind and heart and helps the preacher to see connections among the readings and events in the congregation and in the world. Some preachers read the lessons ahead for several months, especially if one needs to plan for music or special liturgies.

Take notes while reading the lessons. One might start immediately taking notes, or one might read the lessons, let them stew a bit, and then start jotting down ideas. The notes do not have to be formal; they might just be words, ideas, or impressions. One might include stories that come to mind in response to the readings.

The responsibility for choosing music for a worship service may not always rest with the preacher. Often in large churches, the music staff will choose the music, perhaps in conjunction with the pastor, perhaps not. I generally have chosen the hymns for worship services, sometimes in a team with several lay members of the congregation. I find that the process of choosing songs and hymns helps me to ponder the readings, and in the eventual worship service the hymns add an extra dimension to the sermon.

Read commentaries. These come in many guises, whether books, magazines, or online resources. They might be of a scholarly nature, or they might be other preachers' reflections on these passages. Lewallen includes in her book a helpful appendix, "An Annotated Bibliography of Biblical Resources for Preaching."[12]

Give it a rest. Taylor recommends that after all this reading and stewing, to give the preparation a rest. (Taking a break from the sermon is easier to do if the sermon in question is not due in a day or two.) Taylor describes the process this way:

Once I have done all my homework and have a decent idea what the text means, I give it a rest. Understanding is not enough. I do not want to pass on knowledge from the pulpit; I want to take part in an experience of God's living word, and that calls for a different kind of research. It is time to tuck the text into the pocket of my heart and walk around with it inside of me. It is time to turn its words and images loose on the events of my everyday life and see how they mix. . . . This is the gestation period of a sermon, and it cannot be rushed.[13]

Lewallen describes a specific way of approaching the text and the sermon, drawn from homiletics professor William Hethcock. The method consists of four parts: exegesis; describing the human condition of those in the text and for whom the text was written; describing the human condition of those who will hear the sermon and how it is analogous to those in the text; and proclamation—specifically, how the exegesis bears upon the condition of those who will hear the sermon.[14] Once preachers have worked through these four parts, they write a focus sentence that then becomes the essence of the sermon: "a single statement that will be the underlying support for the sermon, the point from which everything will flow and with which everything will be consistent."[15]

Write the sermon. Of course, this stage is also a crucial element of the preacher's rule of life. Will one write a full text of the sermon? Will one simply preach from a few notes? Personally, I advocate preaching from a manuscript so that one can pull together all one's preparation into a coherent whole. Preaching from a few notes might become an excuse for poor preparation, or lead to confusion about what one meant to say, as one tosses in words on a whim that turn out to be inappropriate or irrelevant.

No matter the format of the final product, the preacher then has to prepare the sermon. How will one do it? What will be the discipline one undertakes for this stage? Taylor says this part cannot be taught: "All the parts of preaching can be taught: exegesis, language, metaphor, development, delivery. What is hard to teach is how to put them all together, so that what is true is also beautiful, and evocative, and alive. Life itself is the best teacher."[16]

The method I use after all the reading and thinking and research is to draw a mind-map. One might say this is an outline, but it is not so orderly as an outline, and the process of drawing it allows my thinking and imagination to continue to work. I put the central idea or theme in a circle in the middle of a blank piece of paper. I place various sub-thoughts in circles connected by a line to the central idea. Each of the sub-thoughts then spawns its own ideas, stories, or examples. The end result is a paper with lots of little circles radiating out from the central theme in the center. By the time I finish creating the mind-map, I should be ready to start writing.

Preach. One final piece is necessary for one's rule of life for preaching: How will the preacher deliver the sermon? Will she stand in a pulpit or at a lectern? Will he stand in an aisle in the midst of the people? Will the preacher stand still or pace up and down? The answers to such questions often depend on several factors: the preacher's personality and style, whether the preacher is using a manuscript, and the formality or informality of the specific worship service or the setting. Personally, I almost always preach from a pulpit. As I have often told congregations, when I stand in a pulpit I can see the people much more easily. I can see their eyes and their facial responses, whereas if I stand on the floor, I might be gazing upon a sea of heads.

Many people who preach from a manuscript use a technique to keep themselves from being too focused on the text during the delivery of the sermon. I call it "formatting" the sermon, which I do after I have finished writing it. The technique is to break up the manuscript into "sense lines" of perhaps five words each, indented to varying degrees, with the more important ideas being flush left.

For example, here is how I would format the beginning of the previous paragraph (some people might format it differently):

> Many people
> > who preach from a manuscript
> > > use a technique
> to keep themselves
> > from being too focused
> > > on the text
> > during the delivery
> > > of the sermon.
> I call it "formatting" the sermon,
> > which I do
> > > after I have finished writing it.

The purpose of the technique is so that one is not so tied to the manuscript visually. It means preachers can maintain more eye contact with the congregation, because they can just glance down at the manuscript and see what lines are coming next. Ever since I started using this technique, I have found I cannot go back to preaching from a page set in regular paragraphs: I feel wooden in my preaching.

Exercise: What is your method of sermon preparation? Is there any particular step that especially helps you to prepare a sermon (such as reading commentaries, taking notes, or thinking about the readings for a period of time)? Are there any changes you would like to make to your standard procedure?

We move now to particular issues and questions related to the task of preaching.

Chapter 10

PARADOXES OF PREACHING:

Passing Life Through the Fire of Thought

It is a delicate job for the one in the pulpit, a balancing act between the text, the congregation, and the self. If the preacher leans too far one way, he will side with the text against the congregation and deliver a finger-pointing sermon from on high. If the preacher leans too far the other way, she will side with the congregation against the text and deliver a sermon that stops short of encountering God.
— Barbara Brown Taylor, *The Preaching Life*

PREACHING CAN EASILY FEED the feeling about ministry that "It's all about me." Preachers are the focal point, with all eyes and ears fixed upon them (one hopes). And preachers focus on the reactions of the listeners. Preaching is a prime example of the basic paradox of ministry elaborated at the beginning of this book: the only tool one has is oneself, and yet ministry "is not about you."

183

In fact, preaching involves a number of paradoxes, some of which follow from this basic paradox. Below are some "on the one hand" and "on the other hand" comments about preaching.

Keep yourself out of your sermons vs. "Pass life through the fire of thought"

HOW MUCH PREACHERS SHOULD REVEAL about themselves is a matter of continuing debate. Some say very little; other preachers are fairly self-revelatory in their sermons.

I understand the many arguments for keeping oneself out of one's sermons: The sermon is not about oneself; it is about God. Preaching about oneself can be a distraction to the congregation. The sermon should not be concerned with the vagaries of one's own life; it should be concerned with timeless truths. It is all too easy to present oneself as either the villain or the hero in a personal example, and either illustration is unwise.

Nevertheless, good reasons exist for judiciously inserting oneself into one's sermons. One is that the preacher becomes more human, instead of remaining some distant and seemingly perfect cleric. A second is that a congregation can hear a point more easily if the preacher presents it as a personal example. I started including personal experience in my sermons because I was preaching regularly to a congregation that resisted mightily someone telling them what "truth" is. So I preached what I believed, figuring that no one could argue with the preacher's own experience. It worked. People were not bothered by hearing of my own faith (well, they occasionally left irritated), and some people moved toward faith as a result.

An early influence in my preparation for the ministry

contributed to my belief that a judicious inclusion of oneself in a sermon is appropriate. That influence was Ralph Waldo Emerson's "Divinity School Address." I first attended seminary at Harvard Divinity School, where I heard repeatedly of this famous address that Emerson delivered to the senior class on July 15, 1838. I even lived in the building, then a dormitory, Divinity Hall, down the corridor from the chapel in which Emerson delivered this address. In short, I was steeped in Emerson's thoughts about preaching.

The story goes like this: Emerson and his family attended First Parish in Concord, Massachusetts, a Unitarian congregation. In 1837, First Parish called as its minister the Rev. Barzillai Frost, who served First Parish for twenty years.[1] Emerson found Frost's preaching terribly formal and stilted. Apparently one Sunday, Frost preached while a snowstorm raged outside the windows, but he never mentioned the snowstorm. Such an omission was too much for Emerson. He castigated Frost's preaching in the Divinity School Address, without ever mentioning Frost by name:

He had lived in vain. He had no one word intimating that he had laughed or wept, was married or in love, had been commended, or cheated, or chagrined. If he had ever lived and acted, we were none the wiser for it. The capital secret of his profession, namely, to convert life into truth, he had not learned. Not one fact in all his experience, had he yet imported into his doctrine. This man had ploughed, and planted, and talked, and bought, and sold; he had read books; he had eaten and drunken; his head aches; his heart throbs; he smiles and suffers; yet was there not a surmise, a hint, in all the discourse, that he had ever lived at all. Not a line did he draw out of real history. The true preacher can be known by this, that he deals out to the people his life,—life passed through the fire of thought.[2]

One could dismiss Emerson's views for many reasons. The specifics of one's philosophy are immaterial to one's being able to learn from Emerson's statement about preaching and its application to the ordained ministry in general. "The capital secret" of being clergy, Emerson says, "is to convert life into truth."

The preacher takes the whole of life—including people one has known, places one has been, the books one has read and the movies watched, along with the Scriptures of one's faith—and places it all into a crucible, as it were. One begins to see connections among passages from Scripture and some situation one has encountered in life and what is going on in the world or in the congregation to whom one is preaching. The reason sermon preparation should not be conducted carelessly—the reason that sermon preparation takes an hour of prep time for every minute of preaching—is that one has to pass all this "stuff" through a fire. One passes it all through the fire of thought, so that one can convert life into truth.

To put the point another way: Both Scripture and life contain truth, but not in the form of readily available pithy axioms that one can utter to anyone and have them mean anything. So the preacher's job is to take all this raw material, distill the truth from it, and deliver it to a congregation so that people can see and hear and feel the truth, so that it makes a difference in their own lives. As Taylor says,

Our words are embodied, which means we bring all that we are to their expression.

But this does not mean we are free to turn the sermon into personal show-and-tell time. Those of us who preach do so as representatives. We speak as members of a body and not for ourselves alone, which means that we may not dominate the sermon any more than we may be absent from it. When I speak out of my humanity, I want my listeners to recognize their own. When I say "I" from the pulpit, I want them to say, "Me too."[3]

Exercise: Look back, or think back, through some of your sermons, or sermons you have heard, for examples of personal experience. Were the examples appropriate? Were you, or the other preacher, setting yourself up as a hero or a villain? Were they good examples of "life passed through the fire of thought"?

This paradox of, Keep oneself out of one's sermons vs. Pass life through the fire of thought, and of faith, is another way of stating the fundamental paradox of ministry. On the one hand, ministry is not about us; it is about God. On the other hand, the only tool we truly have to work with is ourselves: who God made us to be, our own personality. This same paradox leads to several others in the realm of preaching.

Preach to yourself, but bleed not upon the congregation

THIS PARADOX AGAIN TOUCHES ON the question of how personal one should be. Someone along my road to ministry said, "Preach to yourself, and someone else will need to hear it." For example, in the book *With Ears to Hear: Preaching as Self-Persuasion*, Robin R. Meyers uses the image of the preacher trying to persuade oneself:

> When ministers talk of the love/hate relationship they have with the pulpit and reflect on one of those moments when something unexpectedly rich or effective took place, perhaps to their surprise, they will often say something like this: *"It was almost like I was preaching to myself."*
>
> . . . In fact, if self-persuasion is the name of the game for everyone who encounters the radical demands of the Gospel, then what the people in the pews need is a *model self-persuader.* In other words, the best way to persuade the people is to persuade the toughest customer the Gospel has: the preacher.[4]

William F. Schulz uses the metaphor of a mirror to illustrate how the preacher's own self is the vehicle through which the message comes alive for the hearers. He says that preachers know that one's words must match one's life and then continues,

> The salve to this anxiety is that the more regularly we preach—particularly to one congregation—the more we are forced to work out our theology, our principles, to resolve its kinks and contradictions and then the more we preach it, the more we may believe and live it for ourselves. "Preach faith until you have it," urged John Wesley, "And then, because you have it, you will preach faith." . . . For a good preacher is never preaching solely to the people; every good preacher preaches also to herself.[5]

I find that when I am wrestling with the Scripture lessons in preparation for a sermon that what might come to me is a message that I need to hear myself. Occasionally, I have even felt, when reading the lessons for a given service, "Oh, God, you aren't giving me *this* to preach about, are you?" For example, the lessons might all seem to be about joy during a week when I am feeling anything but joyful. Or the readings are about family ties during a week when I might be having trouble with family relationships. The given readings, in the midst of personally relevant circumstances, force me to wrestle with them even more than I might otherwise in order to distill their truth and their applicability to everyday life. The result, it seems, is a sermon with more depth and truth than when the readings do not hit home quite so pointedly.

At the same time, preachers must not "bleed" on their congregations. They cannot work out their personal problems in their sermons anymore than clergy can look to members of their congregations to meet their emotional needs in relationships. As Schulz says about the "mirror" image, "Worse even than cold and distant sermons are sermons smarmy with tales of self, wallowing in the glory of the preacher's pain. The best mirrors never lie, it's true, but neither do they tell too much."[6]

In my own practice, a current problem or issue might inform my sermon preparation, to help me understand what the Scripture lessons are saying to such a situation, but I would not say in the course of the sermon something like, "I know about this, because right now in my own life I am dealing with . . ." If I put in a sermon an example from my own life, it would be from some time in the past and about an issue with which I am no longer actively struggling.

189

I have found that when I "preach to myself" that some people inevitably come out of church feeling that I preached to them directly. Perhaps when we dig deep into what Scripture is saying to a given situation, we preach with more passion, and more people in the church that day than just the preacher find it applicable to their lives. Preach to yourself, and someone else will need to hear it.

> **Exercise:** What do you preach about when you encounter lessons for a day that touch a little too close to home for comfort? Do you avoid them and preach about something else? Is there a topic or a type of lesson about which you have a hard time preaching, either right now or ever?

Make people "think" vs. Preaching is not an intellectual activity

When asked what I am trying to do when I preach, I have often responded that "I am trying to make people think." *Think* is the wrong word; it implies an intellectual activity. I might better put the idea this way: I am hoping that through my sermon, people might ponder life anew, that they might look at the world and life and God in a new way. In short, and more specifically, I am hoping to spur people to faith: to see the world through the lens of the Christian faith, to understand their own lives in light of the Christian gospel, to see their own story as connected with God's story. As William H. Willimon says,

> One of the duties of pastors in their preaching is to renarrate our lives in the light of the story of Jesus. Thereby ordinary people have their lives rescripted,

190

caught up in a great drama that is called salvation. People have become the victims of narratives that are inadequate to enable the truthful living of our lives, narratives that are derived from psychology, economics, sociology, and other secular (i.e., godless) means of naming our selves and what happens to us.[7]

As such, to me preaching is more about theology and less about ethics. I want them to *believe*, not simply to *do*. Some preachers say that you have to leave the people with something to "do": some activity they can undertake in the coming week, some change they can make in their own lives. The change that preaching brings about, however, is not simply to prompt someone to undertake a new activity. The change that good preaching brings about, ideally, is *transformation*. People's lives can be transformed.

Joyce H. Smith describes the underlying dynamic of such transformation: "The major function of the sermon is to change the understanding of, or symbolized meaning of, our experience; the pictures in our head which tell us how we can interpret our reality and how we should act as a result."[8] Taylor describes it more poetically: "Preaching is finally more than art or science. It is alchemy, in which tin becomes gold and yard rocks become diamonds under the influence of the Holy Spirit. It is a process of transformation for both preacher and congregation alike, as the ordinary details of their everyday lives are translated into the extraordinary elements of God's ongoing creation."[9]

Some preachers think we have not done our job if a listener does not remember what the sermon said. The hearer has to go out, these preachers would say, being able to restate the point of the sermon and describe something they are going to do as a result of it.

191

It does not matter if people cannot remember what they have heard because preaching, both the preaching and the hearing of the sermon, is not an intellectual activity. This is one reason that printed sermons never quite measure up to the delivered, and heard, experience. Smith describes what might have happened: "Indeed, the sermon which parishioners hear is seldom the one which a minister has preached because the preacher's stories are always modified by the stories of the hearers."[10]

Comfort the afflicted, and afflict the comfortable

THIS WELL-KNOWN PHRASE originally came from Chicago journalist Finley Peter Dunne in 1902, through the mouth of a fictional Irish bartender, Martin Dooley. Dunne was describing what newspapers do, but he was not complimenting them. Dunne was decrying the power of newspapers at the time.

People eventually came to use the phrase to describe the purpose of the Christian gospel message and Christian preaching, although who first used the phrase in a Christian context is uncertain. One website ascribes the first such use to a minister in Latrobe, Pennsylvania, in 1944, as quoted by an editorial writer in the local newspaper.[11]

Often this adage is used to characterize preaching on social issues. Usually the "afflicted" and the "comfortable" are interpreted, respectively, as the poor and the rich, or as the persecuted and downtrodden of war-torn places versus those who live in much, much greater ease and freedom.

If you are the afflicted of the world, then I am to tell you that Jesus Christ will comfort you and lift you out of your afflictions and grant you freedom.

If you are the comfortable of the world, then I am supposed to call you to change your life and help the afflicted.

But these definitions are too easy. Most of us, in truth, are both comfortable and afflicted. All of us are afflicted in the sense that we must deal with life. Just like every other person on the planet, we have to find our way in the world; we have to grapple with growing up, with money, illness, love, heartbreak, birth, death, family, making decisions, taxes, the state—the list could go on and on. The rich might be trapped in an obsession with money or a need constantly to watch their investments. And yes, there are people in the world who truly are afflicted in every sense of the word: people who live in places devastated by war or natural disasters, and people who are persecuted and tormented in all sorts of ways. So we are all both the comfortable and the afflicted, to different degrees.

Maybe one could reword the adage to say that the purpose of preaching is to make people squirm in their complacencies ("afflict the comfortable") while at the same time to peddle hope to all ("comfort the afflicted"). These two aims are not contradictory. Our complacencies, the ways that we shield ourselves from God and God's truth, are the very things that keep us cut off from God and therefore the ultimate, and only real, source of life and hope.

Jesus is speaking to all of us. He challenges what we consider to be important and calls us into greater life. Such a challenge can feel like affliction. And he will comfort us, but he will not allow us to be comfortable. As Frederick Buechner says in his masterful series of lectures on preaching, "The Gospel is bad news before it is good news."[12] We may not like hearing the truth of the gospel until it transforms our lives.

One purpose of preaching, therefore, is to prompt people

to look their complacencies and their blindnesses—their sin, in other words—full in the face, while pointing to another way that provides true sustenance and hope. "Why do you spend your money for that which is not bread," writes the prophet Isaiah, "and your labor for that which does not satisfy? Listen carefully to me, and eat what is good, and delight yourselves in rich food. Incline your ear, and come to me; listen, so that you may live" (Isa. 55:2-3a).

Be aware of current circumstances vs. Sermons are about timeless truths

THE MENTION OF NEWSPAPERS brings us to preaching on current events. Another adage about preaching, this one attributed to theologian Karl Barth, says that preachers should preach with the Bible in one hand and the *New York Times* in the other.

I suggest a more nuanced approach. I have some sympathy for old Barzillai Frost, whose preaching Emerson disliked so intensely. Some preaching focuses heavily on current circumstances, whether it be the snowstorm outside the window or the war halfway around the world, with the preacher telling the congregation what to think about such matters. Preaching ultimately must focus on what is eternal, with current circumstances providing examples, fodder, or background. One problem with tying one's sermon to the *New York Times*, or any other news source, is that news is time-bound. We are not seeing the events of the day in an eternal perspective. Walter C. Klein writes, "The preacher has to close his ears to all the loud discords of the moment if he is to catch the elusive murmur of truth and repeat it for the redemption of the moment."[13]

As a background for preaching, I would much rather read fiction—not so that I deliver a book report, but because fiction teaches me about life, death, and human nature. Sermons should be about timeless truths, and nothing is quite so true, in an ultimate sense, as great fiction. Fiction touches on eternal matters and on human struggles.

When preaching, I do not take stands on controversial contemporary topics, a practice that has annoyed many parishioners. The specifics of controversies come and go. Instead, I seek to find where controversy touches on a more basic concern to human life.

Eugene H. Peterson sums up how one might deal with current events, using Saint John, the author of Revelation, as an example: "He is an alert and alive pastor. He reads and assimilates the Scriptures; he reads and feels the impact of the daily news. But neither ancient Scripture nor current event is left the way it arrives on his doorstep; it is all turned into prayer."[14]

Exercise: How could you better integrate timeless truths into your weekly sermons?

Don't worry about what people think vs. Preach so that people respond

A CONGREGATION MIGHT NOT APPRECIATE the preacher afflicting people in their comforts and complacencies. Yet preachers cannot worry about that attitude. Saint John Chrysostom said that one of the qualities needed in a preacher is "indifference to praise or blame." Graham Neville writes of Chrysostom's thoughts on this matter, "It is still true that the preacher feels the pressure of criticism and the inducement to conform. He still must avoid the twin temptations of preaching to please and ignoring just criticism because he has become content with his own mediocrity as a preacher."[15]

One of my former preaching professors said that if people in the congregation either love the sermon or hate it, then you have probably done your job that day. In other words, a good sermon provokes a reaction. The purpose of preaching is not to make people happy or satisfied. The lukewarm compliment "That was a nice sermon, pastor" is no compliment at all.

On the other hand, one does have to reach the people somehow. If you do not reach the people to whom you are preaching, you might as well be talking to the wall. Still, preachers may be tempted to rely on gimmicks or technology in order to spur people's interest in their sermons. It is true that most preachers today cannot preach for the hour or so that the great preachers of old used to do. But words themselves have the power to transform people's lives without gimmicks or technology.

Accept people's praise, but realize that any positive result of your preaching is God's doing

IF PEOPLE DO PRAISE YOUR SERMON, accept their praise. A simple "thank you" will do. The real trick, especially for someone who can preach well, is not to get caught in the praise. If people *are* transformed as a result of one's preaching, then that is God's doing. It is called grace. We never know how someone will hear something that we preach.

Here lies the catch-22, or even the spiritual trap, of preaching. We have to preach so that people respond; we somehow have to reach them. But when we do, we have to realize that it is not we ourselves who have done the work. If people walk out of a church praising my sermon, I have to remind myself of that prayer with which I began my sermon preparation: "God, these are your people. Help me to preach what you want them to hear."

Indeed, preaching involves the additional paradox that we preach using our own words—words we have put together, words we ourselves speak—but we are meant to be preaching God's word, expounding the readings to the congregation in the circumstances of the moment.

If I have done my job properly, I have gotten out of the way and allowed God to do the work and to receive the praise. God might indeed transform a person in such a way that has nothing to do with any specific thing that I actually said. Remember, how many preachers have had the experience of someone in the congregation telling them how much she appreciated something the preacher said, only for the preacher to discover that he never actually said the words the hearer thinks he said? The preacher and the sermon are always innocent vehicles for God's work.

Part 4
A Pause in Time

Chapter 11

SABBATH:

When Time Stops

But there is something, in the Jewish Sabbath that is absent from most Christian Sundays: a true cessation from the rhythms of work and world, a time wholly set apart, and, perhaps above all, a sense that the point of Shabbat, the orientation of Shabbat, is toward God.
—Lauren F. Winner, *Mudhouse Sabbath*

HERE WE COME to what may be the hardest practice in a rule of life: a proper use of time. More specifically, I refer to the practice of keeping Sabbath. Many clergy (and countless others!) struggle to find a balanced use of time, between work responsibilities, family, friends, and pastimes. Add eating, sleeping, commuting, and the basic necessities of everyday life, and there simply is not enough time in the day.

It is a common problem.

Ironically, the practice that increases one's sense of having "enough time" is to take a Sabbath day: a day, one might say, of doing nothing. It is not exactly doing nothing. It is a day devoted to God in which a person forgets about time and forgets about oneself.

My first real exposure to the concept that I should take a Sabbath day occurred when I was preparing for ordination in the Episcopal Church. I was attending a weekend retreat for those who were in the ordination process in my diocese. We each had to interview with members of various committees, and we each had to meet with the Bishop, who was a new bishop. She had an air of authority about her, and I felt somewhat intimidated. I remember a few things from that interview to this day: the topic that has stayed with me most were her comments about Sabbath. First she asked me, "When do you take a Sabbath day?" I offered some vague answer that as clergy my Sabbath day would be Monday. She made clear that "Sabbath" was different from "a day off" and proceeded to explain that Sabbath is not the day that one runs errands or goes to the dentist. I do not remember whether she explained what Sabbath *is*. Nevertheless, I left the interview with the impression, which has remained with me, that Sabbath is something different from a regular "day off" and that it is necessary and vitally important, in the true sense of the word *vital*: essential for life.

My second real opportunity to consider the notion of Sabbath came about six years later. The notion of "Christian practices" had become popular, and in the congregation I served I was leading a class on the topic during the season of Lent, using the book *Practicing Our Faith*, edited by Dorothy C. Bass.[1] The book describes twelve practices that are part of a Christian way of life. These practices are not what one might think, such as praying and reading Scripture, but rather include such activities as discernment, forgiveness, dying well, and testimony. I asked the participants to vote for the practices they wished to cover in this six-week class, and Sabbath was one of the ones they chose. It turned out to be the most controversial, with some people finding it very attractive and others saying they were extroverts and the notion of sitting around all day struck them as incredibly boring.

Obviously, we were dealing with preconceptions (some unfounded) about what Sabbath is and what it is not.

The Origin of Sabbath

"SABBATH" IS A JEWISH CONCEPT and practice, rooted in the first chapter of Genesis and in the Ten Commandments. Genesis 1 is one of the two creation stories in the Bible; it tells of God creating the heavens and the earth in six days. On the seventh day God rested (Gen. 2:2). It was God's Sabbath day, you might say.

This story serves as the basis for human beings observing a Sabbath day, which is the fourth of the Ten Commandments. The Ten Commandments are delineated twice in the Bible, once in Exodus (20:1-17) and once in Deuteronomy (5:6-21). The Commandment, quoting from Exodus, is this:

> Remember the sabbath day, and keep it holy. Six days you shall labor and do all your work. But the seventh day is a sabbath to the LORD your God; you shall not do any work—you, your son or your daughter, your male or female slave, your livestock, or the alien resident in your towns. For in six days the LORD made heaven and earth, the sea, and all that is in them, but rested the seventh day; therefore the LORD blessed the sabbath day and consecrated it. [Exod. 20:8–11]

Note that this command applies to everyone in a household, including the servants and the animals. The justification for observing the Sabbath hearkens back to Genesis: we are to rest on the seventh day because God rested.

The version in Deuteronomy provides the same basic command, including the instruction that the Sabbath applies to everyone in the household, even one's slaves. But then instead of citing God's resting after the creation of the universe as the reason for observing the Sabbath, Deuteronomy supplies an additional justification:

> Remember that you were a slave in the land of Egypt, and the LORD your God brought you out from there with a mighty hand and an outstretched arm; therefore the LORD your God commanded you to keep the sabbath day. [Deut. 5:15]

Although both versions declare that *no one* is to do any work, the reasoning in Deuteronomy is about freedom. The emphasis in Deuteronomy is that the Lord has delivered the people from slavery in Egypt, and Sabbath is a way of recognizing that one is free. A people in slavery do not have the choice to observe Sabbath.

What does this conception of freedom say about our contemporary ways of life? We laud our many choices. We can choose which of a number of airlines to fly when we want to go on vacation. We can choose from a variety of cell phone providers, Internet service providers, credit card companies, and banks, to name just a few of our options. Our grocery stores and drug stores overwhelm us with choices: we even have the choice of

Oreo cookies with original, chocolate, peanut butter, or mint filling (to name just a few of the options). But can we choose to take a full day with no work responsibilities? Can we take a full day dedicated to God, to simply be—to lose time and to forget about ourselves? To what are we enslaved?

> **Exercise:** Ponder these two justifications for observing Sabbath. Which one is more likely to motivate you to keep Sabbath: the notion of rest or the notion of freedom? How much do you feel enslaved to work and responsibilities? How much are you in need of rest?

What Sabbath Is Not

THE CONCEPT OF "SABBATH" is bandied about quite often these days. The word has become trendy, even. But some of the notions of Sabbath being promulgated are not sabbath at all; they are simply ways to say that one is "keeping Sabbath" without really doing so. In other words, they are ways that we can sound virtuous while not truly getting down to the hard truth of what Sabbath is all about.

Sabbath is not self-care. A favorite practice in the trend of "keeping Sabbath" is to engage in elaborate self-care rituals that make one feel good, such as soaking in a hot bath or getting a massage. The focus in such rituals is not God, however; the focus is simply oneself. As Lauren F. Winner comments, "The Sabbath has come back into fashion, even among the most secular Americans, but the Sabbath we now embrace is a curious one. Articles abound extolling the virtues of treating yourself to a day of rest," with various self-care rituals. Then Winner explains the problem with this approach: "Whom is the contemporary Sabbath designed to honor? Whom does it benefit? Why, the bubble-bath taker herself, of course!"[2]

During the time that I have been in ministry, the Church has increasingly emphasized the need for "self-care" among clergy, often using the term "wellness." Yes, we do have to make sure that we take care of ourselves, but if we are the focus, then we miss out on the values of a day of Sabbath: to forget about ourselves and to orient the day toward God.

"I take little bits of Sabbath." I have heard some people say they take a "mini-Sabbath." In truth, what they are taking is a micro-Sabbath. And what they really do is take a few hours out of a day to do nothing, or whatever their conception of Sabbath might be. I remember two specific instances when I heard someone describe such a practice. One was a conversation with a self-proclaimed extrovert who said she abhorred the idea of spending an entire day in Sabbath; she thought it sounded incredibly boring and proclaimed that she took little snippets of Sabbath, scattered throughout a week.

The other instance was at a conference for clergy and their spouses. One afternoon the leaders broke us into small groups and gave each group a Bible passage to discuss. I have forgotten which passage we were assigned, but my group ended up talking about Sabbath. One of the spouses, a man who himself ran an institution tied to the Church, said that he did not have time for a full day of Sabbath, so he took small bits of Sabbath. I blurted out, "That's a cop-out." I then realized that perhaps I was being too harsh. These days, while I may sympathize, I still think it is a cop-out: a way to avoid the difficult practice of keeping Sabbath and the truths that it teaches us—and the liberation that it offers.

"Little bits of Sabbath" do not work because the practice robs a person of the opportunity to completely forget about one-self and to forget about time. These mini-breaks may restore us to some degree, but they are ineffective because we are still stuck to a schedule. See more on this topic below.

Sabbath is not your day off. As my bishop told me, Sab-bath is not the same as your day off work. It is not the day we clean the house, buy groceries, or go to the dentist. These are all tasks that need to get done, things we can check off a "to-do list." Frequently they are enervating or exhausting. They also do not remind us of God.

For clergy, this has a major implication: we should have two days off a week. Most clergy would say this is impossible. Many clergy do not even take off one day each week. For decades, I have heard clergy say that they have not had a single day off in a number of weeks. Congregations and bishops far too often routinely expect long hours from clergy. I have often heard the language of "half-salaried" clergy rather than "half-time" clergy. The underlying theory is that of course clergy work more than forty hours a week; therefore, we cannot simply expect that a priest receiving half of a full salary will work only twenty hours in a week.

This topic of how we schedule our work time returns us to the "way of life" question raised in chapter 1. If being ordained clergy is truly a way of life, is it possible to demarcate sharply between a "day off" and a day working? To address this question, one might make a distinction between one's vocation of pastor or priest, on the one hand, and one's specific position in ministry, on the other hand.[3] On a day off, one does not stop being the person who exemplifies the Christian parson ("representative person");

for example, one cannot live an exemplary life for five or six days a week and then live a debauched life for one or two days. Still, if pastors work nonstop, they can become burned-out and also become overly focused on their own supposed importance: "It's all about me."

> **Exercise:** Examine how you structure your week. Do you take a Sabbath day, free from chores and errands? Do you even make sure you get a full day off each week? How many hours do you work in a typical week? If you were to take a second day off, how would you schedule it?

What Sabbath Is

THE PREVIOUS SECTION DESCRIBES what Sabbath is not, but what is it? We may look first to the Jewish roots of the practice. Observing Sabbath is one of the fundamental tenets of Judaism, and one of the most loved. The Sabbath is Saturday.[4] Because the Jewish day begins at sundown, the Sabbath starts Friday evening. Families light candles and lay a special meal of food that has already been prepared. Lauren Winner, who grew up a Jew and then became a Christian, remarks that as a Jew, Sabbath was meant to be "the fundamental unit around which I organized my life" and as a Christian, "the piece of Judaism I miss the most."[5]

Christians are unlikely to take up Jewish practices in observing a Sabbath day. We could, however, learn some basic tenets that underlie the Jewish practice. The first is that the Sabbath is oriented toward God. This does not mean that the entire day is spent in worship, although worship should certainly be an integral part of the day (see more on this in the next chapter). It does mean that the entire orientation of the day is toward God.

Two Days Off?

Many dioceses, or other judicatories, have standard Letters of Agreement (by whatever name) for clergy. (Clergy do not sign "contracts," in recognition that the relationship between clergy and congregation is different than that between an employee and an employer.) For many Episcopal dioceses, these templates say that the priest's "scheduled workweek is five days," and that the priest "is expected to preserve at least one continuous twenty-four-hour period each week solely for personal and family use."*

If one reads these lines carefully, one might note that the priest theoretically has two days off, but is guaranteed only one full day (twenty-four-hour period) off work. This wording raises two questions. One is that a twenty-four-hour period theoretically could run from Sunday at 5:00 p.m. through Monday at 5:00 p.m., whereupon the priest attends a church meeting. The priest then is not getting a full day off. To me, a full day means that I can get up in the morning without having in my mind that at some point later in the day I have to concentrate on matters related to my work or have to go somewhere for work.

The second question the wording in the Letter of Agreement raises is this: How does one take that second day off, on which one does chores, goes to the dentist, and so forth? Does one get a full second day off, or does one take that second day piecemeal, in little bits throughout the week? There is a definite advantage to having a full day off, but if the attempt to get one sends us into paroxysms of scheduling trauma, then perhaps a preferable solution is to take a full Sabbath day and then to take

---

* Richard L. Ullman, Commentary to A Model Letter of Agreement, in "Called to Work Together: A Handbook on Letters of Agreement for Clergy and Congregations" (New York: Office for Ministry Development, Episcopal Church Center, 1993), 5.

the second day off in bits scattered through the week.

One suggested method of scheduling a clergy work week that fits with this suggestion is based on calculating "units" of one's work each week. A morning, an afternoon, and an evening each count as a "unit" of work. One decides how many units to work each week, based on how many hours make up a typical unit. For me, in one position I held, a typical unit was about 3.5 hours, based on when I arrived at the office, when I broke for lunch, when I went home, and how long an evening of work typically lasted. In another position, a typical unit was four hours. So, with a four-hour unit, I calculate that I need to work between ten and thirteen units in any given week: thus, between forty and fifty-two hours. Any less than that and I am obviously not being faithful to what I have been called to do and for which I am being paid. Any more than that and I personally am on the road to getting sick, being exhausted, and having insufficient time for my family; I have made the mistake of thinking that the ministry is "all about me" and therefore requires my never-ending attention.

An Episcopal priest has constructed a useful spreadsheet, called "Keep It Collared," that helps clergy to keep track of units worked.† One can specify how many units one wants to work each week, the maximum number of evenings one wants to work, and how many units one wants to spend in reading. There are even special codes one can use in the spreadsheet to keep track of vacation time, sick days, continuing education, and public holidays. If one works more than the specified number of units, or more than the desired number of evenings, a warning appears. Sometimes it is necessary to work more than the ideal number of units (Holy Week comes to mind), and then one takes off a day in a subsequent week. The program specifically warns if one does not have a day off in any working week.

† https://keepitcollared.weebly.com

In a Christian context, one could say that, ideally, the Sabbath day should give us a taste of the kingdom of God.

This "taste" does not mean experiencing what many like to call "the kingdom of God on earth"—an ideal society, free of racism, poverty, disease, war, and all other societal ills. A taste of the kingdom of God means experiencing life as though you were in the presence of Jesus Christ himself and he has transformed your entire way of viewing and living life. You are at rest; there is no need to strive or to accomplish anything. You experience complete freedom.

In addition, you forget yourself—no self-consciousness, no need to boost your own ego, no need to work for something of immense concern to you. Is forgetting about one's work or one's "causes" such a laudable aim? Yes, because it means that you are relinquishing control to God and recognizing that for one day you do not have to do anything—you *should not* do anything—to advance your concerns. You leave them in God's hands for that one day.

And you avoid the temptation to think that this one day of leaving everything in God's hands will make you more productive. Winner calls this "capitalism's justification for Sabbath rest: resting one day a week makes you more productive during the other six. ... And while that may be true, rest for the sake of future productivity is at odds with the spirit of Shabbat."[6] If the concern for future productivity is our motivation, we have not truly relinquished command and control to God.

Experiencing a taste of the kingdom of God also means that we forget the passing of time. In eternity, there is no linear time. We cannot conceive of this; it is beyond our earthly experience. For us, in our earthbound existence, we notice change only because of the passage of time, and we notice the passage of time because things change. The Sabbath day is, ideally, as if time stands still. We avoid doing anything that would make us notice the passage of time. In other words, on a Sabbath day, we do not do anything that is scheduled.

I discovered this one Sabbath day when I decided to make some bread. I love to make yeast bread: to mix the dough, let it rise, shape it, cook it, smell it cooking—and then eat it. But I discovered that once I had mixed the dough, I was required to watch the clock. Not literally—after all, dough rises for a good hour or so. But the day had time markers in it. I had to make sure I did not lose track of time, or my bread would rise too much or burn while it was cooking. So I stopped making bread on the Sabbath. Cooking may be relaxing, for me, but it is also work.

A taste of the kingdom of God also includes connecting with others whom we love, whether in person or, say, in a phone call. I have discovered by officiating at funerals that many people long for harmonious, peaceful interactions with loved ones; for many people, their conception of the afterlife is an eternal existence with those loved ones who have gone before (even if, or perhaps especially if, their earthly interactions with these people were not always harmonious). Forces of evil work through loneliness and isolation. I do not mean that Sabbath observance *must* include interaction with others; perhaps one needs a break from interaction, and loneliness can be most intense when one is in a group of people. What I am suggesting is that Sabbath might well include interactions with others in a spirit of what I can only call *gemütlichkeit*. This is a German word that the dictionary defines as "cordiality" or "friendliness,"[7] but which my German teacher taught cannot truly be translated. It includes experiences of togetherness, unity, enjoyment, and forgetting about oneself in the company of others. It is a taste of the kingdom of God.

One activity fits with all these characteristics of rest, freedom, losing ourselves, being with others, and forgetting the passage of time; that activity is play. I often think that *play* is a word that describes Sabbath. I do not mean, however, organized sports, a favorite Sunday activity in many communities nowadays. Organized sports have underlying intentions that undermine Sabbath: a person often is concerned about individual performance, most sports require the keeping of time, and even if the activity is enjoyable, it is, essentially, work.

Instead, play is spontaneous and unstructured, and it has no goal other than sheer enjoyment. Generally play is a communal, rather than a solitary, activity; thus, we are spending time with people whose company we enjoy. In play, one completely forgets about the passage of time; how often has time seemed to melt away when one is just playing with no thought of goal or schedule? Play also enhances creativity and imagination. These days, between organized sports, after-school activities, and homework, children have little opportunity for true play, much less adults.

I realize it may be radical to conceive of "play" as a characteristic or description of the kingdom of God, or of Sabbath, but perhaps thinking in this way could allow us to ascribe to God a sense of humor and keep us from taking ourselves and our goals too seriously.

Chapter 12

KEEPING SABBATH:

What Do We Do?

Rest and worship. One day a week—not much, in a sense, but a good beginning. One day to resist the tyranny of too much or too little work and to celebrate with God and others, remembering thereby who we really are and what is really important. One day that, week after week, anchors a way of life that makes a difference every day.
—Dorothy C. Bass, *Practicing our Faith*

THE SIMPLEST WAY to keep the Sabbath is to refrain from work. The Puritans, and then some Protestants in general, went further by making the Sabbath day one devoid of play and joy. Observing a Sabbath day, however, as implied in the previous chapter, carries more meanings than simply not working, and it may well include play. Dorothy C. Bass says in *Practicing Our Faith* that practices not good for the Sabbath are "work and commerce and worry."[1]

215

Below are some suggested features of a Sabbath day and the reasons behind them.

Worship

THE SABBATH IS A DAY FOR GOD. It is a day to become steeped again in our identity as God's creatures and God's children, and to forget our identity as priest, pastor, doctor, drug store clerk, truck driver, farmer, stockbroker, what-have-you. So the day should include worship: an intentional turning to and focusing on God. For most Christians, Sunday would be the natural day on which to observe Sabbath—assuming Sunday is for them the principal day of worship, which is not true in all places. One worships in church and then spends the rest of the day keeping Sabbath in other ways. (For suggestions of why it is necessary, for most people, to "worship in church," see chapter 7 on worship.)

These days, churches may want to hold business meetings on Sunday, such as a meeting of the church board, council, or vestry. Laypeople find their weeks too full to give up a weekday evening for such meetings; therefore, many want such meetings on Sunday. (In truth, laypeople in churches are less and less inclined to want to spend any time in meetings, a change that represents a huge shift in church culture over the past few decades.) Ideally, church business is not conducted on Sundays. Sundays are for worship first, and perhaps fellowship and learning.

For clergy, the choice of a Sabbath day can be confusing, because Sunday is a work day—typically one's most intense work day. Most clergy I know, myself included, finish their Sunday activities exhausted. Not only is leading worship "work," because one has to remain aware and focused, but the day also involves one in other ministerial responsibilities. For parish clergy, the day of corporate worship necessarily requires numerous activities related to one's job. It is the day when one sees the greatest proportion of the congregation than in any other activity (one certainly hopes this is true!) or on any other day of the week. People have pastoral concerns. People ask theological questions. People might bring up issues of church business.

Often if someone has a pastoral concern that requires more attention than can be given in a short conversation, the pastor will tell the person that he or she can devote more time and attention to the person at some point during the week and will make an appointment with the person. A minister's attention on Sunday is more on the big picture—two big pictures, in fact: the worship of God and the state of the congregation. Focusing on the personal pastoral concerns of any individual can be difficult; in fact, clergy often might forget what people tell them on a Sunday. However, it is not always possible to set aside or postpone pastoral conversations. Often people are at their most vulnerable on a Sunday after worship, and during the week their defenses might rise again, making beneficial pastoral conversations less likely.

Because Sunday is a work day, clergy need to have some other day than Sunday be their Sabbath day. For many, it is Monday. For many others, it is Friday. I have heard a number of clergy say that they like to work on Monday for the very reason that people's increased vulnerability after the Sunday worship carries over into Monday, but not later into the week; clergy feel that they can do good pastoral work on a Monday.

Take a Break from Work

ON THE SABBATH, one is to refrain from work. This is the original,

217

basic biblical Commandment. What is not so obvious is the answer to the question of what constitutes work. The Jews had to contend with this question, so that "over time, the rabbis teased out of the text [of the Commandment] just what the prohibition on work meant, first identifying thirty-nine categories of activities to be avoided on Shabbat, and then fleshing out the implications of those thirty-nine."[2]

Because Christians probably do not wish to get into such fine detail, I suggest two criteria that define an activity as "work." One is whether it pulls one's focus back onto one's work. For example, I love to read, and reading is a fine Sabbath activity. As I said in chapter 1, anything one reads is potential fodder for ministry. However, if what I am reading begins to make me think about a sermon or something else directly related to my job, then that constitutes "work." It is pulling my mind and focus back into being a priest. It is reminding me of my identity as a priest.

The second criterion is whether the activity changes one's environment. This is the hard one. The implication of this criterion is that some activities that one enjoys, and even finds relaxing, might not be truly suitable for a Sabbath day because they change one's environment. They are items that we can check off on a "to-do" list, which is a definition of work. Examples are gardening and cooking. True, they may be totally unrelated to one's work as a Christian leader, but they are still work. As a Hasidic Jew commented, "What happens when we stop working and controlling nature? … When we don't operate machines, or pick flowers, or pluck fish from the sea? … When we cease interfering in the world we are acknowledging that it is God's world."[3] If we refrain from changing our environment for one day in a week, we are acknowledging that we are not in charge. Thus, if Sabbath means "no work," then we should not do anything that can change our environment.

I do find most gardening relaxing. It is satisfying to be outside, to get one's hands dirty, to see the results of one's efforts. But that last statement is the problem: gardening generates results (we hope!); one is *doing* something, *getting something done*. As much as I enjoy gardening, it is preferable, I have found, to have a whole day in which I do not have to be concerned with accomplishing something. Even if I am not *concerned* about accomplishing something, even if the gardening is just an enjoyable way to wile away an hour or two or three, I have found that to have a day in which I can go without "accomplishing" a single thing brings a feeling of liberation, of relaxation, of rest, of gratitude for God's great gifts, that far surpasses the smaller and momentary satisfaction of weeding the flower bed or trimming the shrubbery. The weeds will grow again, the shrubs will need trimming again. But those feelings of liberation and gratitude grow and feed on themselves over repeated Sabbaths of dedicating the day to God and not feeling compelled to accomplish a thing.

Leave Aside Worry and Anger

THE INJUNCTION "NO WORRY" that Bass mentioned has certain implications. One is to do nothing that would lead to anger or arguments. This may be more easily said than done (as with most things related to keeping Sabbath), since arguments might arise unexpectedly. However, with a certain amount of discipline, one can avoid purposely raising topics that might lead to arguments.

Another implication of "no worry" is to do nothing that involves finances. Money is a huge topic for both worry and arguments, so just leave it aside. Do not use one's Sabbath day to balance the bank account or check on one's investments or go shopping.

An odd implication of "no worrying about money" is that if one's Sabbath is also the day that one attends corporate worship (in other words, goes to church), then whatever offering one gives at church should be automatic. One should already have decided how much one's offering will be. This might mean any of several possibilities, all of which my husband and I have practiced at one time or another: at the beginning of the month write a check for each Sunday in the month and set the checks aside, or cash, until each Sunday comes; have a fixed amount that one automatically gives each Sunday; set up an automatic payment from one's bank account; or write one check at the beginning of the month for that month's portion of one's tithe and then either put nothing in the plate on Sunday or put in some nominal amount—but this should also be pre-decided.

No worry also means leaving aside discussions about, or rumination over, such topics as planning for the future (which involves awareness of time), investments, one's employment or lack thereof, how one will afford the children's college education, what one will do when one's parents' health deteriorates, and all the other topics that can fill our minds and hearts and lives. Yes, these are worthy topics for consideration, but there are six other days to think about them. Leave them aside for one day. Sometimes not thinking about them can then allow one to approach them with fresh insight.

Skip the Shopping

ONE OF THE GUIDELINES for Sabbath is "no commerce." Money

can lead to worry. Engaging in commerce also interferes with other people's Sabbath, because someone has to be working at the store or restaurant one is frequenting. The old "blue laws" in the United States, which required stores to close on Sundays, made it easier to practice "no commerce" on the Sabbath day (if one's Sabbath is Sunday). Nowadays, most stores are open every day of the week, and shopping online is always available. One has to be more disciplined and intentional about observing "no commerce" on one's Sabbath day.

Shopping on Sunday "prompts businesses to hire more Sunday workers, who join the growing percentage of the workforce who toil long, irregular hours."[4] Such a dynamic is hardly a definition of freedom.

Escape from the Digital World

THE USE OF ELECTRONIC DEVICES on the Sabbath is another topic we talked about in our Lenten class. As might be expected, there was wide disagreement, and I suspect there would be even more today. Electronics are ubiquitous, in the form of smartphones, computers, tablets, and televisions. They have become more than just an ever-present backdrop to life; they have become a seemingly essential ingredient. They have become our principal means of communication, information gathering, and entertainment.

In my opinion and experience, there are three primary problems with using electronic devices on the Sabbath. First, as mentioned previously in chapter 2, they make us overly aware of time, the very thing that Sabbath is supposed to counteract. Our electronic devices give us a never-ending stream of things that we are supposed to be doing, and the very speed at which they operate

221

makes us hurry up internally.

A second problem with using electronic devices on the Sabbath is that they do not always work well, even if one has the latest and greatest device with the best software. Little glitches happen: a document or email or photo will not sync properly in the "cloud," a software program will not do what we want or expect it to do, the electricity goes off, or the battery runs out. These events just cause frustration, which is antithetical to the notion of Sabbath.

The third problem is that electronic devices are not as relaxing as we may think they are. In 1978, Jerry Mander wrote a book called *Four Arguments for the Elimination of Television*. One of the four reasons is that the electronic input from a television causes the brain to be stimulated in certain ways that enliven it rather than calm it down. Such an effect explains why using a television or any other electronic device essentially as a babysitter while the parent does something else (such as make supper) is easy but counterproductive: it enlivens, rather than relaxes, the child.[5]

Be Aware of What You Take In

READING IS A GREAT ACTIVITY on the Sabbath. I find, when reading, that I am immersed in something absorbing and enjoyable, and I lose track of time.

Let me qualify this statement, however. If I read on the Sabbath, I read books, not magazines and especially not newspapers. Newspapers are nothing but sources of worry and are completely tied to the passage of time; put them aside for a day and they are already outdated. The world can survive my not knowing what happened on any given day, and if it is truly important, I can find out about it on the next day. In *Surprised by Joy*, C. S. Lewis comments on reading the news. (His observation also would apply to watching the news on television or other electronic device). After explaining why as a schoolboy in Northern Ireland he avoided news about the fighting then happening on the European Continent in World War I, he goes on to comment on news in general:

> Even in peacetime I think those are very wrong who say that schoolboys should be encouraged to read the newspapers. Nearly all that a boy reads there in his teens will be known before he is twenty to have been false in emphasis and interpretation, if not in fact as well, and most of it will have lost all importance. Most of what he remembers he will therefore have to unlearn; and he will probably have acquired an incurable taste for vulgarity and sensationalism and the fatal habit of fluttering from paragraph to paragraph to learn how an actress has been divorced in California, a train derailed in France, and quadruplets born in New Zealand.[6]

What about magazines? I avoid reading them on the Sabbath also. I find magazines enervating. Many magazine articles are filled with things to worry about, or by which to be titillated. Here are some typical examples of the articles one might find in magazines: analysis of the activities of political parties, why the diet one has been following for the past six months has now been shown by scientific studies to be unhealthy, a new diet by which one surely can lose weight, which vacuum cleaner brand is the best purchase, why the mainline church is losing members, an explanation of a country's or the world's dire economic or environmental situation, the latest outrageous behavior by some celebrity figure. Over the years, I have subscribed to several excellent magazines that offer news and social commentary, magazines that have existed for decades, if not more than a century. I have appreciated the generally high quality of their writing, in the sense that the authors know how to construct an essay and they use words well. In reading the magazines, I learn something about events and societies and walks of life that I otherwise would not know. Invariably I find after reading them for any length of time, however, that the worldview many of them portray is negative, nihilistic, and cynical. So I read magazines, but not on the Sabbath.

What Does One *Do?*

AFTER ONE CONSIDERS all the things that are ill-advised on the Sabbath day, the question invariably will arise: What does one *do?* If work, shopping, electronic devices, newspapers, magazines, chores, and so many other of our normal, everyday activities are not recommended, if we are not to change our environment (which rules out many activities), then just how do we spend the day?

To reiterate what was said above: We worship. We let the day pass without thinking about anything we have to do and without being reminded of our work. We spend time with loved ones. We play. We let go of any worries or concerns. We sleep.

Will we be bored? Perhaps we will upon occasion, especially as we first venture into such a practice. But as we continue to keep Sabbath regularly, the feelings of rest and liberation grow as we forget about ourselves and let go of any identity we may have other than being a child and servant of God.

Exercise: What would be the characteristics of your ideal Sabbath day? How would you most like to spend such a day?

Part 5
Daily Life

Introduction to Daily Life

THE LIFE OF CLERGY is not strictly a life of leading worship, providing pastoral care, preparing sermons, and the like. Clergy also must deal with regular life: finances, eating, maintaining a place to live, doing the laundry, exercising, and all the other components of daily life.

How we approach these ordinary tasks must be a part of our rule of life. Simply finding the time to accomplish ordinary tasks can be a challenge amid the demands of ministry. If ministry, however, is a "way of life" rather than a job, then how we fulfill these ordinary tasks expresses who we are and reveals what is important to us. These tasks can be the means through which we discover the presence of God in the midst of daily life.

Several aspects of daily life are crucial to include in a rule of life because they are fraught with difficulties. How we handle money and how we treat our bodies are both arenas that can become minefields in the course of ministry because the ministry itself often presents many traps with regard to money and the body.

Some denominations have programs promoting the well-being of clergy; these programs sometimes are available for lay leaders also. They intend to help clergy recover their sense of call and revitalize their enthusiasm for ministry. Such programs focus not only on spiritual and vocational matters, but also on physical, psychological, and financial health. These programs recognize that health in these arenas of daily life is necessary if clergy and lay leaders are to serve God in ministry with integrity and enthusiasm.[1]

Chapter 13

MONEY:

Relinquishing Money's Hold on Us

*How can I keep from settling into the salary and benefits of
a checkout clerk in a store for religious consumers? How can I
avoid a metamorphosis from the holy vocation of pastor into
a promising career in religious sales?*
—Eugene H. Peterson, *The Contemplative Pastor*

MONEY. Unless clergy live in very rare circumstances, we
have to grapple with financial matters the same as anyone else does. We have to maintain a house, whether
or not it is church-owned housing, pay bills, and perhaps put children through college.

But money is a topic people discourage us from discussing.
Church leaders are not supposed to talk about money—or so
many people say. Many believe that if church leaders talk about
money, then we are being mercenary, we are poking our noses into
people's private business, and we are not focusing on "spiritual"

matters, which supposedly should be our sole focus.

One could view this matter differently, however. Money is an intensely private and personal topic wherever I have worked and lived. In my mind, this fact alone makes money a fair topic for preaching and for conversation in a church. If an issue is so close to the heart, if it raises people's hackles as easily as the topic of money does, then it is linked to the condition of our soul and spirit. The state of our soul is definitely the business of the church. In other words, a connection exists between a person's attitude toward and treatment of money, on the one hand, and one's attitude toward and relationship with God, on the other. Money is a spiritual matter. How we use money reflects who we are and what is important to us.

For clergy, then, what money we have is not strictly a personal matter, disconnected from our work life. How much we earn, how we spend our money, whether we have debt and how much: these seem like private matters. So they are, and we do not necessarily need to reveal all the details about these topics to our parishioners. But because they are also matters that affect our spiritual state, our attitude toward life, and our relationship with God, they are all topics that have a bearing on the work that we do as pastors. If attitudes toward and treatment of money reveal the state of a person's soul, then we clergy need to regard money and how we use it as an integral part of the "way of life" of an ordained leader. "For where your treasure is, there your heart will be also," Jesus says in the Sermon on the Mount (Matt. 6:21).

This tension regarding money makes it easy to take the attitude toward money that "it's all about me." Not only do people consider money to be a highly private and personal matter, but also they often are tempted to regard money as "mine." When I have talked about money in churches, especially about giving money to the church, I have heard people respond, "It's my money. I earned it." (One such person also told me that tithing is not biblical, a statement that I believe made me stare at him open-mouthed in incredulity.)

The implication is that because these people earned the money, they have a right to do with it whatever they want—and this usually means they feel they have a right to spend it on themselves. Thomas Aquinas, according to Rebecca Konyndyk DeYoung, said that our having earned money ourselves makes generosity difficult. Quoting from DeYoung, "the more something feels like our own, the more painful giving it away will be. . . . Earning and owning make us feel important and in control of our lives. Giving stuff away relinquishes those claims."[1]

My husband and I have always felt that we have money only by God's grace. Even if we earn money through the work we do, we believe that we have that work only through the grace of God. We could just as easily be unemployed (and sometimes have been). I have found when I consider the money my husband and I have as coming from God, not as something we have "earned" or that we "deserve," I remain more grateful to God for the work that we have and the money that comes from it. Once I realize that whatever position I may have as a priest is a gift from God, and is also temporary, I am less inclined to carp and whine about troublesome incidents in my work.

We as clergy need to structure a rule of life with regard to money in such a way that money has the smallest possible hold on us. Money can become an obsession, and the point is to live so that it is not. In my rule of life, living in a way that I am not obsessed about money means the following: being content with what we have and structuring our life so that it is "enough," living without debt, and tithing 10 percent to the church. All of these aims are incredibly hard to do, especially in modern life. Society, especially through media and advertising, contradicts all three of these premises. It constantly tells us we "need" many things; thus, no matter how much we have, it is never enough. Credit cards, mortgages, and car loans become the means to acquire all the things we supposedly need, even if we do not have the cash. Thus, society is constructed so that debt is "normal." Our economy is based on consumer spending, such that during financial downturns, a macabre joke is that we are "helping the national economy" by spending money, even if we do not have the money we are spending. Finally, giving away 10 percent of one's income, especially specifically to the church, seems ridiculous in the contemporary environment.

In anyone's life, money issues and conflicts revolve around how much money is coming in (whatever the source or means), how much money is going out, and where it is going. Thus, the place of money in the lives of Christian leaders breaks down, I believe, into three essential topics: income and expenses, debt, and Christian giving. The privacy attitudes toward money also play themselves out in a marriage or indeed in any relationship: Does a couple share their money? Do they have joint or separate bank accounts? How is money distributed if only one person in a couple is earning an income? Clergy have to face these same issues.

Exercise: These questions come from Rebecca Konyndyk DeYoung's book *Glittering Vices,* in the chapter on avarice: "Consider the following thought experiment: Imagine that others had access to all your financial records and spending habits (investment portfolios, savings, checkbook registers, credit card bills, tax returns, receipts, cash flow, etc.) but knew nothing else about you. What sorts of judgments could they make about your character, your loves, your values, your excesses and deficiencies, your ideals and identity? . . . Patterns of getting and giving can reveal our hearts' deepest loves and priorities."[2]

As another exercise, if you are married, consider the questions above about the place of money in your marriage—specifically about bank accounts, how money is distributed, and how decisions are made with regard to purchases, whether for the self or the household.

How much should clergy be paid?

SHOULD CLERGY BE PAID for the work we do? The Apostle Paul was a tentmaker (Acts 18:1-3), but he also received assistance from several of the churches among whom he evangelized (the Philippians, for example; Phil. 4:15–16). When Jesus gave instructions to the Seventy before he sent them out, he said, "Remain in the same house, eating and drinking whatever they provide, for the laborer deserves to be paid" (Luke 10:7).

I have occasionally heard laypeople in the Church say in one form or another, "Don't clergy take vows of poverty?" They usually ask this when challenging why their congregation has to pay their pastor more than they want to pay, or when the pastor has perceived a need for more money in order to meet family needs. When I have heard laypeople ask such a question, they were trying to skimp on offering their clergy a fair wage or some benefit. The answer is, No, clergy do not take vows of poverty. Monks and nuns of certain religious orders, although not all, take vows of poverty.

Churches have conflicting expectations of clergy. At the

same time that churches try to avoid paying clergy, they also expect clergy to have attractive, but not too attractive, clothes, car, and other belongings. If the pastor is driving an old beat-up car, or wearing clothing that has holes in it, then congregations feel embarrassed and expect their pastor to sharpen the image. If the pastor, however, is driving a new high-end sports car, for example, and wears a collectible watch, then the congregation likewise is embarrassed and feels that she is violating Christian standards.

Different traditions will have different attitudes and policies regarding pay for clergy. In Ireland, where I currently live, clergy in the Church of Ireland are paid a "stipend." The Church has chosen the term intentionally, because it has a different connotation than the word *salary*. *Salary* suggests wages paid to a person for doing a job, as a person in another type of workplace might receive. *Stipend* suggests money given to clergy to enable them to live in a place and provide ministry there.

The distinction might seem minor, but each term carries a different attitude attached to it. If I am receiving a salary, then I am inclined to regard my pay as the equivalent to that of a person in a professional career such as, say, an attorney or a principal in a school. I think I am entitled to it. On the other hand, if being clergy is not truly a *job*, but more a way of life, then a stipend is simply the amount of money I am given in order that I might provide ministerial services without the hindrance of having to work another job in order to live. The Church of England describes this approach in this way: "The majority of clergy receive a stipend which is funded by the giving of congregations. It is paid in order to enable the clergy person to exercise their ministry without the need to take another job in order [to] earn their living. It is intended to provide adequately for a clergy person to live during their working years and into retirement." (The explanation then adds: "A significant number of posts are non-stipendiary.")[3]

Such an approach to paying clergy would be anathema to many American clergy, as would the amount of pay received (see sidebar on clergy compensation). I was once in a meeting of the leaders of a diocese in the Episcopal Church, both clergy and lay. We were discussing clergy salaries and how we in the diocese structured the pay scales for parish clergy. Diocesan policy dictated a matrix of salaries, such that how much a priest received was based on the size of the congregation and the number of years that the priest had been ordained. At that time, a priest with twenty-five years of experience, serving a congregation in which 250 people attended worship on a Sunday, for example, would earn about $40,000 more per year than a newly ordained priest serving a congregation with fifty people on a Sunday.

In this particular meeting, we were discussing the possibility of eliminating such a system and paying all clergy the same amount. Several of us made a case for such a system. After all, often clergy in smaller congregations must work harder than clergy in larger congregations; smaller churches have fewer laypeople to help with the tasks that must be accomplished in any congregation, no matter what its size. Paying all clergy the same salary lessens the possibility that pastors will want to serve particular congregations simply because they want a higher salary. But as someone present spoke about the perceived benefits of a single pay package for all clergy, two clergy present suddenly blurted out, "Why would I bother?"

I was surprised. Why would one bother to serve in a parish if one is not going to have salary increases as one's church grows in size and one advances in years? One serves because it is the ministry to which one is suited and to which one is called. Ministry is not based on making money. Call me an idealist, but one "bothers" to serve in a church because one does what is best for the people in one's care and because it is how one can best serve and obey God.

The pay system in many US denominations is constructed to promote the idea that clergy should earn increasingly more money. Clergy earnings are treated the same way as the wages that any professional might make, and clergy are urged to maximize their earnings in order to prepare for their retirement.

During a conference on preparing for retirement, my husband and I began reflecting on the money I earn by being a priest. We had attended several such conferences in the past and had found them helpful, as we learned how the pension fund works, how to budget for retirement, what we can expect from Social Security, and other such topics of financial planning.

As we sat in one conference, however, after I had been a priest for about seven years, the staff person was explaining how one's pension is calculated. One figure in the calculation is one's total years of service. Another is the average of one's salary for seven out of eight consecutive years; this figure is called one's "Highest Average Compensation," or "HAC" (pronounced like *hack*). Clergy routinely talk about their HAC (without naming the figure, of course, believing money to be a private matter). They talk about needing to move to a different ministerial position because they want a higher HAC.

At the conference, the staff encouraged the clergy to try to get our HAC as high as possible. My husband and I heard this advice, and we felt something was wrong with it. We felt that I should take whatever position God called me to take, no matter what the effect on my HAC. Ministry is about doing what God calls one to do, wherever that might be, not doing the "job" that gives one the highest salary possible and thus the highest pen-

238

sion in retirement. A *Christian Century* article makes this clear; the words emblazoned on the issue's cover are enough to get across the point: "God doesn't love your 401(k)."[4]

Clergy Compensation

As a comparison of how much clergy are paid in American and non-American contexts, I offer the following numbers as an illustration of the differing mindsets behind offering a *salary* versus a *stipend*.

In the Episcopal Diocese of North Carolina, for example, the minimum compensation for 2023 for a priest living in church-owned housing, with the parish paying all utilities, was $51,863. If the priest was receiving a housing allowance, the compensation (including salary, housing, and utilities) was $68,726.[*] Across the Episcopal Church as a whole, the median compensation in 2020 for a solo rector was $75,678. For a senior rector, presumably meaning a priest in charge of a congregation who supervises other clergy, the median was $116,537.[†] (I chose North Carolina as the example because it has a fairly large number of clergy, and its median compensation—$77,000 in 2020—is close to that of the Episcopal Church as a whole.)

By contrast, in the Church of England, the minimum stipend in 2020–21 for a priest, with housing provided, was £25,365 (approximately $36,133, using the average exchange rate for

---

[*] Episcopal Diocese of North Carolina, "Minimum Salary Guidelines for Full-Time Clergy," https://www.episdionc.org/minimum-salary-guidelines/, accessed March 24, 2023.

[†] CPG Research Department, "The 2020 Episcopal Clergy Compensation Report," (New York: Church Pension Group, October 2021), p. 16, https://www.cpg.org/globalassets/documents/publications/report-2020-episcopal-clergy-compensation-report.pdf, accessed March 24, 2023.

2021). This is about $15,700 less than the minimum compensation paid to a priest in North Carolina living in church-owned housing.

An even greater contrast exists between the primates (head clergy) of the Episcopal Church versus the Church of England. The salary of the Presiding Bishop of the Episcopal Church as of January 3, 2022, was $318,893.‡ The Archbishop of Canterbury, who is head not only of the Church of England, but also the titular head of the entire Anglican Communion, received a stipend in 2019–20 of £85,070§ (about $109,200, using the average exchange rate for 2020).

Housing plays a huge part in clergy compensation. In the Churches of England and of Ireland, housing is provided. Increasingly, American churches are selling their rectories (or manses or parsonages, depending on the denomination) and paying the parson a "housing allowance," which is a portion of the total package. In areas with high real estate prices (I have worked in two such dioceses), the clergy must use a disproportionately large portion of the total package to pay for housing, leaving little left for the rest of life. I have seen pastors completely unable to afford to live in the town or area in which they serve because the church did not own a house to provide.

———————

‡ Domestic and Foreign Missionary Society, "Salaries of Officers and Principal Employees per Canon I.4.8," https://www.episcopalchurch. org/wp-content/uploads/sites/2/2022/01/Principal-employee-salaries-2022.pdf, accessed March 24, 2023. The source does not indicate whether or not this is a total package that includes housing costs and benefits.
§ Archbishops' Council, "The 48th Report of the Central Stipends Authority," GS Misc 1269, p. 4, https://www.churchofengland.org/sites/default/files/2021-04/Central Stipends Authority %28CSA%29 Report 2020.pdf, accessed March 24, 2023.

On the note of "whatever the position might be," when my husband and I discerned that God was calling me to take a position in the Church of Ireland, the ramifications on my eventual pension were huge. By moving to the Church of Ireland, I was removing myself from my denominational pension fund in the United States and thereby freezing both my HAC in the fund and my years of service. This is not sane preparation for retirement. In fact, my bishop in the United States said to me, "The adventurous side of me thinks this is exciting. The practical side of me thinks you're crazy." Perhaps so, but my husband and I remain convinced that taking this position was precisely what God called us to do.

Debt

"Owe no one anything, except to love one another," Paul writes to the Romans (Rom. 13:8). How difficult it is in today's world to owe no one anything! Many clergy are all too familiar with debt. When I was in seminary, we students heard figures as to how much seminarians typically owed in school debt by the time they graduated: the figure was several tens of thousands of dollars per person. People were graduating with more debt than they could repay based on what a new parish minister earned. Some seminaries are fortunate to have enough financial aid that they can restrict their student loans to amounts that new pastors can repay.

It is wise for a pastor to have no debt, other than perhaps a house mortgage and a car loan, for a number of reasons. Some are purely financial reasons that apply to anyone: one can lose thousands of dollars per year in interest payments on credit cards and loans. Being in debt effectively prevents one from being able to save money, because any "extra" money goes to paying off debt rather than being saved for a future need, such as a down-payment on a house, college tuition, retirement, or even just a good vacation.

Other than these financial considerations, there are at least two other reasons that a pastor should have no debt. First, debt can keep a pastor tied to a position that one rightly should leave. Second, debt is a spiritual weight.

To consider the first reason: Years ago, when I was new in the ordained ministry, several more seasoned colleagues regularly offered me advice. One of them offered this bit of wisdom: "You need to keep your emotional bags packed at all times so that you can leave a position at a moment's notice."

Such advice would seem to contradict the views expressed earlier in chapter 5 on pastoral care that there is a value in staying in one place for an extended period of time so that one can develop deeper relationships with people. How does one develop deep relationships while at the same time keeping one's emotional bags packed so one can depart at any time?

In fact, there is no contradiction: a paradox, perhaps, but not a contradiction. As stated in chapter 6 on relationships, a pastor cannot depend on one's parishioners for emotional support. They may offer such support, and one can be fond of them, but one cannot depend on them. In that sense, therefore, one has to keep one's emotional bags packed.

The advice my colleague offered has another justification, however. Being a priest or pastor requires one to have spiritual freedom. Sometimes one has to take a stand or perform an action that is unpopular or that will cause friction, but that one has discerned is the correct thing to do. (Discernment in such matters is crucial, so that one is doing the will of God, as near as one can determine what that is, rather than launching some personally motivated bandwagon.) Undertaking an unpopular action becomes difficult to impossible if one feels financially chained to one's pastoral position.

To put this another way, a pastor cannot *need* the job. If I need the job, then I cannot do what is necessary for the spiritual health of the people in my care. In some traditions with congregational polity, where a pastor or minister is chosen by a majority vote of the entire congregation (the majority needs to be over 90 percent or one is set for trouble), there is often a tradition of "freedom of the pulpit." Such freedom is a stated and cherished policy. It means that the pastor is free to preach whatever he or she believes is needed for the spiritual health of the congregation without the threat of being fired.

What makes a pastor need the job? Sometimes the pastoral position fulfills some personal need for status. Many times one needs the job because of the money. It is hard enough to need a position in order to meet the basic demands of daily living; such a need is compounded exponentially if one is in debt. One can end up feeling bound to the job.

Several times while in the ordained ministry I have known it was time to leave a position I held. In one instance, I was serving as an interim, and I could tell that my presence was keeping the parish from conducting the search in an efficient manner; they were dawdling. I was in a search myself, but I had received no offers. My husband and I finally made the decision to set a deadline for ourselves. We had an escape route: If by June 30 of that year (about four months away) I had received no offer, we would pack up and move ourselves to a rural area of the United States and live in a friend's barn. With six weeks to go, I received an offer (of two part-time jobs) that allowed us essentially to stay where we were, in the same state and the same diocese.

In two other instances, the decision was harder. In both cases, I was beginning to have philosophical and spiritual conflicts with the position I held. I felt I could not be true to what God called me to do. In truth, I was not being true to God. In both cases, one could say that I needed the job, financially speaking, as I had no other income. In one case, I decided to quit. The decision looked ridiculous, in practical terms. It was one of the wisest decisions I have ever made, and it completely changed my life.

In the second instance, I did not have the courage to quit. I needed the job, for a whole host of reasons. It paid me a good salary. It supposedly fit with my husband's and my plans for the future (except it really did not). Instead, I ended up being fired. And the subsequent move to a new and completely unexpected position again changed my life, and my husband's.

A priest and pastor needs to be free of debt in order to have the greatest flexibility that one can manage. Yes, one might have family obligations; yes, one needs to live; but one also needs to follow God, and as stated before, "God doesn't love your 401(k)." My husband and I have found that as with the stipend I am paid, we have to trust that if we do what it seems God is calling us to do, God will look out for us, even if the results may not be exactly what we had in mind.

The feeling of being chained to a position that one should leave is compounded when one is in debt because one does not have the freedom to make decisions. Even if one loves one's ministerial position, debt is still a spiritual weight. It hangs over one, and one can become preoccupied with thoughts of how to pay it back, if one does not have enough money to cover one's debts as well as one's expenses. If financial concerns dictate our decisions, then we do not have spiritual freedom.

Tithing

Tithing. It is an uncomfortable word. Giving 10 percent of one's income to the church is an uncomfortable practice to consider. Forget the question of whether this means "before or after taxes." People often ask this question about tithing, but in a way, it does not really matter. The attitude and the commitment to tithing are what matter.

Years ago, my husband and I decided to tithe. We managed to keep up the practice for several years, then "fell off the wagon" for a few more. Our ability to tithe has depended on what else was happening in life, such as school expenses or emergency travel. What we have found works best is to give the money without even thinking about it: to pay the tithe as soon as we receive income. Paying it becomes automatic and unquestioned. To waver and waffle about it means that one can always find something else on which to spend the money.

Currently we live in Ireland, where giving to churches is structured in a completely different way than in American churches. Most members of American churches would, I suspect, gladly welcome the expectations that Irish churches place upon their members, for the giving expectations are minuscule in comparison with the demands many American church members face that they will tithe. My husband and I decided after our first year or two in Ireland, nevertheless, to return to tithing.

For most of us, including clergy, giving 10 percent requires sacrifice. Most of us are not independently wealthy. We have to make choices about where our money goes, and spending money on one thing necessarily means that we will not spend money on something else. To give 10 percent to the church, off the top, usually means that we are letting go of something else.

245

In many cases, giving to the church operates this way: A person, couple, or family puts together a budget for the household, with line items for rent or mortgage, car expenses, food, utilities, personal care, and all the other items that make up a household budget, often including credit card debt. They tally it all up, and then giving to the church comes out of whatever is left over. If people have no budget at all, then their giving to the church becomes even more haphazard. Let's be honest: Using this method, rarely would anyone have enough "left over" that they would give 10 percent to the church. Most of us can easily think of places we would gladly spend money if we had it.

The decision to tithe operates differently. As a person or household constructs a budget, the first item entered is the tithe. Other items follow. Then one tallies it all up, and usually one has to make adjustments because projected expenses exceed income. Rarely when one makes the decision to tithe can one pay 10 percent immediately; one might start at 3 or 5 percent per year, for example, and work up to 10 percent by gradually paying off debt and decreasing other expenses.

Tithing is a practice that is "caught more than taught." This same phrase has been used to describe faith itself; the two are related. Tithing is a matter of faith. It means trusting that God will watch out for us. It means trusting that we will survive and even thrive despite freely giving away 10 percent of our income *before* we have determined whether we "need" it. Tithing means diverting attention away from ourselves and what we consider we need and directing our attention to our relationship with God and our responsibility toward God.

I "caught" the practice from several parishioners who tithed in the first Episcopal church that I served. In fact, a significant number of people in that small, challenged congregation tithed.

Some of them had caught the practice from congregations they had attended previously. At least one couple in the congregation had caught the practice of tithing from an event that had happened at the church some months before I arrived. Allow me to describe the event:

One Sunday morning as the congregation was in the church worshipping, a truck drove into the parking lot. Soon thereafter, a noise arose at the far end of the parking lot, as the people in the truck began to root through the dumpster, ferret out any pieces of metal, and put them in the bed of their pickup truck. The noise was disturbing the worship; in addition, the worshippers wanted to know what was going on. So one of the church leaders went out to talk to the people in the truck (who were not parishioners). They were scrap metal dealers, and they were taking from the dumpster any discarded scrap metal. The church leader told them they were welcome to take whatever scrap metal they wished, but asked if they could do it later, after the worship service had concluded. They agreed. The deal suited all involved.

A week later, at the time of the Sunday worship, the truck returned. The people handed the church leader six dollars. They explained that they had been able to sell the scrap metal from the church's dumpster for sixty dollars; they were therefore giving 10 percent of that amount to the church. In other words, they were tithing their earnings.

The church leader who talked to them and his wife were moved by this tithe, as I was when I heard the story. This church couple decided that if these people, who clearly were struggling to make ends meet, could give 10 percent of their earnings to the church, then surely they—who had all they needed—could also tithe.

> **Exercise:** Do you tithe 10 percent to the church? If so, what is your experience doing so? If not, how do you calculate or determine how much to give to the church?

Tithing 10 percent of one's income to the church has two effects. The first is that tithing makes us reexamine what we think we need. One of the clearest examples for me is paying for cable or satellite television service. I have sat in a diocesan meeting in which a priest said that it was difficult for people to willingly pay money to the church because it hampered their ability to pay other expenses, such as their television service, she said. The priest was sympathetic to her parishioners' plight. To me, it is a perfect example of the expenses we are expected to pay that are of dubious necessity. Do I really need 100 or more cable stations? Do I want to spend the amount of time watching television that justifies the monthly expense? The answer to both these questions is "No."

DeYoung says that tithing every week is "perhaps the oldest advice about handling money on record." Tithing helps us handle the paradox that we need possessions, because "(like food) material goods are something nobody can live entirely without," but we must beware of falling prey to the vice of avarice.

> How can we reorder our love of things, calibrating our desire to match need rather than want, without completely forgoing possessions? By regularly giving our money and possessions back to the Giver in return for his gift. Tithing habitually reminds us that our possessions belong first and foremost to God. If we spend on ourselves first and then give away what remains, either to God or to others, we remain entrenched in the

mind-set that it is our prerogative to use our possessions however we see fit.[5]

A second effect of tithing is that it increases joy. These items
that we think we need, but do not, easily become shackles: chains
on our budgets, and therefore on our lives, and eventually on our
spirits. Whittling down our needs, letting go of items that we
think we need, frees us from them. Tithing increases joy by making us depend on God and God's grace. "We realize over time
that we are traveling lighter and breathing more easily, relieved
from the anxiety of always having to manage our possessions. We
can identify virtues like generosity and spiritual disciplines like
simplicity not by percentages given but by their yield in freedom,
lightness, and joy."[6]

I have attended a number of church conferences and workshops over the years. The one in which I felt the most joy among
the attendees was a five-day conference on stewardship. The difference in mood between this and other conferences was palpa-
ble. As I wondered why this would be, it occurred to me that the
focus in the stewardship conference was on God's gift of grace
to us and our response of gratitude. The foci in many other conferences was on our own efforts to make something occur, such
as church growth and church vitality.

One does have to be careful about how one approaches tithing so that it does not end up being about oneself. I have known
people utterly committed to tithing who spoke of its benefits.
They described it almost as a reward system: If they tithed to the
church, then every time they needed something, money suddenly
appeared from somewhere. For example, their car broke down,
and they had no money to fix it. But suddenly, and unconnected
to the car needing service, a person gave them a chunk of money,

and it was exactly the amount needed for the car repair. They believed such events happened to them because they tithed, and they used such stories to encourage other people to tithe.

I freely acknowledge that such events did happen to them, as well as to other people I have known who tithe. They have also happened to my husband and me. But it is dangerous to see any chain of causality between tithing, on the one hand, and positive events happening to us, on the other, including our unexpectedly receiving money we need. To see such a chain of causality is to try to predict and control God's grace, and grace by definition is outside of our control. If we were to tithe because we then expect to be rewarded, it turns tithing into a financial exchange, or similar to getting gold stars for good grades in elementary school. In that circumstance, the giver becomes the focus of tithing, whereas one of the points of tithing is to turn our attention away from ourselves and toward God. It is to help us let go of what we want, live in faith, and accept God's grace, however and whenever it comes.

Chapter 14

The Body:

An Asset and a Liability

Standing your ground awaiting those far away, awaiting the weary in comfort, awaiting the hungry with full stomachs, is mastering strength.

—Sun Tzu, *The Art of War*

S OMEONE ONCE PASSED ON TO ME some advice for ministry drawn from the above quotation from *The Art of War*. The person told me that a warrior should never go into battle hungry, tired, or angry. And since we never know when we will go into battle, we should always be well-fed, well-rested, and not angry.

This admonition is easier said than done—certainly in war, but also in any realm of life, including the ministry. In the ministry, we often either overeat (more on that below) or skip meals. We work long hours and do not get enough time off. We deal with a variety of pressures and conflicts from all sides. In short,

251

we can easily end up hungry, tired, and angry.

Some might say that I should not compare ministry to war. In ministry we have the great privilege of dealing with the mysteries of God and being with people in the deepest concerns of their lives. All the more reason to remain well-fed, well-rested, and not angry. Those very features of ministry, the great privileges it offers, mean that we are also immersed in human conflicts, as well as battling the principalities and powers (Eph. 6:12).

One paradox here is that while we must remain well-fed, well-rested, and not angry, at the same time we cannot become fixated on our physical and mental well-being. Concern over "wellness" can become a trap that easily leads to an attitude, or at least the behavior, "It's all about me."

A second paradox is that the body is both a means to the well-being of clergy and also a minefield of difficulties. On the positive side, good and healthy physical activities can help us balance out the spiritual demands of the job; they can ground us. As I said in chapter 7 on worship, officiants are often tired after leading worship services and may find that food, sleep, or light exercise is necessary. Such things also can be helpful after a difficult or intense pastoral encounter. I used to take walks through my neighborhood after meeting with a difficult parishioner; the walk would exercise my body, clear my head, and revive my spirit. Physical activities can, however, lead to trouble when we push them to excess, such as when we eat or drink too much or engage in inappropriate sexual relationships.

Discussions of clergy wellness include far more issues than those related to the body. They also include concern for additional matters:

- mental, emotional, and psychological well-being, including depression

- isolation, such as being too far from colleagues or having little contact with them
- lack of friendships outside of the parish
- insufficient time for family
- a need for regular contact with a spiritual director

In the several dioceses in which I have worked, I have heard this last item mentioned among clergy more often than one might think. My focus in this chapter is specifically, though briefly, on matters related to the body, particularly food, exercise, alcohol, and sex.

Food and Exercise

IN MANY RESPECTS, the ministry is not a way of life conducive to healthy living. Church life is replete with potlucks and with being invited to people's homes for dinners, or for a delightful dessert with a cup of tea or coffee (in Ireland, these are commonplace in a pastoral visit), or for a beer or a drink, as parishioners gauge whether their pastor will drink alcohol.

When I served in Hawaii, part of my job was to help churches find clergy to serve congregations in this multicultural society. One of the ways that people (and the bishop) would evaluate priests is whether the priest would eat the food at the potlucks held for the priestly candidate after the Sunday service(s). In Hawaii, people would notice if the candidate picked one's way through the potluck, choosing some dishes and disdaining others. If priests were picky about what they ate suggested a squeamishness or a lack of cultural acceptance on their part.

In sum, food is a way that people show hospitality and

welcome, and a pastor can easily overeat.

Then there are the conferences. Clergy often attend conferences, perhaps for diocesan or denominational meetings, perhaps for continuing education. Such meetings and conferences typically consist of sitting in meeting rooms for hours on end, with three solid meals per day, at least one of which is often a three-course meal. Since the schedule of most such events is jam-packed, little time is left for exercise, unless one arises early and runs around the block in whatever neighborhood one happens to be staying, or tries to exercise in a hotel's fitness center. Alcohol also might be rife at such events, which only adds to the calories and potentially presents other problems as well.

On top of all this, the work that we do demands little from us physically. We spend too much time sitting: We sit in a chair to talk to someone or to read; we sit at a meeting or at a desk to work on a computer. We sit while we drive somewhere, perhaps the hospital, perhaps someone's house. Standing or physical activities might be part of our work life, such as if we work in a soup kitchen or a food bank, but if our work is mostly sedentary, we have to be intentional about adding physical activities to our life. In addition, walking the halls of a large hospital on our way to visit people is not the same as taking either a relaxing or invigorating walk outside.

My intention here is not to recommend exercise regimes or dietary patterns. These are for each individual to determine, perhaps in consultation with someone knowledgeable about such matters. My purpose is simply to comment on the need for clergy to be careful and intentional about matters related to diet and exercise.

I will, however, add an endorsement for manual labor, by which I mean physical work, using one's body and hands, according to one's personal abilities. Manual labor is a great way both to exercise the body and to accomplish something tangible and visible. One of the challenges of ministry is that we may never see the results of our labors; yes, we can build buildings and start programs, both of which yield a tangible product. But we may never fully see the effects of our presence on people, which is the real stuff of ministry. Physical labor, by giving us an activity where we see the results, can be a beneficial antidote.

I learned the value of manual labor after attending a meeting about a building project in which two groups in the congregation were battling over the space each would receive. When I went home, feeling a bit annoyed, I cleaned my bathtub (which really needed it) and felt utterly satisfied. It looked better, and the tub did not argue with me or talk back to me while I worked. The task was simple, but helpful.

Working with our hands, whether in labor or in a hobby, also provides a balance to the demands of ministry. Much of ministry involves our minds and our hearts—our intellect, spirit, and emotions—in intense pursuits. Working with our hands offers us a different kind of activity.

The flip side of the concern with healthy living, as suggested above, is that we can become *too* focused on such matters. The trap is that in the interest of "clergy wellness," we become self-absorbed and can spend too much time and energy concentrating on our exercise regimes, for example. Or we might spurn hospitality offered to us because "I don't eat that food; it's not on my diet," instead of balancing out the forbidden item by eating less or differently at another time during the day. In addition, as mentioned in chapter 11 on Sabbath, elaborate self-care rituals may be helpful and necessary, but we should not confuse them with the practice of keeping Sabbath. I, for one, benefit from a regular massage with a skilled massage therapist, but I need to recognize that such treatment is simply an ingredient in good care for mind and body.

The challenge is to determine what is good and healthy for us in terms of food and exercise and to make such practices part of our regular way of life as much as possible, without becoming obsessed with such matters.

> **Exercise:** What types of exercise do you especially like, and how do you (or how could you) include them in an exercise regimen for yourself? What practices have you found help you maintain a healthful way of living? What practices do you need, or what changes do you need to make in your life, so that you are not tired, hungry, or angry as you go about your ministerial duties?

Alcohol

I'LL BE HONEST at the outset: I do not drink. Some people might therefore accuse me of being biased in a discussion of the consumption of alcohol among clergy. I do not try to stop others from drinking, and I do not remove myself from situations where alcohol is being consumed. After all, I live in Ireland and enjoy going to a good pub, mostly for the conversation and the *craic* (Irish for "fun"), although once people start becoming quite intoxicated, being present is no longer as much fun for me.

Each denomination has its own attitude toward alcohol and may stipulate expectations for clergy with regard to alcohol. I had always heard that clergy in the United Methodist Church (UMC) are not allowed to drink (or smoke). The UMC's actual stance appears in the Book of Resolutions:

Alcohol is a drug, which presents special problems because of its widespread social acceptance. We affirm
our long-standing conviction and recommendation
that abstinence from alcoholic beverages is a faithful
witness to God's liberating and redeeming love.

This witness is especially relevant because excessive, harmful, and dangerous drinking patterns are un-
critically accepted and practiced. . . .

Thus, The United Methodist Church bases its
recommendation of abstinence on critical appraisal of
the personal and societal costs in the use of alcohol.
The church recognizes the freedom of the Christian to
make responsible decisions and calls upon each member to consider seriously and prayerfully the witness of
abstinence as part of his or her Christian commitment.
Persons who practice abstinence should avoid attitudes
of self-righteousness that express moral superiority
and condemnatory attitudes toward those who do not
choose to abstain.[1]

This book is about a rule of life for clergy or other Christian
leaders. So what is an appropriate rule of life for the use of alcohol among individual leaders? Anyone can become susceptible
to using alcohol in order to escape the demands of work, not
to mention the need to ease the feelings that can arise from the
intensity of ministry. Alcohol can become an essential ingredient
of the day.

How an individual clergy person uses alcohol is a decision
that requires honesty, reflection on one's temperament and one's
responsibilities and commitments, and discernment before God.

I will not speak for others. I can only say why I decided in my own rule of life to abstain from alcohol:

- I am not an alcoholic, but I have alcoholism in my family history, as do many clergy. I have wanted to make a change from family patterns.
- We tell children and youth, "Don't do drugs." Alcohol is a drug; it is a mind-altering substance. A major influence in my deciding not to drink was leading the youth events at a church family camp and realizing that it was hypocritical to give one message to youth and then use alcohol. I realized that I am called to set an example. If I drink, I feel that I am passing on the message that it is not possible to have fun without a mind-altering substance.
- I found that drinking alcohol has a negative effect on my spirit; drinking damages my prayer life and my discernment. The Anglican Divine Jeremy Taylor, who considered that a moderate use of alcohol could have beneficial effects, wrote in *Holy Living and Dying*, "[Drunkenness] extinguisheth and quenches the Spirit of God, for no man can be filled with the Spirit of God and with wine at the same time."[2]

Exercise: Consider the place of alcohol in your own life, and in the life of your church. What is your own personal practice with regard to alcohol?

Sex

AND FINALLY, WE ARRIVE AT SEX. In a book whose intended purpose is to help clergy, and those preparing for Christian leadership, why would sex come near the end, just before the concluding chapter? Are not issues related to sex crucial to the practice of ministry and the health of ministers? If we are discussing the well-being of clergy and other Christian leaders, then is not sex a critical element in such well-being?

The placement of this topic near the end of the book is purposeful. For the entire time I have been in ministry, which has been several decades, sex has been *the* topic of discussion, whether because of issues around sexual orientation or because of sexual abuse, of children or adult parishioners. A clergy person's opinions on various sex-related topics have become a litmus test for how congregations, colleagues, and judicatories regard that person. I have placed sex near the end of this book because as important and complex a topic as it is, to accord it too much importance is idolatrous. A full discussion of sex in ministry is beyond the scope of this book.

The broader question here is how sex fits into an individual leader's rule of life and how clergy can be faithful to their ordination vows and to any other commitments they have made, including marital vows. One difficulty is that ministry requires a person to give their all to the task: I have been saying that the only tool ministers truly have is ourselves. We are inclined to put everything we are into ministry, but we have to be judicious and discerning in the application of ourselves to ministry. A word that encapsulates what I mean is the word *passion*. Ministry requires passion.

Robin R. Meyers uses the word *passion* to describe an "elusive quality" that "may be responsible for great preaching." He acknowledges that passion is a quality "hard to describe without misunderstanding. . . . It is said to make us interesting on the one hand, dangerous on the other. Without it, life becomes an endless afternoon, a flat, tedious stretch of mindless motion." Applying the word specifically to preaching, Meyers describes passion as "that energy for communicating the Gospel that keeps the call to ministry from becoming a mere profession, and that mysterious compulsion to preach the Word from degenerating into the obligatory duties of an ecclesiastical master of ceremonies."[3] Passion is just as necessary in all of ministry as Meyers insists it is in preaching.

There is a popular misconception that the passion that drives one to seek out God in our lives also demands a parallel sexual expression. I first encountered the public's fascination with this connection of passion to ministry in the late 1980s soon after a certain televangelist was caught in a sex scandal. The Sunday newspaper of a Midwestern US city I was visiting ran an article saying that religious passion and sexual passion tend to go together; both are expressions of deep human impulses, and therefore clergy (including this particular televangelist) might be susceptible to sexual misconduct the more energized and passionate they are religiously.

Whatever one might think about this so-called hypothesis, it does imply that the public demands far more from ministers than they do from other public figures. Clergy must represent God; thus it is especially incumbent on clergy to be responsible and ethical in our relationships with other people, especially in the realm of sex, because of the power that sex has in the realm of human relationships and in our society.

> **Exercise:** What helps you, or has helped you, deal with sexual struggles within ministry and life (assuming you have encountered them)? What are the vows you have taken, and how will you fulfill them? Where do you feel passion, in a broad sense, in your work?

The body is both an asset and a liability in ministry. It can mire us in all sorts of difficulties—overeating, lack of exercise, addictions, and inappropriate sexual relationships. But we can find healthful and wise physical activities, which can provide us a reprieve from the pressures and demands of ministry.

Chapter 15

THE PERSONHOOD OF THE PARSON

All that matters is worshiping God, dealing with evil, and developing faithfulness.
        —Eugene H. Peterson, *The Contemplative Pastor*

The question is not: How many people take you seriously? How much are you going to accomplish? Can you show some results? But: Are you in love with Jesus? . . . In our world of loneliness and despair, there is an enormous need for men and women who know the heart of God, a heart that forgives, cares, reaches out and wants to heal.
        —Henri Nouwen, *In the Name of Jesus*

W HEN I WAS FIRST IN SEMINARY, a number of people—judicatory executives, professors, those newly ordained, even the students—would say, "Don't do this if you can do anything else." In other words, if you can spend your time doing anything other than ministry, if you can make a living in any other way (assuming you expect to be paid to do ministry, which is not always true), then do that thing. Do not go into the ministry.

Let me be clear what these people meant. Most of us can do *something* else. Perhaps we might work in politics, psychology, or drama—those fields I mentioned earlier that seemed to be the backgrounds of most of us seminary students. Some might teach. I have spent a portion of my working years in the publishing industry. People entering ministry have worked in all manner of jobs.

So the purpose of saying, "Don't do this if you can do anything else," is not to say that we who go into ministry are incompetent at other pursuits. God forbid. We are the last generalists, after all, so one might assume we are good at doing *something*. Instead, the admonition is meant to say, Don't go into ministry if you would be at all satisfied doing something else. Don't go into ministry unless your heart burns within you to serve God by serving among people. Don't go into ministry unless you are prepared to give everything you are in the service of the gospel, and in the process, occasionally to have your heart ache and your guts ripped out of you.

And especially, don't go into ministry unless you are truly called to do so, and this decision is confirmed not only by your own very careful discernment, but also by careful discernment on the part of the Church. Otherwise, ministry could destroy you. I have seen several people destroyed by ministry: people whom I saw go through the ordination process and wondered if they were truly called to ordained ministry. I will not easily forget these people, for their destruction was unnecessary, whether the downfall was spiritual, emotional, or financial.

The gut-wrenching starts early in the process that leads toward ordination. Seminarians will often complain about "the process"—all the demands, the requirements, and especially the length of the whole ordeal. But somehow when we undertake the process of being ordained, suddenly we are forced to deal with something, perhaps death, relationships, ambition, desires, our own personality quirks. I have seen it happen to a number of people: they enter the ordination process and it is as though life (or God?) throws something at them that they must confront.

Lest we think this happens only to those headed toward ordination, allow me to say that the same dynamic can happen to anyone who is offering themselves for training for a leadership role in the Church, whether it be liturgical or pastoral, or perhaps with youth. And if we are completely honest, the same dynamic could happen to anyone who ventures into a church truly seeking God's presence and guidance. The process of spiritual growth, the process of being remade in Christ's image, is not an easy one, and therefore many people in a church might resist such transformation and settle instead into some comfortable accommodation to an unoffensive status quo.

But those who offer themselves for leadership, and especially for ordination, must allow themselves to be remade. As repeatedly said in this book, the only tool we have in ministry is ourselves, but ministry demands that we be right before God. Ministry is a way of life, not a job, not a profession, and the minister must embody in one's very being the way of Christ. As Saint Gregory the Great says, "For indeed, the one who is compelled by his position to speak of the highest things is also compelled, by necessity, to show the highest things by his example. For his voice more easily penetrates his listeners' hearts when his way of life commends what he says."[1]

Michael Ramsey, the late Archbishop of Canterbury, also speaks of the importance of the person of the priest, in a series of talks to people whom he is about to ordain to the priesthood, published as the book *The Christian Priest Today*. In one such talk, he says, "Through the years people will thank God for you. And let the reason for their thankfulness be not just that you were a person whom they liked or loved but because you made God real to them."[2]

In chapter 4 on prayer, I quoted Ramsey as saying that the priest is to be a person of prayer, and as priestly intercessors, "we are called, near to Jesus and with Jesus and in Jesus, *to be with God with the people on our heart.*"[3] But the priest is a person not only of prayer, Ramsey says, but also a person of theology, reconciliation, and the Eucharist. These are not just tasks that a priest performs; they are orientations of the priest's entire being. He adds, "I have not made 'pastor' one of the categories, because pastor describes the whole."[4]

It is the task of the pastor to "make God real" in all the situations in which human beings find themselves: in celebrations, in death, and in times of crisis; in work and in love; in family life and in solitude. In preaching, one has the task of connecting the gospel of Christ and the faith of the Church with people's life and experience. In evangelism, one is trying to make Christ real to people who do not know him or the difference he can make in one's life.

To "make God real" is not a task that one can put on and take off; it must be a part of who one is as a person. One cannot be a person of prayer, for example, on a part-time basis (even if one works part-time in ministry), because prayer is a discipline that must permeate one's entire life. One cannot be a person of theology unless one inherently sees connections between the ways of God and regular, ordinary, everyday life, as was said in chapter 8 on reading and study. One cannot be a person of reconciliation if one does not live a life of reconciliation and forgiveness. Otherwise, one's actions and one's words will not integrate with each other. In short, the tool of ministry is who one is as a person.[5]

Ambition

MANY PEOPLE ENTER MINISTRY with high ideals: they will serve God, they can make God real to people, they will preach God's word, they will be agents of transformation, they want to bring Christ and his good news into the terrible situations that people encounter in life.

And then something gets in the way: perhaps the intense demands of the job, the struggle to structure one's days in a way of life that has no inherent structure, the needs of family life, financial woes, depression, health issues. The concern with clergy wellness in denominations and judicatories these days is a recognition that ministry brings a number of pressures that can destroy healthy ministry and, indeed, the minister.

In addition to all of the pressures just named, there is another pressure that can detract significantly from a parson truly being able to serve as the "representative person" who lives a way of life that embodies the gospel of Christ. That pressure is ambition.

Ambition is so accepted, even expected, in many church circles that few people would recognize it as a problem. Ambition is the desire for advancement, the view of ministry as a "career path," the desire for more money, a larger church, a bishopric, or some title that seems to carry prestige. Ambition is the drive that made several of my colleagues say, "Why would I bother?" when someone in a diocesan meeting suggested that all clergy be paid the same amount, regardless of church size or years of experience. Ambition reflects the obsession that one be liked, admired, and respected by parishioners, colleagues, and community.

But there are several problems with ambition in the ministry. The first is that everything—every action, every social media post, every pastoral call—becomes a means to the end of one's ambition. The pastor might treat the wealthy and powerful in the congregation better than the poor and troubled, because the powerful parishioners can be helpful in advancing the pastor's career. (Or conversely, the pastor might treat the poor and troubled better than the wealthy and powerful in order to cultivate the image of oneself as a compassionate seeker after justice.) Walter C. Klein illustrates how everything in ministry can become a means of supporting the ambition of the cleric, especially, in these illustrations, the advancement of the cleric's career:

> A careerist must scheme, calculate, maneuver, and manipulate; he is a politician, and that is the way politicians act. His friendships must be useful, his kindnesses must impose an obligation, his commitments must be conditional, and everything he does must propel him towards the consummation of his ambition. Such a person cannot be at the disposal of parishioners, penitents, and petitioners. Even the advice he gives must contribute to his glorification. Hence he cannot be wholly a priest.[6]

A second problem with ambition is that it robs us of spiritual freedom. If our focus is on fulfilling some ambition, why would we bother to seek direction from God? Ambition makes us susceptible to deluding ourselves with justifications for our actions. Such justifications might even include that we are simply trying to support our family by moving to a parish with a higher salary, or that our sphere of influence will be greater, and therefore we can do much more good, if we are in position with more power attached to it. Perhaps these statements are true, in some circumstances, but they should not be the reasons for seeking a position or title.

Saint John Chrysostom comments on ambition in a chapter of *Six Books on the Priesthood* entitled "The Character and Temptations of a Bishop." We should say first that Chrysostom, who died in the year 407, tried to avoid being made the Archbishop of Constantinople. He starts the aforementioned chapter by saying that the first quality that a priest must have, "and which I lack," is to "purify his soul entirely of ambition for the office."

> For if he is strongly attracted to this office, when he gets it he will add fuel to the fire and, being mastered by ambition, he will tolerate all kinds of evil to secure his hold upon it, even resorting to flattery, or submitting to mean and unworthy treatment, or spending lavishly. . . .
>
> I think a man must rid his mind of this ambition with all possible care, and not for a moment let it be governed by it, in order that he may always act with freedom. For if he does not want to achieve fame in this position of authority, he will not dread its loss either. . . . But those who fear and dread deposition from this office endure a bitter slavery, full of all kinds of evil, and cannot help often offending man and God.[7]

One particular ambition to which clergy are subject is a subtle temptation to take the place of God. Instead of "making God real to people" in who we are and how we live, we instead become a substitute for God. The difference is that when we make God real to people, we are always pointing past ourselves, whereas when we become a substitute for God, the focus is on ourselves. Eugene Peterson says that we can become a substitute because

> people are not comfortable with God in their lives. They prefer something less awesome and more informal. Something, in fact, like the pastor. Reassuring, accessible, easygoing. People would rather talk to the pastor than to God. And so it happens that without anyone actually intending it, prayer is pushed to the sidelines.
>
> And so pastors, instead of practicing prayer, which brings people into the presence of God, enter into the practice of messiah: we will do the work of God for God, fix people up, tell them what to do, conspire in finding the shortcuts by which the long journey to the Cross can be bypassed since we all have such crowded schedules right now. People love us when we do this. It is flattering to be put in the place of God. It feels wonderful to be treated in this godlike way. And it is work that we are generally quite good at.[8]

Peterson's comments now lead us to the ambition that perhaps afflicts more clergy than the desires for career advancement and greater power or prestige. It is simply the desire to be liked. We discussed the danger of such a desire in chapter 5 on pastoral care. I will here add to that discussion a quotation from Susan

Howatch's novel *Glittering Images*. The title comes from the notion that clergy must maintain "glittering images" of ourselves in order to be acceptable. The fictional Charles Ashworth is a widowed young cleric and theologian in the Church of England whom the Archbishop of Canterbury assigns to a commission in the house and cathedral of a controversial bishop; essentially Charles is a spy sent to investigate whether the bishop could be embroiled in a scandal. Charles's presence there, as he attempts to uncover what the "truth" actually is, precipitates a breakdown of sorts, for which he ends up in the care of a monk named Jon Darrow who is an astute spiritual director. The following is from a conversation between Darrow and Ashworth:

> "Charles, would I be reading too much into your remarks if I deduced that liking and approval are very important to you?"
>
> That was an easy question to answer. "Well, of course they're important!" I exclaimed. "Aren't they important to everyone? Isn't that what life's all about? Success is people liking and approving of you. Failure is being rejected. Everyone knows that."
>
> "We'll stop there," said Darrow.
>
> "Success means happiness," I said, "and that's why I'm in fact such a happy person despite these little troubles which are bothering me at the moment. I've always been so successful—a wonderful career, a wonderful marriage—"[9]

I quote this book at some length not only because the passage illustrates the desire to be liked, but also because the novel in its entirety brings out the "gut-wrenching" nature of ministry, the presence and need of passion in ministry and the difficulties associated with its presence, and the inability at times to discern what is true. I have spoken with a number of people who read this book early in their time in ministry and felt as though it hit uncomfortably close to home in what they were having to deal with in ministry. It illustrates the messy, convoluted, ethically questionable situations in which we can find ourselves and in which our various ambitions can easily get in the way of being able to discern God's direction.

In his book *Forgetting Ourselves on Purpose: Vocation and the Ethics of Ambition*, author and teacher Brian J. Mahan invites people (all people, not just clergy) to a life "given over to self-forgetfulness, to the delightfully nonmoral discipline of remembering to forget ourselves on purpose," a phrase he borrows from Thomas Merton. He first challenges us to consider our ambitions:

> Of course, we'd like to believe that our ambition only rarely conflicts with our nobler aspirations, both moral and spiritual, and that we rarely have to choose between them. We would like to believe that our personal triumphs somehow trickle down and enrich the rest of humanity and that when we pursue what we judge best for ourselves, the rest of the universe conveniently falls into place.
>
> But we know better.[10]

Mahan's intention, however, is to encourage us to remember "what we are living for"; his thesis is that we actually *want* something deeper and more idealistic than the usual ambitions for worldly success, social prestige, or acceptance. But to recover those "epiphanies of recruitment," as he calls them—those invitations "to see things differently, to live a different kind of life, to embrace one's unique vocation"[11]—requires forgetting oneself, on purpose.

Exercise: To what ambition(s) are you subject?

The Collar: To Wear or Not to Wear?

CLERGY FACE A DECISION once they are ordained: whether or not to wear a clerical collar, and when. The basic decision gives rise to all sorts of variations: Should one *always* wear a collar when at work? Should one wear a collar in the community, even when not working, such as when shopping at the local grocery store? Should one wear a collar only when performing some sacramental or liturgical function? Should one wear a collar when making pastoral calls in the hospital? Should one dispense with the collar altogether?

My own practice has run the gamut. During my first years of ministry, I never wore a collar. I saw no reason to wear it. Then I served a church whose membership was almost entirely active-duty military. Just as the church members had to wear a uniform when they went to work, I saw the clerical shirt and collar as my "uniform"; I recognized that in such an environment the collar was appropriate and even expected. Since serving in that church, I have tended to wear a clerical collar, but the reasons are not entirely because I consider it a uniform.

Objections to a clerical collar abound: Some people say it makes clergy "different" from other folk. Some say it is alienating, especially to younger people, in a culture that has so little understanding of the Christian faith. Given the discussion above about ambition, one could argue that wearing a clerical collar would only reinforce a focus on oneself and that it is a way to lord it over people. How can we "forget ourselves" if we are wearing something that constantly reminds us that we are clergy?

The collar, however, in an odd way removes the focus from oneself: it directs the focus, for both the wearer and the perceiver, away from the clergy person. A parson in a collar becomes a representative of Christ, rather than simply a nice person doing ministry. The collar offers three helpful reminders.

The collar reminds clergy to whom we belong. I first heard this from a Maori bishop speaking to a group of potential ordinands, people just starting out in the process. He told them that when we wear the collar, it reminds us that we belong to Christ, and Christ will lead us, sometimes where we would rather not go (as Jesus said to Peter in John 21:18). (The potential ordinands, who had great respect for the bishop speaking to them, looked a bit stunned.) I realize that the implication that we are essentially wearing an item comparable to a dog collar with a leash attached might be offensive to some people, but it is reality; otherwise our ministry is based on what we want and perhaps not on discerning what God wants.

In reminding us to whom we belong, the collar also reminds us of how we are supposed to live—that our way of life is meant to reflect who Christ is, that we make God real to people. I remember once driving down a four-lane road and being tempted to drive aggressively; I was in Hawaii, and I was not going to "drive with aloha," as the saying there goes. But I was wearing a collar. I knew people in other cars could see me and that my behavior would send the wrong message about a Christian leader. I realize that this is but a small example of the many actions we might do in life that could detract others from believing in Christ. "Let not those who hope in you be put to shame through me, Lord God of hosts; let not those who seek you be disgraced because of me, O God of Israel" (Ps. 69:7 BCP). The trick, of course, was for me to refrain from driving aggressively because I had no such inclination to do so, rather than that the image I would project would be the wrong one.

Yes, we will make mistakes, because we are not perfect, and for our transgressions we seek the grace and forgiveness of God—but this, in itself, is part of living and modeling a Christian way of life. I have often thought clergy are meant to be "fully and responsibly human"—meaning that we are fully human, with all the foibles, quirks, and sins attached to any particular human being. But we are also meant to be responsible in how we live, for which we seek God's grace and guidance.

The third reminder the collar offers, therefore, is that we are set apart. One of the objections to the clerical collar is that it makes us "different" from others. We may not *want* to be set apart, and we may think that to be set apart is unwise because it puts us out of touch with others. But the reality is that we *are* set apart to be different from what society and the world consider to be real and true; we are set apart so that we might better show in how we live the new heaven and the new earth that God intends for us all.

Again, our tool in ministry is who we are, but we are always meant to be pointing past ourselves to God.

Exercise: What is your practice and experience with a clerical collar? If you wear one, what criteria do you use for when to wear it?

To Conclude . . .

I END THE WAY I BEGAN: I have good news and bad news. Ministry is not about us, as clergy or any other Christian leader. This is bad news if we wish to be the focus of people's attention. It is bad news if we wish for all the results of ministry to be under our control. It is bad news if we truly wish to spend all our time and energy fulfilling every expectation that others, or we ourselves, have of the kind of pastor we should be.

Ministry is not about us as ministers. This statement is, in fact, good news, because it means that the results of what we do are not, in the end, up to us. We have a way of life in which we deal with the messiness and complexity of life and human relationships. We also must live in the midst of the majesty and mystery of God, as much as we are able. We encounter people in all the joys and vicissitudes of life. We have the work of communicating both the hard demands and the overwhelming love and grace of the Christian gospel.

How do we do it? As I have attempted to state throughout this book, we develop a rule of life—guidelines for how we will live—so that we can remain true to our ordination, baptismal,and other vows. And then we let go of results. We cannot control the effects of our ministry; we may never even know what effects we have had on others through our work and our living. We point past ourselves to God, forget ourselves, and look always to God for guidance and grace, plus compassion and forgiveness when we mess up, as we inevitably will.

I turn to words of Jesus in the Gospel according to Mark:

He called the crowd with his disciples, and said to them, "If any want to become my followers, let them deny themselves and take up their cross and follow me. For those who want to save their life will lose it, and those who lose their life for my sake, and for the sake of the gospel, will save it. For what will it profit them to gain the whole world and forfeit their life? Indeed, what can they give in return for their life?" [Mark 8:34–27]

It is tempting to think that the cross we take up in the life of ministry is the difficulty of the work, or the sacrifices we inevitably make in order to be in ministry. But in this way of life, the cross we must take up ultimately is a loss of control. In ministry, we may be "in charge" in many of our ministry settings, but we are not in control. When we die to our life in this world, as Jesus says in the Gospel, and instead follow him as his servant, we give up control. We do not know what will happen. We do not know where God will lead us. And this loss of control is completely antithetical to the messages we receive in a world that tells us we must be in control of our life and our work, or else something is the matter with us.

In truth, to give up control and follow where God leads us, to take up the cross of Christ and to do what it commands, whatever that may be at any moment of our lives and ministry: this *is* demanding, yes, but it is also liberating and exciting. And it is never boring. It means always being open to wherever Christ leads us and to whatever God offers to us in each and every moment, because we have no idea what that will be. We have to die to what we want, as Jesus indicates in the Gospel. We have to give up anything that we would boast in: our own abilities, even if they are God-given; our own success, even if it is in God's service; the good things of our lives, even if we recognize they are blessings. We cannot boast in these things. We boast only in Christ, who is our wisdom and righteousness, and the source of our sanctification and redemption, as Paul says (1 Cor. 1:30). *That* is to give up control, and truly, it brings a life that is exciting and mystifying.

A rule of life is not a means of being in control. A rule of life does not give us control of life and ministry. It is simply a way to outline for ourselves a structure in a way of life that has no inherent structure. It helps us maintain integrity in the midst of complex and ethically demanding situations. It keeps our focus on God instead of on a whole host of external criteria by which we could judge ourselves. And it helps us "redeem the time": to live our whole life in relation to God, guided and inspired by the Christian gospel.

That is good news.

NOTES

Notes to the Introduction

1. Anthony C. Meisel and M. L. del Mastro, trans. and ed. *The Rule of St. Benedict* (Garden City, NY: Image Books, an imprint of Doubleday, 1975), 32–39.

2. Barbara Brown Taylor, *The Preaching Life* (Norwich, UK: Canterbury Press, 2013), 32.

3. William Law, *A Serious Call to a Devout and Holy Life*, in *A Serious Call to a Devout and Holy Life; The Spirit of Love,* ed. Paul G. Stanwood, Classics of Western Spirituality (New York: Paulist Press, 1978).

4. My mentor was drawing from Byron David Stuhlman, *Redeeming the Time: An Historical and Theological Study of the Church's Rule of Prayer and the Regular Services of the Church* (New York: Church Hymnal Corporation, 1992).

Notes to Chapter 1: What Is a Rule of Life?

1. Paul Vitello, "Taking a Break from the Lord's Work," *New York Times*, 1 August 2010; http://www.nytimes.com/2010/08/02/nyregion/02burnout.html?_r=0.

2. Walter Conrad Klein, *A Priest Forever* (New York: Morehouse-Barlow, 1964), 64.

3. Episcopal Church, "The Ordination of a Priest," in *The Book of Common Prayer, and Administration of the Sacraments and Other Rites and Ceremonies of the Church* (New York: Seabury Press, 1979), 531–32.

4. This, and the questions and answers that follow, come from Episcopal Church, "Ordination of a Priest," 532.

5. Klein, *Priest Forever,* 64.

6. Episcopal Church, "Ordination of a Priest," 532.

7. Klein, *Priest Forever,* 64.

8. John Chrysostom, *Six Books on the Priesthood*, trans. Graham Neville, Popular Patristics Series 1 (Crestwood, NY: St. Vladimir's Seminary Press, 1964), 135.

9. Episcopal Church, "Compline," in *Book of Common Prayer*, 133.

10. These cycles are described in detail, with their liturgical, historical, and theological connections, in Byron David Stuhlman, *Redeeming the Time: An Historical and Theological Study of the Church's Rule of Prayer and the Regular Services of the Church* (New York: Church Hymnal Corporation, 1992).

Notes to Chapter 2: Don't Hurry

1. Dave Crenshaw, "Switchtasking is a thief," exercise in *Time Management Fundamentals*, Lynda.com, accessed 2 September 2016.

2. Tanza Loudenback, "Commuting to work has a negative effect on job satisfaction," *Business Insider UK*, October 23, 2017, http://uk.businessinsider.com/commuting-work-job-satisfaction-2017-10?r=US&IR=T

3. Marcus Buckingham and Donald O. Clifton, *Now, Discover Your Strengths* (New York: Free Press, 2001), 83.

4. Eugene H. Peterson, *The Contemplative Pastor: Returning to the Art of Spiritual Direction* (Grand Rapids, MI: William B. Eerdmans, 1989), 48.

5. Lyle E. Schaller, *Innovations in Ministry: Models for the 21st Century*, Ministry for the Third Millennium series (Nashville: Abingdon, 1994), 59–60.

6. Donald V. Romanik, *Beyond the Baptismal Covenant: Transformational Lay Leadership for the Episcopal Church in the 21st Century* (New York: Episcopal Church Foundation, 2010), 47, 49. See also Stewart C. Zabriskie, *Total Ministry: Reclaiming the Ministry of All God's People*, (Washington, DC: Alban Institute, 1995) for a description of an approach to ministry in which the traditional duties of the clergy are divided among a number of people, some ordained and some lay.

7. William H. Willimon, *Pastor: The Theology and Practice of Ordained Ministry* (Nashville: Abingdon, 2002), 72.

8. Willimon, *Pastor*, 72.

9. William Law, *A Serious Call to a Devout and Holy Life*, in *A Serious Call to a Devout and Holy Life; The Spirit of Love,* ed. Paul G. Stanwood, Classics of Western Spirituality (New York: Paulist Press, 1978), 78.

10. Willimon, *Pastor*, 62.

11. Peterson, *Contemplative Pastor*, 23.

12. Peterson, *Contemplative Pastor*, 22.

13. Peterson, *Contemplative Pastor*, 17.

14. Peterson, *Contemplative Pastor*, 17.
15. Peterson, *Contemplative Pastor*, 18.
16. Willimon, *Pastor*, 61.
17. Willimon, *Pastor*, 63.
18. I recognize that some jobs or professions require people to act quickly and efficiently, such as emergency room personnel or ambulance drivers. With regard to ministry, I recall a story of a pastor serving several churches who was stopped by a police officer on Christmas morning as he sped from one church to the next. The pastor told the police officer that he was speeding so that he could start his next church service on time, to which the police officer replied, "Christmas has been around for 2,000 years. I think it will still be here if you're a few minutes late."
19. Willimon, *Pastor*, 62.
20. C. S. Lewis, *The Screwtape Letters*, illus. Papas (New York: William Collins, 1979), 90–91.

Notes to Chapter 3: God and People

1. General Synod of the Church of Ireland, Psalm 62:8–10, *The Book of Common Prayer* (Norwich, UK: Canterbury Press, 2004, 2018), 660.
2. Michael Ramsey, *The Christian Priest Today*, rev. ed. (Boston: Cowley, 1987), 14. Italics in original.
3. George E. Demacopoulos, trans., introduction to *The Book of Pastoral Rule*, by Gregory the Great, Popular Patristics Series 34 (Crestwood, NY: St. Vladimir's Seminary Press, 2007), 16.

Notes to Chapter 4: Prayer

1. Walter Conrad Klein, *A Priest Forever* (New York: Morehouse-Barlow, 1964), 62.
2. 1 Thessalonians 5:17.
3. Eugene H. Peterson, *The Contemplative Pastor: Returning to the Art of Spiritual Direction* (Grand Rapids, MI: William B. Eerdmans, 1989), 20.
4. Thomas H. Green, *Weeds Among the Wheat: Discernment: When Prayer & Action Meet* (Notre Dame, IN: Ave Maria Press, 1984), 100. This book is a good introduction to Ignatian discernment.
5. Ignatius of Loyola, "Rules for the Discernment of Spirits," *The Spiritual Exercises*, #313–27, in *The Spiritual Exercises and Selected Works*, ed. George E. Ganss, Classics of Western Spirituality (New York: Paulist Press, 1991), 201–205.

6. Klein, *Priest Forever*, 72.

7. Byron David Stuhlman, *Redeeming the Time: An Historical and Theological Study of the Church's Rule of Prayer and the Regular Services of the Church* (New York: Church Hymnal Corporation, 1992), 42.

8. Stuhlman, *Redeeming the Time*, 42.

9. Stuhlman, *Redeeming the Time*, 42.

10. Klein, *Priest Forever*, 68.

11. Stuhlman, *Redeeming the Time*, 17, 18.

12. Michael Ramsey, *The Christian Priest Today*, rev. ed. (Boston: Cowley, 1987), 13–14. Italics in original.

13. Ramsey, *Christian Priest Today*, 14.

Notes to Chapter 5: Pastoral Care

1. Roy M. Oswald, "How to Minister Effectively in Family, Pastoral, Program, and Corporate-Sized Churches," Alban Institute, *Action Information* 17, no. 2 (March/April 1991): pp. 1–7, and 17, no. 3 (May/June 1991): pp. 5–7. Available as a reprint at https://static1.squarespace.com/static/54c7d7ede-4b03a45e09cd270/t/5aa00b43652dea8c73c46299/1520438089615/How-ToMinisterEffectivelyInFamilyPastoralProgramandCorporate-SizedChurches.pdf. The theory comes from Arlin Rothauge, *Sizing Up a Congregation for New Member Ministry* (New York: Episcopal Church Center, 1986).

2. William H. Willimon, *Pastor: The Theology and Practice of Ordained Ministry* (Nashville: Abingdon, 2002), 96.

3. George E. Demacopoulos, trans., introduction to *The Book of Pastoral Rule*, by Gregory the Great, Popular Patristics Series 34 (Crestwood, NY: St. Vladimir's Seminary Press, 2007), 11–20.

4. Demacopoulos, introduction, *Pastoral Rule*, 17.

5. Gregory the Great, *The Book of Pastoral Rule*, trans. George E. Demacopoulos, Popular Patristics Series 34 (Crestwood, NY: St. Vladimir's Seminary Press, 2007), 3.26, 3.29, and 3.34.

6. Gregory, *Pastoral Rule*, 2.7.

7. Gregory, *Pastoral Rule*, 2.7.

8. Gregory, *Pastoral Rule,* 2.6.

9. Martin Bucer, *De Ordinatione Legitima*, in E. C. Whitaker, *Martin Bucer and the Book of Common Prayer*, Alcuin Club Collections 55 (Great Wakering, Essex: Mayhew-McCrimmon, 1974), 179. The ordination rite for the priesthood in the Church of Ireland still includes such an exhortation: "Yet remember in your heart that if it should come about that the Church, or any of its mem-

bers, is hurt or hindered by reason of your neglect, your fault will be great and God's judgment will follow." General Synod of the Church of Ireland, "The Ordination of Priests," *The Book of Common Prayer* (Norwich, UK: Canterbury Press, 2004, 2018), 566.

10. Bucer, *Ordinatione*, 179.

11. Marion J. Hatchett, "The Ordination of a Bishop, of a Priest, of a Deacon," in *Commentary on the American Prayer Book* (San Francisco: HarperSanFrancisco, 1995), 521; Timothy F. Sedgwick, "On Theology, Ministry, and Holy Orders," *Anglican Theological Review* 69 (April 1987): 168; Standing Liturgical Commission, *The Ordination of Bishops, Priests, and Deacons*, Prayer Book Studies 20 (New York: Church Hymnal Corp., 1970), 31.

12. The discussion of the Anglican ordinal is adapted from Elizabeth Parish Beasley, "Conclusion: Authority, Responsibility, and Humility," in *God Willing and the People Consenting: The Theology of the Ordinal of the Episcopal Church* (Master of Sacred Theology thesis, School of Theology, University of the South, Sewanee, TN, 2004).

13. Beasley, "Conclusion," *God Willing*.

14. John Chrysostom, *Six Books on the Priesthood*, trans. Graham Neville, Popular Patristics Series 1 (Crestwood, NY: St. Vladimir's Seminary Press, 1964), 56.

15. Chrysostom, *Priesthood*, 56.

16. Gregory, *Pastoral Rule*, 2.6.

17. Gregory, *Pastoral Rule*, 2.6.

18. Gregory, *Pastoral Rule*, 2.8.

Notes to Chapter 6: Relationships

1. Episcopal Church, "The Reconciliation of a Penitent," in *The Book of Common Prayer, and Administration of the Sacraments and Other Rites and Ceremonies of the Church* (New York: Seabury Press, 1979), 446.

Notes to the Introduction to Central Tasks of Ministry

1. Methodist 2017-2020_Ordinal-FINAL.pdf, p. 20. https://gbod-assets.s3.amazonaws.com/legacy/kintera-files/worship/2017-2020_Ordinal-FINAL.pdf

2. Episcopal Church, The Examination, "The Ordination of a Deacon," in *Book of Common Prayer, and Administration of the Sacraments and Other Rites and Ceremonies of the Church* (New York: Seabury Press, 1979), 543–44.

Notes to Chapter 7: Worship

1. William H. Willimon, *Pastor: The Theology and Practice of Ordained Ministry* (Nashville: Abingdon, 2002), 75.

2. A good introduction to, and argument for, the value of congregational singing is Keith and Kristyn Getty, *Sing! How Worship Transforms Your Life, Family, and Church* (Nashville: B&H Publishing Group, 2017). The book contains appendices with questions for pastors, worship leaders, singers and musicians, and songwriters—questions that essentially lead to writing a customary with regard to music for a congregation.

3. Willimon, *Pastor*, 80.

4. Conrad Wright gives an excellent discussion of congregational polity, as practiced in one tradition, in his book *Congregational Polity: A Historical Survey of Unitarian and Universalist Practices* (Boston: Skinner House, 1997). He addresses the issues that arise in such a tradition, including authority, the boundaries of membership, and the role and authority of denominational organizations.

5. C. S. Lewis, *The Screwtape Letters*, illus. Papas (New York: William Collins, 1979), 71.

6. Walter Conrad Klein, *A Priest Forever* (New York: Morehouse-Barlow, 1964), 20–21.

7. J. Neil Alexander, Liturgy I class, School of Theology, Sewanee, TN, Spring 1998.

8. Kamehameha IV, "He Olelo Hoakaka: The Teaching Explained," Preface to the *Book of Common Prayer* (Honolulu, 1863), http://justus.anglican. org/resources/bcp/Hawaii_BCP_preface.htm.

9. Klein, *Priest Forever*, 49.

10. Annie Dillard, *Holy the Firm* (New York: Perennial Library, Harper & Row, 1988), 59.

11. Klein, *Priest Forever*, 34.

12. Thomas G. Long, "Preaching as Bearing Witness," in *Pastor: A Reader for Ordained Ministry*, ed. William H. Willimon (Nashville: Abingdon, 2002), 109.

Notes to Chapter 8: Reading and Study

1. Walter Conrad Klein, *A Priest Forever* (New York: Morehouse-Barlow, 1964), 66.

2. Klein, *Priest Forever*, 11.

3. Craig Dykstra, "Pastoral and Ecclesial Imagination," in *For Life Abundant: Practical Theology, Theological Education, and Christian Ministry*, eds. Dorothy

C. Bass and Craig Dykstra (Grand Rapids, MI: William B. Eerdmans, 2008), 52.

4. Dykstra, "Imagination," 51–52.

5. Dykstra, "Imagination," 53.

6. Dykstra, "Imagination," 54.

7. Graham Neville, trans., Introduction to *Six Books on the Priesthood*, by John Chrysostom, Popular Patristics Series 1 (Crestwood, NY: St. Vladimir's Seminary Press, 1977), 32.

8. William H. Willimon, *Pastor: The Theology and Practice of Ordained Ministry* (Nashville: Abingdon, 2002), 71.

9. Willimon, *Pastor*, 101.

10. Willimon, *Pastor*, 125.

11. Willimon, *Pastor*, p. 21.

12. Klein, *Priest Forever*, 73.

13. Herbert O'Driscoll, *A Doorway in Time: Memoir of a Celtic Spiritual Journey* (San Francisco: Harper & Row, 1985), 42.

14. With the adjectives we are using, my husband and I actually are both paraphrasing and conflating two passages. Matthew 16:4 quotes Jesus as using the adjectives "evil and adulterous" to describe the generation seeking for a sign; in Philippians 2:15, Paul exhorts his readers to be "blameless and innocent, children of God without blemish in the midst of a crooked and perverse generation."

15. Episcopal Church, "The Great Vigil of Easter," in *The Book of Common Prayer, and Administration of the Sacraments and Other Rites and Ceremonies of the Church* (New York: Seabury Press, 1979), 284–95. The readings, with their accompanying psalms or canticles and collects (prayers) are on pages 288–291.

16. Willimon, *Pastor*, 126.

17. Thomas G. Long, "Preaching as Bearing Witness," in *Pastor: A Reader for Ordained Ministry*, ed. William H. Willimon (Nashville: Abingdon, 2002), 107.

18. Willimon, *Pastor*, 115.

19. Willimon, *Pastor*, 119–20.

20. C. S. Lewis, *The Screwtape Letters*, illus. by Papas (New York: William Collins, 1979), 100.

21. Neville, Introduction, *Priesthood*, 32.

22. Dykstra, "Imagination," 52.

23. Klein, *Priest Forever*, 84.

Notes to Chapter 9: Preaching

1. William H. Willimon, *Pastor: The Theology and Practice of Ordained Ministry* (Nashville: Abingdon, 2002), 67.

2. Episcopal Church, Examination, "The Ordination of a Priest," in *The Book of Common Prayer, and Administration of the Sacraments and Other Rites and Ceremonies of the Church* (New York: Seabury Press, 1979), 531.

3. Eugene H. Peterson, *The Contemplative Pastor: Returning to the Art of Spiritual Direction* (Grand Rapids, MI: William B. Eerdmans, 1989), 19–22.

4. Jerrilee Parker Lewallen, *Making Your Way to the Pulpit: Hethcock's Homiletics Goes to the Parish* (Eugene, OR: Wipf & Stock, 2011), 2.

5. Thomas G. Long, "Preaching as Bearing Witness," in *Pastor: A Reader for Ordained Ministry*, ed. William H. Willimon (Nashville: Abingdon, 2002), 106.

6. Joyce H. Smith, "The Wizardry of Words: Preaching and Personal Transformation," in *Transforming Words: Six Essays on Preaching*, ed. William F. Schulz (Boston: Skinner House, 1984), 51.

7. Graham Neville, Introduction to *Six Books on the Priesthood*, by John Chrysostom, Popular Patristics Series 1 (Crestwood, NY: St. Vladimir's Seminary Press, 1964), 30.

8. Many denominations use the Revised Common Lectionary (RCL), perhaps with their own variations. A good introduction to the RCL may be found here: https://lectionary.library.vanderbilt.edu/faq2.php.

9. Lewallen says that she preaches on the Gospel "at least 90 percent of the time." Lewallen, *Making Your Way*, 14.

10. C. S. Lewis, *The Screwtape Letters*, illus. Papas (New York: William Collins, 1979), 71.

11. Barbara Brown Taylor, *The Preaching Life* (Norwich, UK: Canterbury Press, 2013), 85–90.

12. Lewallen, *Making Your Way*, 103–109.

13. Taylor, *Preaching Life*, 87.

14. Lewallen, "Making Your Way Through the Four Boxes," in *Making Your Way*, 10–55.

15. Lewallen, *Making Your Way*, 45.

16. Taylor, *Preaching Life*, 89.

Notes to Chapter 10: Paradoxes of Preaching

1. History of First Parish, website of First Parish in Concord. https://firstparish.org/wp/about/history-of-first-parish/.

2. Ralph Waldo Emerson, "Divinity School Address," delivered before the Senior Class in Divinity College, Cambridge, Sunday Evening, July 15, 1838; https://emersoncentral.com/texts/nature-addresses-lectures/addresses/divinity-school-address/.

3. Barbara Brown Taylor, *The Preaching Life* (Norwich, UK: Canterbury Press, 2013), 84.

4. Robin R. Meyers, *With Ears to Hear: Preaching as Self-Persuasion* (Cleveland: Pilgrim Press, 1993), 6.

5. William F. Schulz, "Mirrors Never Lie?: The Existential Demands of Preaching," in *Transforming Words: Six Essays on Preaching*, ed. William F. Schulz (Boston: Skinner House, 1984), 43.

6. Schulz, "Mirrors," 43.

7. William H. Willimon, *Pastor: The Theology and Practice of Ordained Ministry* (Nashville: Abingdon, 2002), 104.

8. Joyce H. Smith, "The Wizardry of Words: Preaching and Personal Transformation," in *Transforming Words: Six Essays on Preaching*, ed. William F. Schulz (Boston: Skinner House, 1984), 56–57.

9. Taylor, *Preaching Life*, 91.

10. Smith, "Wizardry of Words," 57.

11. "The Duty of Newspapers Is to Comfort the Afflicted and to Afflict the Comfortable," Quote Investigator, February 1, 2019. https://quoteinvestigator.com/2019/02/01/comfort/. Accessed February 18, 2023.

12. Frederick Buechner, *Telling the Truth: The Gospel as Tragedy, Comedy, and Fairy Tale* (San Francisco: HarperSanFrancisco, 1977), 7.

13. Walter Conrad Klein, *A Priest Forever* (New York: Morehouse-Barlow, 1964), 73.

14. Eugene H. Peterson, *The Contemplative Pastor: Returning to the Art of Spiritual Direction* (Grand Rapids, MI: William B. Eerdmans, 1989), 42.

15. Graham Neville, Introduction to *Six Books on the Priesthood*, by John Chrysostom, Popular Patristics Series 1 (Crestwood, NY: St. Vladimir's Seminary Press, 1964), 31.

Notes to Chapter 11: Sabbath

1. Dorothy C. Bass, ed., *Practicing Our Faith: A Way of Life for a Searching People* (San Francisco: Jossey-Bass, an imprint of John Wiley & Sons, 1997). A second, revised edition was published in 2010 by Wiley, and a third edition published in 2019 by Fortress Press.

2. Lauren F. Winner, *Mudhouse Sabbath* (Brewster, MA: Paraclete Press,

2003), 10–11.

3. Richard L. Ullman, Commentary to A Model Letter of Agreement, in "Called to Work Together: A Handbook on Letters of Agreement for Clergy and Congregations" (New York: Office for Ministry Development, Episcopal Church Center, 1993), 5. https://www.ecfvp.org/uploads/vestry_papers/files/Called_to_Work_Together,_a_Handbook_on_Letters_of_Agreement_for_Clergy_and_Congregations_-_Loren_Mead.pdf

4. Technically, this is true even in Christianity; Christians worship on Sunday because it is the day of Christ's Resurrection. One of the names for Sunday in the Christian faith is "the eighth day." In other words, Saturday is the seventh day of the week. The collects [prayers] for Saturday in the Episcopal Church's Book of Common Prayer state explicitly that the day is a day of rest. I have always felt a little odd saying these prayers when leading morning or evening worship at a church meeting taking place on a Saturday, because obviously we are not resting, much less observing Sabbath!

5. Winner, *Mudhouse Sabbath*, 9, 3.

6. Winner, *Mudhouse Sabbath*, 11.

7. *Merriam-Webster*, s.v. "gemütlichkeit (*n.*)", accessed March 24, 2023, https://www.merriam-webster.com/dictionary/gemutlichkeit.

Notes to Chapter 12: Keeping Sabbath

1. Dorothy C. Bass, "Keeping Sabbath," in *Practicing Our Faith: A Way of Life for a Searching People*, ed. Dorothy C. Bass (San Francisco: Jossey-Bass, an imprint of John Wiley & Sons, 1997), 86.

2. Lauren F. Winner, *Mudhouse Sabbath* (Brewster, MA: Paraclete Press, 2003), 5.

3. Lis Harris, *Holy Days: The World of a Hasidic Family* (New York: Touchstone Books, 1995), 68-69; quoted in Winner, *Mudhouse Sabbath*, 6–7.

4. Bass, "Keeping Sabbath," in *Practicing Our Faith*, 84.

5. Jerry Mander, *Four Arguments for the Elimination of Television* (New York: HarperCollins, 1978), Kindle ed., pp. 166–68.

6. C. S. Lewis, *Surprised by Joy: The Shape of My Early Life* (New York: Harcourt Brace & Company, 1984), 159.

Notes to Introduction to Daily Life

1. One such program is CREDO, initiated by the Church Pension Fund of the Episcopal Church in 1997: https://www.cpg.org/retired-clergy/learning/credo/about-credo/. Other denominations then adapted the CREDO

program for their own use. For the Presbyterian Church (U.S.A.), see https:// www.pensions.org/your-path-to-wholeness/credo. For the United Church of Christ, see https://www.pbucc.org/images/pbucc/ministerial_assistance/ CREDO/2018_UCC_CREDOBrochure.pdf, the last date for which information is available.

Notes to Chapter 13: Money

1. Rebecca Konyndyk DeYoung, *Glittering Vices: A New Look at the Seven Deadly Sins and Their Remedies*, 2nd ed. (Grand Rapids, MI: Brazos Press, 2020), 117.

2. DeYoung, *Glittering Vices*, 121.

3. Church of England "Clergy pay and expenses," https://www. churchofengland.org/resources/clergy-resources/national-clergy-hr/clergy-pay-and-expenses, accessed January 4, 2023.

4. Jonathan Wilson-Hartgrove, "Economics for Disciples: An Alternative Investment Plan," *Christian Century* 126, no. 18 (September 8, 2009), https://www.christiancentury.org/article/2009-09/economics-disciples.

5. DeYoung, *Glittering Vices*, 131.

6. DeYoung, *Glittering Vices*, 132.

Notes to Chapter 14: The Body

1. United Methodist Church, "Alcohol and Other Drugs," *The Book of Resolutions of the United Methodist Church*, 2016, https://www.umc.org/en/content/book-of-resolutions-alcohol-and-other-drugs, accessed March 24, 2023.

2. Jeremy Taylor, *Holy Living and Dying* (London: George Bell & Sons, 1883; reprinted in the Elibron Classics Series, Adamant Media Corporation, 2005), 53.

3. Robin R. Meyers, *With Ears to Hear: Preaching as Self-Persuasion* (Cleveland: Pilgrim Press, 1993), 4.

Notes to Chapter 15: The Personhood of the Parson

1. Gregory the Great, *The Book of Pastoral Rule*, trans. George E. Demacopoulos, Popular Patristics Series 34 (Crestwood, NY: St. Vladimir's Seminary Press, 2007), 2.3.

2. Michael Ramsey, *The Christian Priest Today* (Boston: Cowley, 1987), 81.

3. Ramsey, *Christian Priest Today*, 14.

4. Ramsey, *Christian Priest Today*, 7–10.

5. A portion of this section about the comments of Michael Ramsey is

adapted from Elizabeth Parish Beasley, "Conclusion: Authority, Responsibility, and Humility," in *God Willing and the People Consenting: The Theology of the Ordinal of the Episcopal Church* (Master of Sacred Theology thesis, School of Theology, University of the South, Sewanee, TN, 2004).

6. Walter Conrad Klein, *A Priest Forever* (New York: Morehouse-Barlow, 1964), 89.

7. John Chrysostom, *Six Books on the Priesthood*, trans. Graham Neville, Popular Patristics Series 1 (Crestwood, NY: St. Vladimir's Seminary Press, 1964), 80, 81.

8. Eugene H. Peterson, *The Contemplative Pastor: Returning to the Art of Spiritual Direction* (Grand Rapids: Eerdmans, 1989), 43.

9. Susan Howatch, *Glittering Images* (New York: Fawcett Crest, 1987), 228.

10. Brian J. Mahan, *Forgetting Ourselves on Purpose: Vocation and the Ethics of Ambition* (San Francisco: Jossey-Bass, an imprint of John Wiley & Sons, 2002), xx.

11. Mahan, *Forgetting Ourselves*, 20.

Resources

Below are the primary works that I have used in the writing of this book, whether or not there is a specific reference to them, or that I recommend as helpful in fashioning a rule of life.

Augustine of Hippo. *Confessions.* Translated by R. S. Pine-Coffin. London: Penguin, 1961.

Bass, Dorothy C., editor. *Practicing Our Faith: A Way of Life for a Searching People.* San Francisco: Jossey-Bass, an imprint of John Wiley & Sons, 1997.

Benedict of Nursia. *The Rule of St. Benedict.* Translated and edited by Anthony C. Meisel and M. L. del Mastro. Garden City, NY: Image Books, an imprint of Doubleday, 1975.

Buechner, Frederick. *Telling the Truth: The Gospel as Tragedy, Comedy, and Fairy Tale.* San Francisco: HarperSanFrancisco, 1977.

Chrysostom, John. *Six Books on the Priesthood.* Translated by Graham Neville. Popular Patristics Series 1. Crestwood, NY: St. Vladimir's Seminary Press, 1977.

Dawn, Marva J., and Eugene H. Peterson. *The Unnecessary Pastor: Rediscovering the Call.* Edited by Peter Santucci. Grand Rapids, MI: William B. Eerdmans; Vancouver: Regent College, 2000.

DeYoung, Rebecca Konyndyk. *Glittering Vices: A New Look at the Seven Deadly Sins and Their Remedies.* 2nd edition. Grand Rapids, MI: Brazos Press, 2020.

Dykstra, Craig. "Pastoral and Ecclesial Imagination." In *For Life Abundant: Practical Theology, Theological Education, and Christian Ministry*, edited by Dorothy C. Bass and Craig Dykstra, 41–61. Grand Rapids, MI: William B. Eerdmans, 2008.

Episcopal Church. *The Book of Common Prayer, and Administration of the Sacraments and Other Rites and Ceremonies of the Church.* New York: Seabury Press, 1979.

Evagrius Ponticus. *The Praktikos and Chapters on Prayer.* Cistercian Studies Series 4. Translated by John Eudes Bamberger. Trappist, KY: Cistercian Publications, 1972.

General Synod of the Church of Ireland. *The Book of Common Prayer.* Norwich, UK: Canterbury Press, 2004, 2018.

Green, Thomas H. *Weeds Among the Wheat: Discernment: Where Prayer and Action Meet.* Notre Dame, IN: Ave Maria Press, 1984.

Gregory the Great. *The Book of Pastoral Rule.* Translated by George E. Demacopoulos. Popular Patristics Series 34. Crestwood, NY: St. Vladimir's Seminary Press, 2007.

Grudin, Robert. *Time and the Art of Living.* New York: Ticknor & Fields, 1982.

Guenther, Margaret. *At Home in the World: A Rule of Life for the Rest of Us.* New York: Seabury, an imprint of Church Publishing, 2006.

Howatch, Susan. *Glittering Images.* Church of England Series. New York: Fawcett Crest, 1987. I also recommend the rest of the series, especially the second book, *Glamorous Powers.*

Ignatius of Loyola. "Rules for the Discernment of Spirits." In *The Spiritual Exercises and Selected Works.* Edited by George E. Ganss. Classics of Western Spirituality. New York: Paulist Press, 1991.

Jerome. Letter 52. In *Early Latin Theology.* Translated and edited by S. L. Greenslade. Library of Christian Classics, Ichthus Edition. Philadelphia: Westminster Press, 1956.

Kierkegaard, Soren. *The Sickness Unto Death: A Christian Psychological Exposition for Edification and Awakening by Anti-Climacus.* Translated by Alastair Hannay. London: Penguin, 2004.

Klein, Walter Conrad. *A Priest Forever*. New York: Morehouse-Barlow, 1964.

Law, William. *A Serious Call to a Devout and Holy Life*. In *A Serious Call to a Devout and Holy Life; The Spirit of Love*. Edited by Paul G. Stanwood. Classics of Western Spirituality. New York: Paulist Press, 1978.

Lewis, C. S. *The Great Divorce*. New York: Macmillan, 1963.

————. *The Screwtape Letters*. Illustrated by Papas. New York: William Collins, 1979.

Lischer, Richard. *Open Secrets: A Spiritual Journey Through a Country Church*. New York: Doubleday, 2001.

Long, Thomas G. "Preaching as Bearing Witness," in *Pastor: A Reader for Ordained Ministry*, edited by William H. Willimon, 103–10. Nashville: Abingdon, 2002.

Mahan, Brian J. *Forgetting Ourselves on Purpose: Vocation and the Ethics of Ambition*. San Francisco: Jossey-Bass, an imprint of John Wiley & Sons, 2002.

McIntosh, Mark A. *Discernment and Truth: The Spirituality and Theology of Knowledge*. New York: Herder & Herder, an imprint of Crossroad, 2004.

Nouwen, Henri J. M. *Creative Ministry*. New York: Image Books, an imprint of Doubleday, 1971.

————. *In the Name of Jesus: Reflections on Christian Leadership*. New York: Crossroad, 1989.

Peterson, Eugene H. *The Contemplative Pastor: Returning to the Art of Spiritual Direction*. Grand Rapids, MI: William B. Eerdmans, 1989.

Placher, William C. *The Domestication of Transcendence: How Modern Thinking about God Went Wrong*. Louisville: Westminster John Knox Press, 1996.

Placher, William C., ed. *Callings: Twenty Centuries of Christian Wisdom on Vocation*. Grand Rapids, MI: William B. Eerdmans, 2005.

Ramsey, Michael. *The Christian Priest Today*. Rev. ed. Boston: Cowley, 1987.

Servan-Schreiber, Jean-Louis. *The Art of Time*. Translated by Franklin Philip. Reading, MA: Addison-Wesley, 1988.

Simmons, David. "Keep It Collared: Time Management for Clergy." https://keepitcollared.weebly.com/

Stuhlman, Byron David. *Redeeming the Time: An Historical and Theological Study of the Church's Rule of Prayer and the Regular Services of the Church*. New York: Church Hymnal Corporation, 1992.

Taylor, Barbara Brown. *The Preaching Life*. Norwich, UK: Canterbury Press, 2013.

Willimon, William H. *Pastor: The Theology and Practice of Ordained Ministry*. Nashville: Abingdon, 2002.

Willimon, William H., ed. *Pastor: A Reader for Ordained Ministry*. Nashville: Abingdon, 2002.

Winner, Lauren F. *Mudhouse Sabbath*. Brewster, MA: Paraclete Press, 2003.

———. *Real Sex: The Naked Truth about Chastity*. Grand Rapids, MI: Brazos, 2005.

It's Not About You: Paradoxes of Christian Leadership

Text set in 12/15 Garamond
Headings in Optima
Titles in Book Antiqua
Ornament in Zooland

Book Design by Parish Hall Co.
Printed in Wales by Gomer Press.

P R E S S